The German Wars

The German Wars

A Concise History
1859—1945

Michael A. Palmer

ZENITH PRESS

First published in 2010 by Zenith Press, an imprint of MBI Publishing
Company, 400 1st Avenue North, Suite 300, Minneapolis, MN 55401 USA.

Zenith Press titles are also available at discounts in bulk quantity for
industrial or sales-promotional use. For details write to Special Sales
Manager at MBI Publishing Company, 400 First Avenue North, Suite 300,
Minneapolis, MN 55401 USA.

To find out more about our books, join us online at www.zenithpress.com.

ISBN-13: 978-0-7603-3780-6

Design Manager: Brenda C. Canales
Layout by: Cindy Samargia Laun
Cover designed by: Simon Larkin

Front cover image: Olemac/Shutterstock

Library of Congress Cataloging-in-Publication Data

Palmer, Michael A.
    The German wars : a concise history, 1859-1945 / Michael A. Palmer.
        p. cm.
    Includes bibliographical references and index.
    ISBN 978-0-7603-3780-6 (hbk. w/jkt)
    1. Germany--History, Military--19th century. 2. Germany--History,
Military--20th century. 3. Europe--History, Military--19th century.
    4. Europe--History, Military--20th century. 5. United States--History,
Military--19th century. 6. United States--History, Military--20th century.
    7. Europe--History--1871-1918. 8. Europe--History--1918-1945. 9.
United States--History--19th century. 10. United States--History--1901-
1953. I. Title.
    DD103.P35 2010
    355.020943'09041--dc22
                                2010026090

Printed in the United States of America

To my father, Howard V. Palmer,
who quit high school to serve
in the Second World War and
died on 23 June 2008

Contents

Introduction

W ARFARE BEGAN A GRADUAL TRANSITION from what strategist Bernard Brodie termed the age of muscle to the age of the machine during the Renaissance, centuries before the advent of the Industrial Revolution. At first, gunpowder weapons had a minimal tactical impact on the battlefield, although large but immobile cannon did prompt a revolution in siege craft. At sea, as on land, cannon did not immediately herald a new age of naval warfare. Not until the sixteenth century did the square-rigged, carvel-built man-of-war, armed with broadside cannon, become the state-of-the-art seagoing weapons system.

As Europe meandered into the Industrial Revolution—the mechanization of production, a shift from cottage-based industries to large-scale factory manufacturing, specialization, concentration of capital and labor, and concomitant socioeconomic changes—in the second half of the eighteenth century, its impact on warfare remained fairly limited. From the late seventeenth century into the middle of the nineteenth century, increased industrial output allowed the European states to field ever larger armies. The numbers of troops on battlefields rose from the tens of thousands to often over 100,000. But while the capability to produce sufficient materiel to maintain these larger armies in the field increased, the actual movement of supplies and reinforcements to the front, and the strategic movement of troops, changed little from the days of Alexander the Great and Julius Caesar. Men moved from point to point and from the rear to the front, by foot and by horse. Armies were often, as had always been the case, supplied locally, either through requisition or outright looting. Smooth-bored, muzzle-loading muskets remained the dominant infantry weapon. There were improvements in the production of locks (match, flint, and percussion) and fitted bayonets (plug, ring, and socket), along with marginal increases in rate of fire. The same was true of smooth-bored, muzzle-loading artillery. Improved carriages increased battlefield mobility while massed production and standardization allowed armies to field ever more cannon. But the rifling of muskets and artillery remained the exception and had minimal impact on battles. At sea, wooden ships of war remained wind driven.

The Industrial Revolution did not transform warfare until the second half of the nineteenth century. Rifling and breech loading altered the character of infantry weapons, artillery, and battlefield tactics. Initially, rifling slowed the reloading process; only after the American Civil War had ended did rate of fire begin an almost steady increase. The railroad allowed for the more rapid mobilization of troops, along with the movement of supplies, to the frontier, encouraging the development of reserve systems that led to a massive increase in the size of armies. To manage these ever-larger deployed forces and meet the new demands of the battlefield, officer corps became more professionalized, and the European states began to develop general staff systems. The growing European industrial infrastructure generated increasing wealth—Cicero's "sinews of war"—to support large-scale industrial conflict.

How marked were these developments? Imagine a Prussian army of 50,000 men from 1756 being mysteriously transported through time to an 1806 battlefield, there to confront another comparably sized Prussian army of the latter date. Despite the advance of fifty years, the 1756 force would still give a good account of itself. If better led, it might conceivably triumph. But imagine a similar event carrying a French army of 100,000 men from 1870 onto a battlefield of 1920, there to combat a comparably sized French force equipped with quick-firing 75-mm field guns, long-range howitzers, poison gas, flamethrowers, machine guns, and tanks, and supported from above by ground-attack aircraft. The 1870 force would be slaughtered.

A similar contrast can be seen between the armies of Europe and those of the non-Western world. The growing inability of local African, Middle Eastern, and Asian forces to compete with those of Europe, even when the former possessed a large numerical advantage, became increasingly marked. While indigenous forces on occasion overwhelmed European armies, the Zulu victory over the British at the battle of Isandlwana (1879) being an example, such defeats were so notable because they were so rare. Increased rate of fire combined with other Industrial Revolution advances—steam power that opened river systems to navigation and medical advances that contained the threat of heretofore debilitating diseases such as malaria and yellow fever—allowed European imperialists to advance from the coastal regions of Asia and Africa, where they had remained for centuries, deep into the interiors of these continents.

Within Europe the military impact of the Industrial Revolution arrived in force during the mid-nineteenth century, but under false colors. Most general staffs and commentators believed that the increasing industrialization of warfare would make conflicts more decisive. A few thought otherwise, citing examples from non-European wars, such as the American Civil War (1861–1865) and the Boer War (1899–1902). But the seeming decisiveness of the short wars of German unification (1866–1871), fought by the Prussian army against the Danes, Austrians, and French, suggested that "first-class" armies, once engaged, would quickly battle to a decision. Moreover, the direct and indirect economic expense of a conflict made the concept of a long war unthinkable to some critics. The costs of an extended clash would most certainly outweigh the likely gains. Economic competition was overtaking military rivalry. Surely, the European states, with their seemingly ever-expanding prosperity and popular governments, had entered a new and enlightened era.

But in 1914, the realities of industrial-era warfare shattered the self-confidence of the Europeans, dealing them a psychic blow from which they have never truly recovered. They soon discovered that conflict among modern industrial powers was more destructive and costly than pre-industrial warfare and far from decisive. The attritional nature of warfare reasserted itself, and the targets for that attrition were not only the opposing military force, but also the enemy state and supporting society. While neither of the two world wars lasted as long as the Seven Years' War (1756–1763), the somewhat shorter chronological extent of the conflicts was more than offset by colossal casualty lists, widespread destruction, enormous economic costs, and often societal disintegration. The first of the two world wars (1914–1918) led directly to the collapse of the German, Austro-Hungarian, Russian, and Ottoman empires. The Second World War led to the redivision of Germany (united in 1871), the physical destruction of most of central and eastern Europe, and the deaths of not only millions of combatants, but also scores of millions of noncombatants, often as the result of campaigns of intentional and industrialized genocide.

Central to the history of this entire period is Germany. Between 1859 and 1945, there were few inter-European wars, and none of them general, that did not directly involve the Germans. Several peripheral conflicts took place in the Italian and Balkan peninsulas. The Second War of Italian Independence (1859) pitted France and Sardinia against the Austrian Empire. The Third War of Italian Independence (1866) pitted the newly unified national state of Italy against Austria and was fought as part of the latter's struggle against Prussia. The Serbo-Turkish War (1876), Russo-Turkish War (1877–1878), and the First and Second Balkan Wars (1912–1913) completed the process, underway since the late seventeenth century, of rolling back the European frontiers of the "the sick man of Europe"—the Ottoman Empire.

Germany set the military example for the states of industrial Europe. By the 1870s, the successes of the Germans were influencing not only the militaries of Europe, but also those of the entire world. General staffs modeled on the German system proliferated. Reserve systems multiplied. The Ottomans, who had survived the nineteenth century primarily through the support of Great Britain, looked to the German Empire as their new ally. Even the American military shed its fascination with things Napoleonic and French, epitomized by the kepis of the Civil War period, and embraced the *pickelhauben*. The Prussian-German general staff was the first modern bureaucracy to become the object of fascination, imitation, and eventually fear and loathing. At the end of the Great War, the Entente outlawed its reestablishment. At the end of the Second World War, the victorious Allies dismantled the entire Prussian state apparatus.

Throughout the period of this study, Europe, and much of the rest of the world, stood in awe of the Prussian-German military. Innumerable states sought to emulate what Robert M. Citino has termed "the German Way of War," albeit often with rather limited success. Little wonder: even the Germans, to their great dismay, could not equal the results they achieved in 1866 and 1870.

The conventional images of the world wars remain subject to a degree of confusion and distortion. In general, people view the First World War as an indecisive struggle marked by attrition and outright slaughter, and epitomized by trench warfare and inconsequential "big pushes." By contrast, we often think of the Second World War as a conflict notable for its decisiveness and mobility. You can visit Europe and easily spot the scars of the western front and its trenches on the physical landscape. But that is only because Europeans did not rebuild fields in Flanders the way they rebuilt central European cities leveled by aerial bombing between 1939 and 1945. The reality is that both world wars were horribly destructive struggles of *attrition*. Maps are nothing more than spatial data—a measure of a conflict's progress. Maps of the western front during the 1914–1918 war reinforce the popular image of deadlock, whereas maps of the 1939–1945 war reveal rapid changes of position and blitzkrieg. But if you examine other and more important measures of data—calendars, casualty statistics, civilian deaths, wholesale physical destruction, and wealth expended—the Second World War was a longer and far more costly war of attrition that ended only with the final collapse of the German National Socialist state.

In fact, the German-dominated near century from 1859 to 1945 was the bloodiest of eras, if not also the cruelest, in the history of mankind. In the two world wars alone, at least seventy-five million people—military and civilians—died. Countless others, numbered in the millions, met their ends in other small, and not-so-small, wars in Europe, Asia, Africa, the Middle East, and the Americas. Great empires such as the Hapsburg, Romanov, Hohenzollern, and Ottoman collapsed. When Adolf Hitler's rapacious Third Reich threatened to plunge the world into a savage dark age, only history's bloodiest and most costly conflict delivered mankind from the abyss of a global Dachau. The Soviet Union and its archipelago of Gulags survived, born in 1917 with the demise of the Tsarist empire, only to collapse a half century and tens of millions of lives later.

Even after 1945, despite Germany's defeat in a pair of world wars, the fascination with the German military nevertheless continued. United States military professionals read Carl von Clausewitz and studied the wartime operations of their former enemy. American army officers became fluent in the jargon of what could be termed *germilspeak*, spewing tongue twisters in the original German—*bewegungskrieg, schwerpunckt, auftragstaktik, fingerspitzengefuhl*, and phrases such as *klotzen nicht kleckern*. Even the helmets of the American soldiers fighting in Iraq and Afghanistan share (albeit, for sound safety reasons) the basic shape of the successor of the pickelhauben, the *stahlhelm*. For the foreseeable future, like it or not, we will associate the Germans with the world wars and European warfare in the industrial age.

Unfortunately, the military legacy of the Germans is often overstated, at times grossly. The German military performed exceptionally at the tactical and operational levels of warfare. There is, as a result, much to be learned from the study of German doctrine and methods. But at the strategic level, despite the reputations and seeming brilliance of Clausewitz and the famed German general staff, Germany's military strategy failed to evolve along with the growing power of the state. That failure undermined, and eventually undid, whatever miracles the Germans achieved at the tactical and operational levels. The proverbial bottom line was that the Germans convinced themselves and many others that quick and decisive victories were achievable in the age of industrialized warfare. They were not. The belief that such victories were possible led the Germans to plunge Europe, and the entire world, into a pair of ghastly world wars that killed millions of people, nearly destroyed Europe, and in 1945 left Germany shrunken and once more divided. It is impossible even to speculate how history would have progressed and how different the world would look today had the Germans been more cautious in their employment of military power.

Walter Millis wrote in his 1956 classic *Arms and Men* that by 1815 war had begun "to lose its one virtue—its power of decision." Millis, of course, had the advantage of retrospection, writing as he did after the end of the Second World War. But there were others who in the decades before the Great War foresaw the realities of modern inter-European war. In 1898, Ivan Bloch, a Pole who had helped develop the Russian railway system, published *La Guerre Future* (which appeared in English as *Is War Now Impossible*), a six-volume study of contemporary warfare. Bloch argued that a combination of new weaponry and entrenchments would benefit the defender to the extent that maneuver and assault would become hopeless. If war did begin, it would quickly become a stalemate that would only be won after an extensive process of attrition and the exhaustion of the society of one of the belligerents, perhaps to the point of famine, collapse, and political revolution. In 1910, Norman Angell published *The Great Illusion*—the "illusion" being the belief held by many who saw a grand European war on the horizon. Angell argued that the nature of the international financial system would either prevent an outbreak of war or force a conflict to a rapid conclusion.

Admittedly, there were many reasons to discount the warnings of Bloch and Angell, writing in Europe at the turn of the century. Neither were professional soldiers; they wrote as amateurs. There were many details in their works that were simply wrong, demonstrably so at the time and, especially, in retrospect. Angell's warning could be rejected as those of a pacifist. But there were also soldiers who proffered similar warnings, most notably Field Marshal Helmuth von Moltke (the elder), the victor of Germany's wars of unification, who, in his final speech to the Reichstag in 1890, noted:

> The age of cabinet war is behind us—all we have now is people's war. . . . Gentlemen, if the war that has been hanging over our heads now for more than ten years like the sword of Damocles—if this war breaks out, then its duration and its end will be unforeseeable. The greatest powers of Europe, armed as never before, will be going into battle with each other; not one of them can be crushed so completely in one or two campaigns that it

will admit defeat, will be compelled to conclude peace under hard terms, and will not come back, even if it is a year later, to renew the struggle. Gentlemen, it may be a war of seven years' or of thirty years' duration—and woe to him who sets Europe alight, who first puts the fuse to the powder keg.

Obviously, Bloch, Angell, and others who considered a major war a near impossibility were mistaken, because war not only began, but also failed to end quickly. Nevertheless, Bloch's and Angell's rational analyses of why war should have been unthinkable *were* accurate; by the twentieth century, the prospect of an industrialized war resolving in some cost-effective manner any of the great-power problems in Europe was an illusion. The tragedy was that it took two world wars and millions of deaths before Europeans reached that same conclusion. And the fact remains that it was primarily, though by no means exclusively, the Germans who through their excellence managed to convince themselves and many others—not once, but twice—that the possibilities of rapid and relatively inexpensive decision were not chimerical, but within reach. The wars that afflicted Europe and the world between 1859 and 1945 were, undeniably, the German wars.

CHAPTER I

The Wars of Italian and German Unification

DURING THE MID-NINETEENTH CENTURY, the industrializing world struggled with innumerable problems—rapid industrialization, population expansion, growth of the state, and political turmoil. The United States descended into a bloody civil war. In Europe, the principal political factor undermining stability was not the issue of slavery, but the question of nationalism. The rise of nationalistic sentiments undermined the legitimacy of the old dynastic regimes, many of which—most notably the Ottoman, Romanov, and Hapsburg empires—were multinational in character. National forces ultimately shattered the European empires at the close of the 1914–1918 war, and nationalism as a political force continues to play a major role in European, and non-European, politics to the present day.

In 1859, only one of the major continental European powers could be termed a true nation-state—France. Its population was overwhelmingly French, and the majority of French-speaking Europeans found themselves within the borders of their state. Prussia could be termed a nation-state, but only to a degree because its population included a sizeable minority of Poles. Moreover, millions of German-speaking Europeans found themselves living as members of other states, both small and large. The Austrian Empire was a polyglot realm, ruled by German-Austrians (primarily) and Hungarians, but containing millions of Czechs, Poles, Slovaks, Ukrainians, and assorted other Slavic peoples in the Balkans. Other Christian Slavs in the Balkans still lived under the heel of the Ottoman Turks. To the east, the Russian Empire was an enormous multinational operation, containing within its European borders Finns, Latvians, Estonians, Lithuanians, Poles, Byelorussians, Ukrainians, and other minorities.

The increasing tendency of European peoples to identify themselves, and often to organize themselves, politically along ethnic lines threatened the stability of the existing European order. Nationalism had come to the fore during the period following the French Revolution, and it had played a significant role in the revolutions that had swept across the continent in 1848. The political reaction that followed only temporarily squelched the forces at work. A decade later, stronger nationalistic forces emerged. These forces triggered a series of wars in central and eastern Europe that continued until the very eve of the Great War in 1914 that remapped the boundaries of the continent. The most significant of the national struggles centered on the question of the leadership and national political organization of the German-speaking people of central Europe. Would they be united? And if so, would it be under the banner of the Prussian or Austrian empires?

The first of the national wars began in 1859 when the Italian kingdom of Piedmont and Sardinia began its ultimately successful attempt to unify the states of the Italian peninsula. The Piedmontese undertook their efforts with the support of the French Empire of Napoleon III. The emperor, a nephew of Napoleon I, had pretensions of imperial greatness, but lacked virtually all of his uncle's talents. Italy had been the scene of General Bonaparte's early triumphs over the Austrians, who still dominated northern Italy.

In June 1859, at the battles of Magenta and Solferino, the French and their Italian allies defeated the Austrians and set in motion the convoluted and prolonged process that led to the unification of Italy under Piedmontese rule.

The campaign in northern Italy revealed that the two major European powers involved had thus far not only failed to grasp the realities of warfare in the middle of the nineteenth century, but also had forgotten far too many of the lessons learned more than a half century earlier on the bloody battlefields of Europe. The poorly prepared French army moved into northern Italy without its supply trains. Initially, little effort was made to exploit the logistical advantages offered by railroads. Staff work was shoddy. Despite the forethought given to French policy, the military campaign was one of improvisation, at which the French at least proved themselves superior to the Austrians. The battle of Solferino, one of the first to be fought by two armies equipped with rifled muskets, was a contest in mutual butchery that shocked even the vainglorious Napoleon III.

As the Austrians and French bludgeoned each other south of the Alps, to the north the Prussians carefully observed the progress of the campaign. The Prussian military had just completed a round of reorganization overseen by its then acting chief of the general staff, General Helmuth von Moltke. As a cautionary response to the French victories, the Prussians mobilized troops along the Rhine, employing for the first time their railroad net for that purpose. The result was less than spectacular, but Moltke and the Prussian general staff learned innumerable and invaluable lessons from the exercise.

The Prussians had established a general staff as one element of a series of military reforms in the aftermath of their defeat at the hands of Napoleon in 1806–1807. The purpose of the general staff was to compensate for the military talents that army commanders, be they of royal blood or not, might lack. A general staff was, as one historian termed it, an attempt to "institutionalize" in a collective body the brilliance, or something

Military Medicine in the Mid-Nineteenth Century

The technological and scientific advances of the Industrial Revolution that made the battlefield so lethal an arena initially failed to produce comparable advances in the area of military medicine. The major breakthroughs of the nineteenth century came later and primarily from scientists, not doctors. Concepts such as "germ theory," developed separately by the German Robert Koch and Frenchman Louis Pasteur, had yet to achieve full scientific acceptance, let alone be applied by military surgeons. The latter remained mostly amateurs (though often very caring and conscientious) in their approach to their craft, for they were as yet only on the threshold of true professionalism.

Military surgeons trained in medical schools of uneven quality. The typical school term might last only a few months, usually during the winter when the cold weather allowed study and practice on cadavers that would otherwise rot.

The good military surgeon would work with commanding officers to insist on hygiene within the camp. Cleanliness was a boon to healthiness, even if the intent was to prevent "bad air" from infecting the men. Nevertheless, infectious diseases could, and on occasion did, sweep through armies, especially in the tropics.

For the wounded soldier, treatment remained limited. Flesh wounds would be cleaned and dressed, and, if the job were done well and infection did not set in, there was a good chance the soldier would survive. Major wounds to the head or torso usually resulted in death, if not immediately, then in a matter of hours or, if the soldier were particularly unlucky, days. Survival after a wound to a limb was problematic. The large-caliber, soft lead bullets of the day would shatter the bones of an arm or leg. Surgical techniques were not advanced enough to repair such damage, and the usual practice was to amputate.

Fortunately for the soldiers of the mid-nineteenth century, surgeons did rely on anesthesia when it was available. A generation earlier, amputees were restrained and, if they were fortunate, plied with alcohol as they suffered through the brutal operation that could take between five and fifteen minutes, depending on the limb in question and the skill of the surgeon. Amputees in the mid-century wars were often (though not always) anesthetized with ether or chloroform. Such practices eased the already difficult tasks of the surgeon and lessened the chance that the amputee would succumb to shock. In the American Civil War, men whose limbs were amputated within twenty-four hours of their wounding had a survival rate of better than 50 percent.

A major development in the area of military medicine followed the June 1859 battle at Solferino, the bloodiest engagement fought in Europe since Waterloo. Among the civilian observers was the Swiss Jean Henri Dunant, who organized help for French and Austrian wounded. Dunant was so shocked and moved by the suffering of the wounded after the battle that he published *A Memory of Solferino* (1862), recounting his experiences and calling for the establishment of voluntary relief societies in all countries. The book's publication led, the following year, to the establishment of the International Committee for the Relief of the Wounded (subsequently called the International Red Cross) and in 1864 to the first Geneva Convention, at which the signatory states agreed to care for wounded soldiers, both friendly and enemy.

approximating it, of a commander such as Napoleon. The various divisions of the general staff spent their time preparing the army and themselves for war. They planned, they mapped, they studied, and they wrote.

Moltke, who after December 1859 became the formal chief of the general staff, was a reflective man who studied the Italian campaign closely and even published his own account of the Franco-Austrian war. He drew several lessons from the campaign, among them the need for rapid mobilization, improved coordination of the large armies taking the field, the development of comprehensive doctrine reinforced by training, and the promotion of aggressiveness and initiative at all levels of command.

As Moltke and the Prussian general staff prepared their army for war, Otto von Bismarck became the central political figure in the Prussian state in 1862. Over the next decade, he adroitly handled Prussia's diplomacy in a manner that allowed the state to unify most Germans under the Prussian crown through a series of short and localized wars.

Central to Bismarck's diplomacy was his effort to keep his most likely opponents diplomatically isolated. When revolution erupted in the Polish lands of the Russian Empire in 1863, the French and British attempted to convince the Austrians to intervene on behalf of the Poles. Bismarck countered by supporting the Russians and mobilizing an army to prevent the movements of Polish rebels across the border. This policy of aid to the tsar assured the Prussians of Russian neutrality during the coming decade.

By the 1860s, German nationalists had recovered from the shock of 1848 and were clamoring for political reform along nationalist lines. The first crisis came in Denmark, where two duchies, Schleswig and Holstein, became the focus of a dynastic struggle with international complications. The people of neither province wished to become part of Denmark proper, a development that seemed to be in the offing. And the fact that Holstein, along with Prussia and Austria, was a member of the German Confederation made war likely. Bismarck demonstrated his diplomatic dexterity, using the theme of pan-Germanism, to maneuver Austria into an alliance against Denmark—moreover, one powerful enough to deter other European powers from intervening on the Danes' behalf. The conflict thus remained isolated. In January 1864, the allies struck, and in six months the war was over. It mattered little to Bismarck that Prussia had to share the spoils with Austria. The latter controlled Holstein, while the Prussians took Schleswig. Bismarck knew that this Austrian prize would fall to Prussia during the course of the war that would soon follow the triumph over tiny Denmark.

Bismarck was already hard at work in his efforts to isolate the Austrians, as a preliminary move to a new war. In October 1865, the Prussian leader met the French emperor Napoleon

III at Biarritz. Bismarck may have suggested possible territorial gains along the Rhine or elsewhere if the French remained neutral in the event of war between Prussia and Austria. Bismarck next turned his attention to the Piedmontese, who had yet to drive the Austrians out of Venetia in northeastern Italy. Prussia concluded an offensive-defensive military alliance with Piedmont in April 1866.

No sooner had the ink dried on the agreement with the Piedmontese than Bismarck began a series of political maneuvers within the German Diet to provoke a war with Austria. By June 1866, the die was cast. While the Austrians were able to gain the support of several of the larger independent German states, most notably Hanover, Bavaria, and Saxony, France and Russia would stand by while the Prussians struck. The stage was set for the Austro-Prussian War, or Seven Weeks' War, of June–August 1866.

Even with the enemy isolated, the Prussians were outnumbered. The Austrians could mobilize nearly 250,000 men in Bohemia, while their German allies could put another 200,000 in the field. Almost another 300,000 troops were spread about in garrisons or in Italy. The Prussians could mobilize 400,000 men, although garrisons would consume about a quarter of these and another 50,000 were required to take the field against Hanover in the northwest. Moltke could hope, then, to mobilize about 250,000 men in the south against the Austrians and their Saxon allies. Despite the arithmetic, Moltke was confident of victory.

Moltke was perhaps the first truly modern—that is to say, nineteenth-century—military commander. He grasped the realities of the mid-century battlefield, if not completely, then certainly more deeply than most of his contemporaries. The advent of the modern industrial state meant that armies were larger and their firepower more deadly than heretofore. These two factors raised the risk that wars could easily become prolonged attritional struggles of the type that Prussia could not afford. To avoid such an outcome, which had been evident in the course of the American Civil War, he sought to use the fruits of

continued on page 23

Naval Warfare in the Age of Steam and Steel

By the late 1850s, the impact of the Industrial Revolution on navies and naval warfare brought the age of fighting sail to a close, albeit slowly. Steam propulsion, the screw propeller, armoring, shell guns, rifling, and iron and steel construction transformed the ship of war. Steam freed the warship from dependence on the wind, at first only in battle, but then gradually at the operational and strategic levels. The French launched their first armored steam warship—the *la Gloire*—in 1859. The British countered in 1861 with the *Warrior*, an iron-hulled, 400-foot-long, steam-driven man-of-war capable of fourteen knots and mounting thirty-eight 68-pounder naval guns.

During the American Civil War, the navies of the North and the South reflected the revolutionary changes overtaking naval establishments. The Federal navy continued to employ wooden sailing men-of-war, albeit outfitted with auxiliary steam power. The infamous Confederate raiders, such as the *Alabama*, likewise relied on their sails for cruising and steam as a combat auxiliary. The principle armament of these raiders, and the ships that hunted them, was massive, centrally mounted, rifled pivot guns capable of firing to port or starboard. For coastal defense, the South clad many of its wooden ships, such as the *Virginia*, with iron and dispensed with sails. The North countered with its own ironclads, as well as several classes of iron-constructed and -armored "monitors" that mounted heavy, muzzle-loading cannon in powered turrets.

This contest between the gun and armor placed a premium on penetration, not explosive power. To defeat armor, navies adopted ever-larger rifled cannon capable of hurling shot, increasingly designed to pierce armor plate, with greater range, accuracy, and penetrating ability. Rifling, in turn, led to longer barrels, which promoted a shift to breech-loading mechanisms in the 1860s.

During the decade after the American Civil War, the "modern" warship began to emerge. In 1872, the Italians launched the *Duilio* with armored decks and echeloned turrets. The following year, the British commissioned the *Devastation*, which established the basic pattern followed into the twentieth century.

As engagement ranges increased, sighting naval guns of different size became next to impossible. The chaotic patterns of splashes made the correction of individually sighted guns impractical. The solution involved salvo firing by batteries of uniform type, a development that led inexorably to the all-big-gun battleship—the most famous of which was the Royal Navy's *Dreadnought*, launched in February 1906. The 17,900-ton ship mounted ten twelve-inch guns in its main battery and was the first man-of-war powered by steam turbines. The *Dreadnought* pattern remained unchanged for forty years.

The industrial age also wrought a revolution in ship types and tactics. Dreadnoughts replaced the wooden ship of the line; protected and armored cruisers took up the frigate's role as commerce raider and scout. New types of light, fast, but deadly smaller ships milled about the battle line, waiting for the opportunity to disrupt and to weaken the enemy's formation.

Central to this revolution was the self-propelled, or "automotive," torpedo. In the late 1860s, the Englishmen Robert Whitehead refined an Austrian design and manufactured the first automotive torpedo. Until the development of effective internal combustion engines later in the century, the preferred means of delivering the new automotive torpedo was small, steam-powered surface craft termed "torpedo boats." The ability of these smallish ships to sink a ship of the line, a capability lesser sailing-age warships had never possessed, added a new dimension to naval tactics. To screen the battle line, navies developed "torpedo-boat destroyers" and "light" cruisers, whose job was to counter the destroyers and which, armed with their own torpedoes, eventually supplanted the torpedo boats.

By the beginning of the Great War in 1914, navies had assumed a new pattern. Warships were steel constructed and steam driven. Dreadnoughts mounted long-ranged, rifled breechloaders, while new classes of smaller ships screened and scouted for the fleet.

The Industrial Revolution also dramatically changed strategic geography. Steam power shortened cruising radii: gone were the days of the six-month cruise under sail. Navies now needed overseas bases, particularly coaling stations, and this factor had a regressive impact on strategy and planning, and accelerated the centuries-old trend toward European imperialism.

Because the new ships were more expensive, fleets became smaller. The Industrial Revolution also spawned a new European challenger to British naval supremacy, Germany, and two non-European centers of naval power—the United States and Japan.

At the tactical level, technology offered solutions to old problems while simultaneously presenting new threats. Dreadnoughts could cover their vulnerable bows and sterns and apply a substantial portion of their fighting power forward and aft, although commanders still arranged their fleets in a line-ahead formation to maximize firepower. Steam power eased the problem of maneuvering a fleet. Wider arcs of fire made crossing the enemy's *T* a favored fleet tactic—one permitting a deadly concentration of firepower against the head of an enemy column in a manner impossible during the age of sail. But an enemy fleet armed with big guns, once within visible range, posed an immediate, rather than a potential, threat. While sea battles remained two dimensional (until the advent, later in the century, of effective submarines and aircraft), the presence of torpedo boats and destroyers made the first late-nineteenth- and early-twentieth-century naval encounters complex affairs. Every man-of-war possessed the capability to strike a deadly blow. The smallest and most inexpensive torpedo boat could sink the most powerful and costly dreadnought.

If the advent of the new industrial technology at sea increased the demands on naval commanders, that same technology offered few compensating advances in the area of command and control. At the strategic and operational levels of warfare, the telegraph revolutionized the contours of naval command and control. For the first time in history, the submarine telegraph offered admiralties, and the governments they served, the prospect of commanding and controlling fleets and squadrons operating on distant stations. But into the twentieth century, signal flags and doctrine remained central to fleet command and control at the tactical level.

The first major European test of the new tactics for steam-powered and armored ships came off the Adriatic island of Lissa on 20 July 1866, during the Austro-Italian War. The battle, the largest naval encounter since the 1827 battle of Navarino, was a confused affair from which naval officers drew few lessons.

The Italian admiral Count Carlo Pellion di Persano was a pusillanimous man who ranks as one of the worst commanders in the annals of naval history. He decided that the island of Lissa offered an excellent forward base for a blockade of the Austrian coast. Persano sailed south and reached the island on 17 July. He foolishly waited several days before cutting the telegraph cable that linked the island to the Austrian mainland. On 20 July, as Persano finally prepared to land his invasion force, one of his scouts appeared on the horizon making the signal for "suspicious" ships to the northwest. The Austrians, alerted by the uncut telegraph, had arrived.

While Persano's force was the stronger, outnumbering the Austrians in every quantitative category, the Italians were in trouble. Their fleet steamed toward the southwest in line-abreast formation as the Austrians came into view, heading on a southeasterly course. Persano made the signal for his ironclads to reform into line ahead on a course toward the northeast—directly across the path of the Austrian fleet.

Rear Admiral Baron Wilhelm von Tegetthoff, a generation younger than Persano, commanded the Austrians bearing down on the Italian line. The Austrian commander was an aggressive man who, despite being outnumbered and outgunned, intended to bring on a mêlée. Tegetthoff deployed his ships into three successive wedges.

Tegetthoff's decisiveness was matched by Persano's vacillation. The Italian commander at the last moment decided to switch his flag from the *Re d'Italia* to the new British-built *Affondatore*, a powerful ship that carried two turreted 300-pounder muzzle loaders and a twenty-six-foot-long ram. As the Italian flagship, the fourth vessel in line, slowed to allow the transfer, the three ships ahead continued on course, while those behind the *Re d'Italia* reduced speed. As a result, a wide gap opened in the Italian line. Worse yet, Persano's captains were unaware that their admiral had changed ships and continued to look to the *Re d'Italia*, from which Persano's flag still flew, for signals that never came. Nor did the *Affondatore* carry a complete set of signal flags.

Tegetthoff did not rely on signals; he personally led his fleet. His flagship—the *Archduke Ferdinand Max*—was at the point of the leading wedge. As the Austrians bore down upon the Italian line, Tegetthoff made only two signals:

"Ironclads, charge the enemy and sink him," followed by "Ram everything gray!" Once the battle began, Tegetthoff trusted to the initiative of his captains.

About 1050 that morning the Austrians broke the Italian line, or, to be accurate, steamed through the gap created by Persano. What followed was a chaotic battle; smoke produced by the heavy guns and more than a score of steam-powered men-of-war cast a blackened pall that reduced visibility to, at best, 200 yards. Amidst the confusion, Persano steamed about in the *Affondatore*, signaling madly to subordinates intently watching the *Re d'Italia*.

After about thirty minutes of action, neither fleet had secured an advantage. Despite an excess of expended shot and shell, few ships were actually hit. The tide finally began to turn when the Austrians concentrated their attack against the rear of the Italian line. The old Kaiser, a ninety-two-gun wooden ship of the line, rammed the *Re di Portogallo*, shocking its crew, though not damaging the Italian ironclad. Under heavy Austrian gunfire, the Italian armored gunboat *Palestro* caught fire. Then Tegetthoff's flagship rammed the American-built *Re d'Italia*, punching a hole in the side that in minutes sent the Italian flagship to the bottom, where it was soon followed by the *Palestro*.

Persano withdrew; the battle of Lissa was over. Tegetthoff, his fleet slower and weaker than the surviving Italian force, chose not to pursue. The Austrians had 38 men killed and another 138 wounded. The Italians lost two ships and suffered nearly 800 casualties, including over 600 dead.

The symbol of the battle of Lissa immediately became the ram bow. Because the Austrians won the day following the ramming of the Italian flagship, ramming became an accepted, and in some quarters the principal, tactic in naval warfare. Such tactics appear idiotic in retrospect; at Lissa the Austrians and Italians actually had little success ramming opponents under actual battle conditions. But the reality was that they had an even more difficult time sinking ships with gunfire.

The lesson that the gun had taken the measure of armor became evident during the Sino-Japanese War of 1894–1895. At the battle of the Yalu, 17 September 1894, the Japanese fought and won a long-range battle during which gunnery predominated.

> Given the remarkable advances in the technology of warfare at sea, the practice of actual naval combat during the century that followed Trafalgar (1805) was too limited to draw many clear lessons, although a few trends were apparent. The tempo of the naval battle under steam was faster. The end of reliance on the wind for mobility, the marked increase in the speed of ships, and the ever-lengthening ranges of the big guns placed a premium on quick decision-making. Steam-driven and armored line-of-battle ships dominated, but no longer monopolized, the engagement. Torpedo boats and destroyers, while they had no place in the line, were important and deadly fleet assets. The era of "combined arms" had come to naval warfare. In the battles of the Russo-Japanese War, the largest of the era, battleships, cruisers, destroyers, and torpedo boats played important roles in a contest in which a rising Asian power defeated a European empire.

the Industrial Revolution, namely the railroads and telegraph, to mobilize his armies quickly along the frontier. Those forces would then advance aggressively to engage the enemy army along its front, but always seeking its flanks and rear in an effort to encircle and destroy it.

Moltke knew, through a simple study of the railway systems of the two states, that he could mobilize his armies far more quickly than the Austrians, giving the Prussians an enormous initial advantage. On the diplomatic front, Bismarck could calmly allow the Austrians and their German allies to mobilize first, making them appear to be the aggressors, thereby lessening the likelihood that the war would spread. Militarily, Moltke, despite the delay, expected to be able to knock Saxony out of the war, force the mountain passes into Bohemia, and then to concentrate superior numbers against the Austrian forces moving north.

In 1866, the Prussians had the best railway system on the continent. In many cases, military, and not commercial, considerations had determined the direction and extent of these developments. Five double-tracked Prussian railways led to the border with Austrian Bohemia, whereas the paucity of Austrian railways on the other side of the border would force the Austrians to detrain further south and to march their own forces into Bohemia.

If the Prussians held the advantage at the strategic and operational levels, the same was not true at the tactical level. Prussian infantry was superior to the Austrian. Prussian soldiers carried the rifled and breech-loaded Dreyse "needle gun." The advent of breech-loaded rifles increased the rate of fire of the Prussian infantry and, in theory, allowed the weapon to be fired while its owner was prone and under cover. But the "needle," or firing pin, of the Dreyse weapon tended to bend or break. The tolerances of the breech were such that after a few firings, gas and flame escaped to such an extent that they would burn the face of any soldier foolish enough to raise the weapon for well-aimed fire. As a result, the Prussian rifles were often fired from the hip, thereby wasting much of the accuracy gained by rifling. Nevertheless, rates of fire remained high, and, whatever the faults of the weapon, it was superior to the rifled, muzzle-loaded muskets carried by the Austrians. Their tactics revolved around shock and the use of the bayonet, rather than firepower. Conversely, the Austrians fielded more effective cavalry and artillery units than the Prussians. Austrian horsemen traditionally received excellent training and equipment, and they were markedly superior to the cavalry arm fielded by the Prussians. One lesson the Austrians had learned during their campaign in northern Italy in 1859, where Napoleon III's gunners had demonstrated their excellence, was the need to reform their artillery. This they did, adopting rifled, though still muzzle-loaded, artillery and developing more aggressive tactics to employ these guns in direct support of the infantry. On the eve of the war, the Prussians had developed a technologically superior steel, breech-loaded artillery piece, but they had yet to deploy these new guns in great numbers or to determine how the guns could best be used on the battlefield.

Nevertheless, in Moltke's mind, Prussian superiority lay primarily with the training of the officer corps and, more broadly, the army. He believed that his army was better prepared for the war it was about to face and that its commanders, from top to bottom, would prove to be more able than their Austrian counterparts to adapt to the contingencies of war as they developed.

On 2 June 1866, Moltke received permission from the king to issue orders direct to the armies in the field. On 7 June the Prussians overran Austrian Holstein. On the twenty-ninth, the army of Hanover surrendered to a Prussian force.

The main campaign, of course, was that waged in the south. Moltke had three armies moving along converging axes into Bohemia. On the right wing, the Army of the Elbe marched through Saxony; the First Army moved due south from Gorlitz; the Second Army moved southeast from Schweidnitz. Dresden, the Saxon capital, fell on 19 June, and the Saxon army retreated south into Bohemia to join the Austrians. In Berlin, Moltke monitored the movements of the three armies via the telegraph, watching anxiously, afraid that he might have miscalculated and that a concentrated Austrian force would emerge from the fog of war to fall upon a single, isolated Prussian column.

The initial skirmishes in Bohemia began on 27 June. Tactically, the Prussians experienced few marked successes and, in several cases, got the worst of the engagement. But collectively, the reports from the front indicated to Moltke that the Austrians had yet to concentrate their army.

To the Austrian commander, Alexander von Benedek, the pattern of these skirmishes revealed that his own plans for concentration, and by extension the campaign, had been overtaken by events. The troubled Austrian field marshal ordered his army to concentrate near the town of Königgrätz, along the upper Elbe River.

Because of the superiority of the Austrian cavalry, the Prussians kept their own in reserve instead of deploying it forward to scout. As a result, their armies stumbled forward without a clear picture of the Austrian movements. When Moltke, by this time at a forward headquarters in Bohemia, learned that the Austrians were reportedly concentrating near Königgrätz, he assumed that

continued on page 28

The Battles of Mars-la-Tour and Gravelotte-St. Privat, 16–18 August 1870

In mid-August 1870, the French armies commanded by marshals Bazaine and MacMahon had escaped the trap Moltke had set for them near Saarbrucken and were retreating toward the fortresses of Verdun and Toul. Three Prussian armies marched westward, hoping to engage the French before they could escape. On 16 August, the Second Army's III Corps, commanded by Lieutenant General Constantine von Alvensleben, having bypassed Metz to the south, marched north to cut the roads leading west from the town. Along the stretch of road from Vionville to Mars-la-Tour, the Prussians encountered large bodies of French troops. Initially, Alvensleben suspected that he had caught up with the French rear guard, but as the situation developed, he quickly concluded that he had unwittingly placed his corps into the retreat path of Bazaine's army.

Alvensleben knew that the 30,000 men of his corps had to be heavily outnumbered. In fact, during the course of the day, the French would throw nearly 100,000 men at the exposed Prussian corps. Nevertheless, given the situation, the immediate task of III Corps was to attempt to hold firm, block the road, and wait until reinforcements arrived. This Alvensleben proceeded to do, personally and at great risk, directing the battle while his chief of staff raced back to bring up the rest of the army.

Despite the fact that little support reached Alvensleben during the day, III Corps clung to its exposed position. Alvensleben, well aware of the capabilities of the Chassepot-armed French soldiers, husbanded his own infantry whenever possible and relied on his Krupp guns—the quick firing, steel breech-loaders—to hold the French at bay. When the situation looked grave late in the day, Alvensleben launched elements of a Prussian heavy cavalry division against the French line near Mars-la-Tour. The Prussians suffered 50 percent casualties, but the charge—the last successful charge in European military history—broke the French line and helped to secure the town and anchor the Prussian left. At the end of the day, both sides had suffered about 16,000 casualties, a figure that represented slightly more than half of the strength of III Corps. But Alvensleben had held his position, the road remained blocked, and reinforcements were beginning to arrive.

On 17 August, elements of Moltke's First and Second Armies closed on III Corps and took up positions in support along an east-west axis that paralleled the road. But Bazaine, in a move that surprised Moltke, although it made a French escape somewhat less likely, pulled his line back toward Metz and established a strong position that ran from St. Privat in the north to Gravelotte in the south.

On the morning of 18 August, the Germans had to redress their lines and wheel their corps to face east. This took several hours. When the action finally began, somewhat prematurely, elements of the Prussian IX Corps advanced in a fashion that left several artillery batteries exposed. A sharp and effective French counterattack cost the Prussians four of their Krupp guns.

The loss of the guns seemed to presage a sorry day for Moltke's armies. Throughout the rest of the day, the Prussians, ignoring the experience gained earlier at Spicherin and Wörth, launched fruitless and costly frontal attacks against the French left and center. The Chassepot-armed French troops, dug in or under cover in ravines and villages, shredded the attacking Prussian infantry.

Not until the afternoon did the tempo of the battle begin to shift toward the Prussians. The German left wing swung into action with the support of massed batteries of artillery. Gradually, the French line showed signs of weakening, and late in the afternoon the Prussian Guard Corps advanced. But the French were not yet ready to crack, and the Guards suffered horrendous casualties.

Nevertheless, under unremitting pressure the French right gradually collapsed, and the center ultimately gave way as the day ended. Moltke expected a French counterattack the following morning, but Bazaine instead chose the safety of the fortress of Metz.

Tactically, the battle of Gravelotte-St. Privat could be considered a draw. The Prussians lost over 20,000 men, 8,000 of them Guardsmen. French losses numbered between 12,000 and 13,000. Nevertheless, Moltke had achieved his purpose. Bazaine's force, the larger of the two French armies, was now trapped in Metz. Operationally and strategically, the series of battles fought between 16 and 18 August had all but ensured an ultimate Prussian victory.

they would do so on the east bank of the Elbe, lest they be forced to fight a battle with a river to their rear. Moltke directed the movement of his three armies accordingly, expecting to bring on a climactic battle of encirclement on the third or fourth of July. But Benedek had, in fact, concentrated on the west bank of the Elbe. As the Prussian right wing advanced, it collided unexpectedly with the Austrian left late on the afternoon of 2 July.

The battle that developed the next day—known as Sadowa or Königgrätz—was not fought according to Moltke's grand plan. Amidst the confusion, the Austrians held off, and occasionally even drove back, the attacking Prussian units. Nevertheless, in these encounters, the Austrian infantry generally suffered the heavier casualties, and gradually Benedek's army began to give way. The Austrian commander wisely ordered a retreat, which was ably covered by the Austrian cavalry. When the battle ended, the Austrians had 20,000 men killed or wounded and as many taken as prisoners. Prussian casualties had been lighter— about 10,000 men. But Moltke's plan to encircle and to destroy Benedek's army had failed.

The survival of the main Austrian army, combined with the defeat of the Piedmontese in northern Italy and rumblings from Paris that could presage a French intervention, convinced Bismarck to seek a quickly negotiated peace. The Prussian chancellor had made his point and humbled the Austrians; there was little to be gained by dismantling their empire or so humiliating them that they would seek revenge, possibly in alliance with Russia or France. In fact, Bismarck was already looking ahead to the possibility, if not likelihood, of a war with France. As a result, he accepted Napoleon III's 5 July offer of mediation.

Not surprisingly, the Austro-Prussian treaty, the Peace of Nikolsburg, of 26 July was far from draconian. The agreement involved subtle changes of political orientation for the German states—changes that left Prussia the dominant power. But the quest for German unification remained, and that unification would come only following a war with France.

The drift toward that struggle had already begun. In June and July 1866, Napoleon III attempted to exploit his position by negotiating for some German territory in return for his neutrality. Bismarck quickly rejected these efforts. The French next sought to gain German support for a takeover of Belgium. When the French foolishly agreed to place their proposals in writing, Bismarck saw that the missives made their way to London, thereby improving the chances of British neutrality should France and Prussia go to war.

Over the next several years, Bismarck continued his effort to tie the smaller German states politically, economically, and militarily to Prussia. Simultaneously, Moltke prepared the army for war with France. In 1867, a crisis over Luxembourg nearly brought France and Prussia to war. But the months passed as Bismarck worked to isolate France diplomatically. The following year, a new crisis developed, concerning a dynastic transition in Spain. The details of the complicated question of the "Hohenzollern candidacy" are unimportant. The relevant facts are simple: Napoleon III mishandled the affair, and Otto von Bismarck exploited those mistakes. By the summer of 1870, both France and Prussia eagerly sought war, each determined to humiliate the other. On 19 July 1870, France declared war on Prussia.

In the four years since the Austro-Prussian war, both France and Prussia had been digesting what they viewed as the most important lessons of that conflict. The Prussians focused on the superiority of the Austrian artillery and cavalry. By 1870, they had reequipped their artillery with steel, rapid-firing, breech-loading cannon and developed an aggressive tactical doctrine to employ these guns forward in support of the infantry. The Prussian cavalry arm likewise underwent marked improvement and was deemed capable of employment up front, both as a screening and a reconnaissance force. The French focused on the inferiority of the Austrian infantry arm. In response, they reequipped their infantry units with the Chassepot breech-loading rifle, a weapon far superior to the Prussians' Dreyse needle gun. The range of the French rifle was 1,600 meters, compared to the 600 of the Prussian weapon. Moreover, the Chassepot breech sealed securely, allowing the rifle to be aimed and fired more accurately from the shoulder. The French also adopted a new weapon, the mitrailleuse—an early machine gun. Fortunately for the Prussians, the French viewed these new weapons as artillery and organized them accordingly into batteries deployed in the rear.

So armed, both the French and Prussians entered the war optimistic about its outcome. Napoleon III decided to risk a confrontation on 15 July and declared war four days later. He planned to concentrate and deploy about 300,000 men in two wings and to advance toward the Rhine. The Prussians planned to mobilize about 475,000 men (including reservists) in three armies along a front running from the Moselle to the Rhine. Moltke, fully expecting a French advance, planned to encircle and to destroy Napoleon III's army near Saarbrucken.

Moltke's plan might well have succeeded had not the French stumbled into a skirmish with advance elements of the Prussian right wing near Saarbrucken. The two armies met in a meeting engagement at Spicheren on 6 August. The confused battle continued until nightfall; the Prussians suffered heavier casualties, but nevertheless held the field. That same day, on the French right, near Wörth, the armies also clashed in a second bloody engagement.

Napoleon had expected to find the Prussians along the Rhine, and their appearance near Saarbrucken was a cause for alarm. So, too, were the weight of the Prussian assaults early in the campaign. Because of the more efficient Prussian mobilization, Moltke already had 462,000 men at hand, while the French fielded only 270,000. Moreover, the French mobilization was chaotic, and the units at the front were often missing certain specialists, most notably their medical staffs.

Napoleon halted his advance and reorganized his forces into two armies commanded by marshals Patrice MacMahon and Achille Bazaine. Unfortunately, the French army organization, with its roots in the era of Napoleon I, did not include headquarters staffs between the corps level and that of the overall commander-in-chief—that is the emperor himself. As a result, MacMahon's and Bazaine's corps staffs had to double as army staffs, a role they would be expected to learn in the midst of a chaotic campaign.

The French were now in full retreat: Bazaine through Metz toward Verdun, and MacMahon farther south toward Toul. As the Prussians advanced, elements of their right wing found the gap between the French and swung around behind Bazaine. On 16 August, along the road from Vionville to Mars-La-Tour, an isolated Prussian corps held off the much stronger elements of Bazaine's army. The Prussian victory, owed primarily to its superiority in artillery, had not only driven a wedge between the two French armies, but also trapped Bazaine in Metz.

On 18 August, elements of Moltke's First and Second Armies attempted to drive the French into the city to complete their encirclement. In *the* major pitched battle of the war—Gravelotte-St. Privat—the Prussians launched initial attacks that stalled in the face of the superior firepower of the French infantry. Nevertheless, weight of numbers and better use of the Prussian artillery late in the day gave the Germans the victory they sought.

The French were now beset by grave uncertainty. Napoleon believed that the proper course of action was to retreat with MacMahon's army to Paris. But several of his advisors, most notably his wife, the empress Eugenie, advised against such a move for political reasons: an admission of defeat would bring the regime to an end. Instead, Napoleon directed MacMahon to attempt the relief of Metz, where the larger of the two French field armies was trapped.

Unfortunately for the emperor, Moltke was well served by both his cavalry and reports in French newspapers; he was able not only to check MacMahon's moves, but also to outmaneuver the French and to trap them in the small fortress town of Sedan, astride the Meuse River.

On 1 September, the Prussian Third Army maneuvered to complete the encirclement, while the French made several heroic but vain efforts to break out. MacMahon was severely wounded early in the day, furthering the confusion in the French ranks. By late afternoon, the superior Prussian artillery turned Sedan into a deathtrap. Napoleon III drew the proper conclusions and surrendered. French casualties totaled over 100,000, most of whom, including the emperor himself, were prisoners of war. German losses totaled 9,000. Moltke finally had won the annihilative (*vernichtungsschlacht*) battle of encirclement he had sought since 1866.

Nevertheless, the Prussian victories did not bring an immediate end to the war. Revolution broke out in Paris as the empire of Napoleon III disintegrated. The Prussians and their German allies conducted a prolonged siege of the French capital. On 27 October, Bazaine surrendered Metz and another 140,000 men. On 18 January, in the Hall of Mirrors at King Louis XIV's palace at Versailles, the Prussians proclaimed the establishment of the Second German Empire. On 28 January, the French garrison of Paris, its food supplies all but expended, surrendered.

The results of the Franco-Prussian war were many. France, an empire, became a republic. The Prussian king became the emperor of a new national German empire. The destruction of French power allowed the Italians to complete the unification of their country. But whereas Bismarck had been reluctant to humiliate the Austrians in 1866, he showed far less restraint with the French. The Germans levied an indemnity of 5 billion francs and annexed the French provinces of Alsace and Lorraine.

The technologies of the Industrial Revolution had a substantive, though uneven, impact on the wars fought in the mid-nineteenth century. Economic and demographic expansion enabled states to raise ever-larger armies and to sustain them in the field. The railroad and the telegraph permitted those states to mobilize troops and to deploy them with incredible rapidity. On 6 August 1870, elements of the East Prussian I Corps were in action at Spicherin thirty-six hours after entraining at Königsberg, in far away East Prussia. On the battlefield itself, the greater rates of fire, accuracy, and lethality of infantry and artillery weapons created innumerable tactical dilemmas.

Nevertheless, not all states shared evenly in these developments. The Prussians were the first to master the use of railways and a general staff, but the French fielded the most effective infantry weapon of the era. This uneven development was true within Europe and even more so beyond the continent, where native troops proved increasingly unable to compete with even small well-armed European forces. There were also gaps in the impact of the new military technology. The gaps were most acute at the tactical level, where commanders, despite the increased complexity of battle, had no new means at their disposal for controlling the armies they commanded, and still relied on messengers and aides.

Military asymmetry (i.e., falling behind in the technology race) became a grave danger. The Austro-Prussian War of 1866 was the first modern inter-European war in which technological disparities could be said to have influenced the outcome of the conflict.

The mid-century wars fought in Europe, as well as in North America, also demonstrated the increasing superiority of the defensive. Europeans had not ignored these warnings. As early as 1865, Moltke had accepted the superiority of the defensive at the tactical level. His continued emphasis on the offensive reflected not ignorance, but a calculated decision to trump the tactical realities at the operational and strategic levels of warfare. There remained flanks to be turned. The infliction of high casualties could still gut an opponent's army. And Prussian military successes in 1866 and 1870 all but ensured that the major European armies emerged from the era likewise committed to the offensive. In so doing, they were not, as it is often said, ignoring the lessons of the mid-century wars, but embracing them. By 1914, all the major European states had developed a Prussian-style general staff, integrated reserve systems, and railroad nets constructed for military use; they had improved their infantry and artillery arms, and expanded the size of their field armies. These developments precluded technological asymmetry, but in the resultant symmetry lay the risks of stalemate. Larger armies could mean that there would be no flanks to be turned. Effective reserve systems made it difficult to kill soldiers more quickly than they could be replaced. Extensive alliance systems barred the diplomatic isolation that had left France and Austria so vulnerable.

CHAPTER II

The Road to Sarajevo

ON 18 JANUARY 1871, WITH THE PROCLAMATION OF THE Second German Empire in the Hall of Mirrors at Versailles, the balance of power within Europe came undone. The swift Prussian defeats of Austria and France had secured German unification, sans Austria, but had also demonstrated that no single European power could hope to check the newly unified empire on the battlefield. Worse yet for the balance of power, over the next forty years, the population of Imperial Germany would expand by 50 percent and virtually every measure of growth would increase between 300 percent (exports) and 1,200 percent (steel).

Nevertheless, the newly unified Germans found themselves anxious rather than secure; they were surrounded by potential enemies. To survive, Germany's leaders understood that they needed to continue to improve the general effectiveness of their military forces vis-à-vis those of neighboring countries, to further expand their army and the railway net that served it in wartime, and to conduct an active and adept foreign policy to prevent an anti-German alliance of major powers. Each of these issues posed significant challenges for the generals and statesmen of the Second Empire.

The German army maintained its qualitative edge during the decades after the Franco-Prussian War. The Germans continually reequipped their army with the newest infantry and artillery weapons, including more machine guns than any of the other powers had. They stressed realistic and large-scale maneuvers, the initiative of officers throughout the entire chain of command, aerial reconnaissance, and wireless technology. The army experimented with new tactics and a more open order on the battlefield to reduce casualties. The reserve system continued to expand and improve to the point that reserve infantry divisions would be employed in the front lines at the start of any major war. The army that took the field in 1914 was far superior to that of 1870. But so, too, were the opposing armies aligned against the Reich. The French, Russians, and British, after witnessing the German victories of the mid-century, mimicked the German way of war to various degrees. The Russian and French armies, most especially, followed the German lead and improved their military effectiveness markedly. While the Germans continued to hold a distinct qualitative edge in 1914, it was not as great a margin of superiority they had possessed in 1870.

Railroads were a key measure of military preparedness in the industrial age. Rail systems remained central to mobilization and the various war plans of the major powers. All the continental powers increased the size of their standing armies and reserve components by lengthening soldiers' time of service or by expanding the number of reserve cadres. Larger armies required more railways, locomotives, and rolling stock for both deployment and supply. As Germany, Austria-Hungary, Russia, Great Britain, and France expanded their reserve systems, they likewise expanded their rail systems. These expansions lessened the amount of time it took forces to mobilize, and they increased the number of troops, especially reserve formations, which would be available for operations in the initial stage of a conflict. Overall, the length of European railways nearly tripled between 1870 and 1914—from 105,000 kilometers to 290,000 kilometers. But the rate of increase for the Germans was less marked than that of France and Russia. As an example, the number of German soldiers moved each day over the various lines reaching the frontier with France in 1914 was over 400 percent larger than the number moved in 1870. But the count of French troops moving along the lines increased by between 600 and 700 percent. By 1914, the Russians could move 360 trains per day toward the frontiers facing the Austro-Hungarian Empire in Poland and Galicia; the Austrians could move only 153. In short, as the decades passed, French and Russian improvements outpaced those of the Germans, who were unable to maintain the margins of superiority they had held in 1870.

The Germans faced their greatest challenges in the diplomatic realm. As long as they could prevent the other great powers from forging an anti-German alliance, the Reich would remain secure, even if the French or Russian militaries improved, expanded, and mobilized more quickly. No single power could hope to take on Germany.

The competing alliance systems that gradually emerged, with Germany and Austria-Hungary aligned against France, Russia, and Great Britain, were neither "natural" nor preordained. For example, the Germans had innumerable opportunities between 1870 and 1914 to prevent the formation of the Franco-Russian alliance, to lessen British hostility, and to avoid a war on multiple fronts.

Several factors did shape, and stress, German diplomacy. Prussia had been lenient with the defeated Austrians but did not treat the French in a similar fashion. The latter were stripped of the provinces of Alsace and Lorraine, which had been part of France since the reign of Louis XIV, and saddled with a large reparations bill. The French, after their defeat in 1870–1871, established their Third Republic and began to reform their military, fortify their border, and organize for a war of *revanche* against the Germans. Nevertheless, France alone could not threaten German security. France would need a major continental ally, either Austria or Russia, to challenge militarily the German Empire. French expectations of finding an ally were realistic. The Germans faced a difficult time trying to remain simultaneously on good terms with France's potential allies, since both multinational empires often, although not always, pursued competing interests in the unstable Balkans.

And then there was Great Britain. Late in the nineteenth century, as Germany pursued an overseas empire in Africa and Asia and constructed a world-class navy, tensions arose between the British and the Germans. Anglo-German friction, in many ways, epitomized the extent to which German policies were largely responsible for the predicament in which the Reich found itself in 1914. Prussia and Great Britain had a long history of cooperation, dating back to the eighteenth century. The British, historically, had spent far more time worrying about threats from France and Russia. Even during the period after 1870, the British and Russians were often at odds with each other in the Far East, central Asia, and over the question of the future of the Ottoman Empire. The Russians posed the greatest threat to the survival of the Ottoman Empire; the British had been the sultan's primary protector since Napoleon I's invasion of Egypt in 1798. In 1904, Russia went to war with Japan, Britain's ally since 1902, and the British perceived the ever-deeper Russian penetration into central Asia as a threat to British India. The Germans, rather than building on their relationship with Britain, instead chose to pursue an overseas empire in Africa and Asia, and constructed a modern dreadnought-based navy that challenged British naval supremacy in European waters. And to what end? The German colonies were virtually useless—imperial afterthoughts. And the German navy's powerful dreadnoughts—described by one historian as a "luxury fleet"—accomplished little, if anything, during the 1914–1918 war. In short, there was nothing "natural" about Britain's adherence to the Entente; it was primarily a reaction to inane German policies.

The Austrians, stung by their defeat in 1866, initially had clung to hopes of revenge, and in that sense were candidates for diplomatic advances from Paris. But the crushing Prussian victory over France caused a prompt reassessment in Vienna. The new reality led to rapprochement with the German Empire, a shift of

continued on page 41

Schlieffen and the Battle of Cannae

At the start of the Second Punic War, Hannibal Barca led a Carthaginian army from Hispania across Gaul, over the Alps, and into the northern Italian plain. In December 218 BCE, he inflicted 75 percent casualties on a defeated Roman army of 42,000 at the battle of Trebia. In June 217 BCE, in Etruria, Hannibal again defeated the Romans at Lake Trasimene, killing over a third of the 40,000 Roman and allied troops arrayed against him. The following year, on 2 August 216 BCE, Hannibal won his greatest victory at Cannae in Apulia, about nine miles southwest of modern Barletta. In a single day, Hannibal's army of 50,000 defeated a Roman army of 86,000, inflicting 53,000 casualties on the Romans for the loss of 15,000 men. Hannibal achieved this victory through a crushing double envelopment—an encirclement of both Roman flanks. In Alfred Graf von Schlieffen's study of Cannae, he noted that even though Napoleon Bonaparte and Carl von Clausewitz had cautioned against a weaker force fighting a concentric battle, which by definition offered the larger army the advantage of interior lines, Hannibal had nevertheless achieved one of the most crushing victories in history. "A battle of complete extermination had been fought," Schlieffen wrote, and won by a numerically inferior army. He admitted:

> Arms and the mode of combat have undergone a complete change during these 2,000 years. No attack takes place at close quarters with short swords, but firing is used at thousands of meters range; the bow has been replaced by the recoil gun, the slingshot by machine guns. Capitulations have taken the place of slaughter. Still the greater conditions of warfare have remained unchanged. The battle of extermination may be fought today according to the same plan as elaborated by Hannibal in long forgotten times. The hostile front is not the aim of the principal attack. It is not against that point that the troops should be massed and the reserves disposed; the essential thing is to crush the flanks. The wings ought not to be sought at the advance flank points of the front,

but along the entire depth and extension of the hostile formation. The extermination is completed by an attack against the rear of the enemy. The cavalry plays here the principal role. It need not attack "intact infantry," but may wreak havoc among the hostile masses by long range fire.

In Schieffen's Cannae studies, he discussed that battle and many others fought over the intervening 2,000 years by Frederick the Great, Napoleon, and Moltke. To this day, militaries study Cannae. Schlieffen's studies, for example, can be found on the website of the Combined Arms Research Library of the U.S. Army's Command and General Staff College at Fort Leavenworth, Kansas.

But there was a major aspect of the battle that Schlieffen and many of the students of military history, both civilian and in uniform, who followed him did not address. Following Hannibal's "complete extermination" of the Roman force arrayed against him on 2 August 216 BCE, the war continued *for another fifteen years*: thirteen in southern Italy and another two years in Africa, to which Hannibal's army was recalled in 203 BCE to defend Carthage. There, on 19 October 202 BCE, a Roman army led by Scipio Africanus defeated Hannibal at a hard-fought battle near Zama. Unlike Hannibal's victory at Cannae, Scipio's victory, while stylistically somewhat less notable (and not included in Schlieffen's battle studies), was decisive, leading to the surrender of Carthage and the end of a seventeen-year-long war of attrition.

Clearly, "a battle of complete extermination" did not guarantee ultimate victory. Cannae, while an example of a perfectly executed double envelopment, could with greater justification have been presented as a lesson in the futility of the quest for a "decisive" battle—the idea that a major war could be won quickly in some climatic engagement. The belief that the Prussian nineteenth-century victories over Denmark, Austria, and France represented some new norm in warfare, rather than an exception to the rule, was mistaken and ultimately costly—and not just for the Germans. After 1870, the other major powers were so enamored with things German, that all the European militaries prepared themselves for short wars and sought victory through quick, decisive, and climatic battles. Unfortunately, the European militaries were chasing a chimera. Despite the painful and obvious lessons of the First World War, the Germans would continue that pursuit for another bloodied generation.

attention to the Balkans, and more of an internal focus on holding the multinational Austro-Hungarian Empire together.

That left Russia. But there, too, the conservative German monarchy held an edge over Republican France. In 1872, Bismarck forged an alignment of the three conservative monarchies in central and eastern Europe—the German, Austro-Hungarian, and Russian—into the *Dreikaiserabkommen* ("Accord of the Three Emperors"). He followed the agreement in 1873 with a German-Russian military convention, establishing a comparable agreement between the Austrians and the Russians, and even negotiating a loose association between the Italians and the *Dreikaiserabkommen*. France continued to rearm, but remained isolated and without a continental ally.

Bismarck recognized the potential dangers posed by a Franco-Russian alliance. In 1875, France's rapid military recovery led to public concern in Germany, prompting press rumors of a possible German preventive war and an ensuing European war scare. Bismarck, to his dismay, saw both Great Britain and Russia fall into alignment and pressure Germany to avoid such a strike. While no such attack was in the offing, the German chancellor recognized the reality of a possible British-Russian alliance should Germany move offensively against France. Just as important, the scare focused French attention on securing an agreement with Russia. For the time being, however, any such alliance, be it with Russia or Austria, remained more of a dream than likelihood.

The situation in the Balkans further complicated German efforts to prevent either Austria or Russia from moving toward the French. By the second half of the nineteenth century, the Ottoman Empire was more than the sick man of Europe; it was the terminal man of Europe. The various Christian ethnic groups in the Balkans—Greeks, Bulgarians, Romanians, and even Muslims in Bosnia and Albania—sought independence. The Serbs, independent since 1867, wanted more territory and an outlet to the Adriatic. This reality caused perpetual instability in the region that complicated the diplomacy of not just Germany, but also the rest of the European powers. To further complicate matters, as Bismarck sought to navigate Balkan intrigues while maintaining ties with Russia and Austria, he simultaneously worked to extend German influence in the Ottoman Empire.

Austria and Russia, especially the latter, had their own designs on the Balkans and the Ottoman Empire. The Austrians feared that unrest and nationalist sentiments in the Balkans could undermine their own rule over the non-German and mostly Slavic peoples—Poles, Czechs, Slovakians, Croatians, Slovenes, Serbs, and the mixed Slavic populations of Montenegro and Herzegovina—of their own empire. Russian policy was driven by two forces: a long-standing desire to control the Turkish straits and pan-Slavic sentiment that meant support for Bulgarian and Serbian nationalists, which presumed a new political alignment in the Balkans and the probable collapse of the Ottoman Empire.

In July 1875, as the war scare swept European capitals, an insurrection erupted in Herzegovina, and then another in Bosnia, against Ottoman rule. The following May, the revolt spread to Bulgaria. In June, the Serbs joined the conflict against the Turks, and in July, the Montenegrins entered the battle.

The Ottomans still had some fight left in them and, compared to their Balkan enemies, were well armed and equipped. By September, the Turks had soundly defeated the Serbs, who turned to Russia for help. The Russians approached the Germans for support, but Berlin refused. On 31 October, the Russians moved unilaterally and issued an ultimatum that forced the Turks to halt their offensive. A congress convened in Istanbul in December

1875, but failed to reach an accord. In January 1876, the Russians, eager to avoid a broader war, reached a bilateral accord with the Austrians and on 24 April 1877 declared war on the Ottoman Empire. On 10 May 1877, the principality of Romania, which, despite being under nominal Turkish rule, had granted permission to the Russians to cross its territory, declared its independence from the Ottomans.

The Ottoman Empire, despite its state of decline, was not entirely outclassed by Russia. Wartime reports from foreign military observers traveling or serving with the tsar's army documented its innumerable flaws, including lackluster leadership and planning by an amateurish officer corps, abysmal medical care for the ranks with regard to the treatment of combat casualties and the avoidance of disease, notable weaknesses among the transport service and supply corps, and poor discipline among the Cossack units. Geography also worked against the Russians. Neither railroads nor adequate sea transport in the Black Sea basin connected the two theaters of war—the Caucasus and the Balkans. To reach Istanbul, the Russians had to march over 450 miles and cross the Lower Danube and the Stara Planina (the Balkan Mountains). Moreover, in an industrial-era war in which troops, supplies, and ammunition were usually transported by rail, the Russians had to move nearly everything overland. There were no direct rail connections running between the Russian and the Ottoman empires. There were rail systems in both Romania and Bulgaria, but they were not well interconnected. Worse yet, the Russian rail gauge was wider than that of the Romanian railroads. As a result, rail transport required frequent offloading and reloading, until the Russian engineers could convert the existing net, assuming the Turks did not have time to destroy it. During the American Civil War, the Union army rarely moved more than fifty miles from a sea or rail head; the Russians had to operate 450 miles from theirs. Given their difficulties, it took the Russians ten weeks to reach the Danube; by comparison, the Austro-Prussian War of 1866 and the Franco-Prussian War of 1870 were both decided in only seven weeks.

While the Turks enjoyed interior rail lines, they gained no benefit because their own rail system did not extend into the eastern reaches of Anatolia, nor of their control of the Black Sea. Nevertheless, the Ottomans had established a system of depots throughout the Balkans, especially in Bulgaria, and had the advantage of a rail net, albeit somewhat primitive, running from Istanbul toward the front, giving them the logistical advantage.

The Turks also enjoyed a weaponry advantage over the Russians, just as they had over the Serbs. By the 1870s, the Ottoman Empire had given up efforts to develop its own armaments industry and had accepted the reality of dependence on foreign sources. The Russians, conversely, were developing an indigenous arms industry, although not without difficulties. Most Russian infantryman carried the Krinka, a converted muzzle-to-breech-loading rifle with a range of 1,000 yards, while other Russian soldiers carried imported, American-made Berdan rifled breechloaders, which had a range of 1,200 yards. By the start of the conflict, the Ottomans had imported about 300,000 American-made Peabody-Martini breechloaders for their army, and the Americans shipped another 200,000 during the war. Other Turkish troops carried English-made Snyders. The Peabody-Martini rifles, the same weapons used by the British army during the Anglo-Zulu War in 1879, had a range of 1,500 yards. While the Turkish artillery was a hodgepodge assortment of cannon, including some museum pieces, each Turkish battery was equipped with a few Krupp 4- and 6-pounder steel, rifled breechloaders. The Russians outnumbered the Turks in guns by three to one, but the more modern Krupp rifles outranged the Russians' best cannon by more than 2,000 yards.

On the night of 26–27 June, ten weeks into the campaign, the Russians crossed the Danube at Svistov. After the crossing, the Russian western column struck west along the southern bank of the river and at Plevna ran into the advance guard of the main Ottoman army of about 60,000 men. The Turkish force, which had previously defeated the Serbs, easily drove off an attack.

Had they pursued the defeated Russians, they might well have advanced to the Russian bridgehead, but the Turkish commander, Osman Nuri Paça, held his ground, entrenched, and waited for the rest of his force to close up. The Russians approached again and launched another assault of 19 July, but were again driven off with heavy casualties. After a third failed assault, the Russians moved to encircle and besiege the Turks. The siege of Plevna, which came to epitomize the Russo-Turkish War, lasted until the Ottoman surrender on 10 December, following a failed Turkish breakout attempt.

The human costs of the war were high. Neither army did a good job of maintaining casualty statistics. Each army probably suffered about 150,000 military casualties. The cost to local civilians was also high, since both sides committed atrocities, and the Bulgarians resorted to what today would be termed ethnic cleansing. Estimates for the number of Bulgarian Christians killed following the April 1876 uprising vary from 15,000 to 100,000. The Christian Bulgarians responded even more harshly, killing over 250,000 Muslims, while another 500,000 refugees fled to Istanbul. A Bulgarian pogrom against Jews prompted their flight toward Istanbul, alongside the Turks. In the east, where the Armenian Christian population under Ottoman control was clearly pro-Russian, the Kurds attacked, with Ottoman encouragement, and massacred about 30,000 Armenians.

On 12 December, the Turks, beaten and running up additional debt, asked for mediation. When that brought little diplomatic action, the Ottomans appealed directly to the Russians for an armistice on 9 January 1878. On 31 January, the Russians, aware that a British fleet was on its way to the Dardanelles Straits, agreed. The Russian army was by that time camped on the approaches to Istanbul.

The Russians and Ottomans reached an agreement on 3 March 1878 at San Stefano (now Yeşilköy), a town along the front line between the Russian and Ottoman armies. Montenegro nearly doubled in size and became independent. Serbia gained territory in the south. Romania gained its independence, and

Bulgaria became autonomous, though effectively independent, with its own government and army and access to the Black Sea and the Aegean. In exchange for reparations, the Russians picked up the towns of Ardahan, Kars, Batumi, and other territory along the Caucasus border with the Ottoman Empire. The Turks also agreed to allow neutral ships to pass the Straits, even in wartime.

Unfortunately, the other European powers, especially the British, who now had a fleet in the Straits, were dissatisfied with the accord. With Bismarck's assistance, the powers convened a congress in Berlin in June. In this congress, Bulgarian autonomy was markedly weakened and its territory along the Aegean—and, along with it, the Russian position in the Balkans—reduced. Austria-Hungary gained the right to occupy and administer Bosnia and Herzegovina. In a separate agreement with the Ottomans, the British occupied Cyprus.

While the Austrians, British, and Ottomans were satisfied with the outcome in Berlin, other powers and several of the Balkan states were not, thus setting the stage for yet another round of wars. The Italians had participated in the congress, but come away with nothing. The Bulgarians were unhappy, given the weakening of their autonomous status. The Greeks were pleased to see the Bulgarian borders rolled back along the Aegean coast, but were disappointed to see the territory returned to the Ottomans. And although Bismarck did his best to play the role of honest broker, the results had clearly favored the Austrians over the Russians and spelled doom for the *Dreikaiserabkommen*.

Militarily, the Russo-Turkish War of 1877–1878 had not followed the patterns of the Prussian victories of the preceding decade. Operations had proceeded slowly. There were no climatic battles comparable to Königgrätz or Mars-la-Tour. The fighting at Plevna lasted for months and was marked by entrenchments akin to the final stage of the campaign in Virginia at the end of the American Civil War, but it was believed these siege conditions came about only because the Russians had failed to maneuver and foolishly attacked head on.

Since the pattern of the conflict did not fit the experiences of the German wars of unification, the consensus in Europe was to consider the Russo-Turkish War, with its mutual butchery, a non-European affair, with few, if any, lessons to be learned. As the Prussian king Frederick II sarcastically remarked, the conflict was "a war between the one-eyed and the blind."

Both the Russian and Ottoman armies were, in fact, in the process of reform and transition, and both were far less sophisticated than the Prussian army of 1870. Observers considered both the Russian and the Turkish soldiers to be hardy and brave, but their officers to be barely competent. The siege warfare waged around Plevna was not the result of modern firepower on the battlefield, but of the poor quality of command and leadership. The Ottomans fought the war not with a general staff, but with a council located in Istanbul. The effectiveness of Turkish long-range and often unaimed rifle fire, which caused the Russians heavy and constant casualties, was considered proof of the superiority of infantry weapons over artillery and the mitrailleuse. One of the few lessons the European armies did identify and respond to was the need for infantrymen to carry their own entrenchment tools.

A French study completed in 1902 which reviewed the Russo-Turkish War noted that the conflict "occurred in an epoch when people were still too completely under the exclusive influence of the campaign of 1870 for it to be possible to study its consequences with all the desirable open-mindedness." As a result, the European powers missed an opportunity to rethink new realities, even if the war itself did not make things perfectly clear.

The Russo-Turkish War, occurring as it did on the heels of the 1875 war scare, upset the pattern of German diplomacy. In October 1879, Bismarck concluded the Dual Alliance, a defensive treaty between Germany and Austria-Hungary aimed primarily against Russia. But the Iron Chancellor had not given up on a relationship with Russia. In June 1881, Germany, Austria-Hungary, and Russia reached a formal agreement generally termed the

Three Emperors League (*Dreikaiserbund*). Italy, annoyed by French actions in Tunisia, joined the league in 1882.

The short-termed changes in the German diplomatic position had an impact of military planning. Through the mid-1870s, Moltke, who remained chief of the Prussian general staff, had focused on a one-front war against France. There were contingency plans for a war on two fronts, but in that case, the Germans intended to strike an overwhelming blow to knock France out of the war. The French were busily constructing a network of frontier fortifications around Verdun, Toul, Epinal, and Belfort. Then the Russians, who recognized the inadequacy of their railroad system during the Russo-Turkish War, began to expand their rail network within the empire and toward their western frontiers, into Poland and Galicia—a development that threatened both Germany and Austria-Hungary. As a result, Moltke considered a two-front war probable and a quick decisive blow against the French unlikely. The changed situation called for a defensive effort on both fronts, and the Germans and their Austrian allies taking the offensive when the situation warranted, most likely along the eastern front. Throughout the 1880s, German strategy followed this basic form. Until his death in 1891, Moltke, despite his victories, had grave doubts about the situation facing Germany.

Throughout the 1880s, German political leaders, most notably Otto von Bismarck, worked to prevent German diplomatic isolation and to diffuse the situation in the Balkans. In 1881, the Austrians reached a secret accord with the Serbians, seemingly separating the Serbs from Russia. In 1882, Italy joined the Dual Alliance, alongside Germany and Austria-Hungary, turning it into the Triple Alliance. In 1883, the Austrians negotiated yet another accord with one of Russia's Balkan allies, Romania.

But the Balkans were . . . the Balkans. In September 1883, the Bulgarians rose in revolt against the Turks and set out to form a fully independent state that included Eastern Rumelia, setting off another eastern crisis. The Turks, despite the loss of additional territory along their European border, chose not to resist.

Instead, the reaction to the Bulgarian move came from Belgrade; in November, Serbia declared war. By the end of the month, the Bulgarians—who were becoming known as the Prussians of the Balkans—had shattered the Serbian army in a series of battles. When the Greeks threatened to intervene alongside the Serbs, the Ottomans countered by cutting a deal with the Bulgarians in February 1886. The Ottomans decided that rather than continue to resist Bulgarian national aspirations, the Porte (as the Ottoman government was called) would be more secure with a powerful Christian state, increasingly hostile toward Russia, along the northern border. Under the accord, Bulgaria became fully independent, while Eastern Rumelia remained ostensibly part of the Ottoman Empire, but as a fully autonomous region administered by the Bulgarian prince. Under British pressure, the Greeks subsequently backed down, but the Russians continued to interfere with Bulgarian affairs. They kidnapped the Bulgarian ruler, Prince Alexander of Battenberg, in a well-orchestrated coup and prevented his return to power. The Bulgarians responded with a national assembly that chose a new prince, Waldemar of Denmark, but he rejected the offer of the Bulgarian throne. As the crisis continued, the prospect of a Russian invasion grew and with it, the prospect of an Austro-Russian conflict. Amidst the diplomatic confusion— political division and chaos in France and growing Franco-Russian pressures against Britain—Bismarck negotiated a new treaty, called the Reinsurance Treaty, with Russia, seeking to secure the status quo in the Balkans, a veritable impossibility.

In July 1887, the Bulgarian assembly elected Ferdinand of Saxe-Coburg as prince. Once again the Russians protested. In December, as Bismarck stood aside trying to avoid antagonizing the Russians, the British, Austrians, and Italians reached an agreement of their own, calling for the maintenance of the status quo in the Balkans and support for the Ottoman Empire as long as it protected its rights in Bulgaria and the Straits. In the event the agreement was breached, the three powers declared themselves justified to occupy those parts of the Ottoman Empire.

The agreement was clearly aimed at Russia. In January 1888, the Germans negotiated an agreement with the Italians that called for the dispatch of several Italian corps across the Alps to guard the German border with France in the event of a Franco-German war, thus freeing German troops for deployment to the east against Russia. Later that year, the Germans leaked news of their heretofore secret alliance with Austria, yet another warning to the Russians. As Germany, Austria, Turkey, Italy, and Great Britain fell into alignment, it was the French and, especially, the Russians who found themselves isolated.

On 1 February 1888, Kaiser Wilhelm I, who had reigned over the German Empire since 1861, died. Wilhelm the Great, as he was often known, was born in 1797, had overseen the unification of the German Empire, and, like Moltke, had lived through the perilous years of the early nineteenth century. Young Wilhelm witnessed the Prussian defeats at the hands of Napoleon in 1806–1807 and the subsequent French occupation; he fought in the campaigns of 1814 and 1815, including the battle of Waterloo. His Prussia-Germany was one that had risen like a phoenix from the ashes of defeat.

With Wilhelm's death, his son, Frederick III, became emperor. Frederick was far more liberally inclined than his father or Bismarck. But Frederick's reign was cut short—at ninety-nine days—by throat cancer. With his death, his son, Wilhelm II, became emperor in June 1888.

Space does not permit a full biography of Wilhelm II. At the time of his accession to the throne, he was only twenty-nine years old. Unlike his grandfather, little Willy reached maturity at the zenith of German power, and unlike Bismarck (born in 1815) and Moltke (born in 1800), did not recall a time before Germany was considered *the* major continental European power. Wilhelm always did his best to cut a martial figure, usually dressing in military uniforms, in an effort to appear as imposing as the state he ruled. But he was born with a withered left arm, the result of a difficult breech birth. He hid his deformity by resting his left hand on the hilt of his sword or carrying a pair of gloves to make the arm appear longer. Early in his reign, most considered him temperamental, and a few of his critics thought the kaiser a megalomaniac.

Historians debate Wilhelm II's impact on German policy, which clearly underwent dramatic shifts during his rule. Wilhelm sought to regain those elements of monarchal authority that his immediate predecessors had yielded to powerful military and political figures, most notably Moltke, Bismarck, and the Reichstag. But Wilhelm lacked the tact, wisdom, self-control, and political realism to meet the demands he placed on himself.

In March 1890, he forced the resignation of Otto von Bismarck. In June, the Germans allowed the Reinsurance Treaty, which ensured Russian neutrality in the event of a French attack, to lapse, despite sincere Russian efforts to renew it. The Germans' stated reasons for the lapse were many; these reasons included the Germans' fear that knowledge of the treaty would undermine their relationship with Austria-Hungary and the alliance with Romania, as well as the fact that Bismarck's critics and enemies were able to convince the kaiser of the wisdom of the new course. That course assumed that the war Bismarck had worked so assiduously to prevent was inevitable. The following year, in May 1891, the Germans secured an early renewal of the Triple Alliance.

The Russian response to this shift in German policy was to turn increasingly toward France. In July 1891, a French naval squadron visited Kronstadt. In August, France and Russia agreed to a diplomatic convention. The French sought hard guarantees of military assistance, proposed in a draft military convention, but the Russians remained reluctant to commit to a course that they were coming to understand meant war perhaps more than it meant security. They agreed only to consultation in the event of a crisis and a loose military arrangement "in principle." In October 1892, a Russian squadron visited Toulon. Then from December 1893 to January 1894, France and Russia exchanged notes formalizing a Franco-Russian alignment against the Triple Alliance, calling for mobilization and probably war, if Germany, Austria-Hungary, or Italy mobilized.

It was in this changed environment in 1891 that Alfred Graf von Schlieffen became chief of the German general staff. Initially, Schlieffen did not fundamentally change Moltke's plan for a two-front defensive-offensive war, with the eastern front the most likely scene of offensive operations. But in 1894, in response to the formalization of the Franco-Russian entente, Schlieffen embarked on a major shift in German military strategy. He, like Moltke, feared the prospect of a two-front war. Moltke had trusted in Bismarck's diplomacy to avoid such a conflict. But by 1890, Bismarck was gone, and Schlieffen inherited a very different situation.

Schlieffen assumed that Germany could not fight and win an extended two-front war. In fact, he considered a long war "impossible in our time, in which the very existence of the nation depends upon trade and industry; a quick decision is required to set the wheels in motion once again. A strategy of attrition is impossible if it requires the support of millions and an expenditure of billions." Moreover, Russia was too large and populous to be defeated quickly. The French had markedly improved their army, especially its size, but the Germans retained a qualitative advantage. Thus, the French posed the greatest immediate threat and ought to be the focus of Germany's initial offensive operations. The dilemma, which Moltke had identified, was the French system of border fortresses, which made a quick victory in the west problematic. That consideration had led Moltke to turn toward the east. But Schlieffen's response to the problem was to consider, and ultimately to adopt, the concept of a march around the northern flank of the French fortress line. That move meant, however, violating the neutrality of the one or more of what we today term the Benelux countries. Luxembourg, a small state with virtually no military, was an easy mark, but presented broken and wooded terrain and offered little room for maneuver. The Belgian plain offered better ground and more space, but Germany was a guarantor of Belgian independence, and a violation of the country's neutrality would likely lead to British intervention. Nevertheless, Schlieffen decided that the risk was worth the opportunity. The German move would lead to a quick victory either before the British could intervene or, in the event of a hasty British response, allow the Germans to round up British forces along with the French in an even greater victory. Later, Schlieffen further extended his right wing to march through the southernmost region of the Netherlands—the Limburg appendage. Schlieffen planned to deploy 90 percent of the German army in the west. The remaining 10 percent, aided by the Austro-Hungarian army, would hold off the Russians, who were expected to mobilize slowly. After achieving victory in the west in about six weeks, the Germans would use their interior lines and railroad network to shift forces east to meet and defeat the Russian advance.

Schlieffen's plans encompassed many flaws, both political and military. Since he assumed that Russia could not be defeated quickly, did it not logically follow that if the Germans initially struck west, they would still have to fight a prolonged war in the east if Russia refused to surrender? Ought not this observation have led to planning for an extended war, if only on one front? Invading Belgium and Holland involved major political issues. But in Wilhelm II's Reich, no political leaders emerged to rival Bismarck or to challenge the self-assured and increasingly belligerent kaiser. As a result, Schlieffen was able to turn on its head Carl von Clausewitz's principle, voiced in *Vom Krieg*, that said war was an extension of policy, and German policy became an extension of military strategy. There were also logistical questions, ably identified by historian Martin Van Creveld in his book *Supplying War*: Could the Germans supply an industrial-age army overland as it made its sweeping right hook around the French flank, perhaps even swinging west of Paris? And what of Schlieffen's fascination with double-envelopments, most notably, the August 216 BCE battle of Cannae?

So it was that Europe blundered along, with the kaiser leading the way. The outbreak of war in 1914 was not the fault of the kaiser alone. But he played a leading role, aided by the archaic and patchwork governmental structure of the Second German Empire, which provided few checks on the kaiser's myriad imbalances.

In January 1896, following the Boer defeat of the British irregulars responsible for the ill-fated Jameson Raid, Wilhelm sent his infamous "Kruger telegram" to Stephanus Kruger, president of the Transvaal Republic. The message encouraged anti-British sentiment amongst the German public and infuriated the British. Two years later, in March 1898, the Reichstag passed the first of several naval appropriation bills at the behest of the kaiser and Admiral Alfred von Tirpitz, secretary of the Naval Office. The British viewed the German naval building program as a challenge to the Royal Navy's command of the sea.

Sea power is an expensive commodity, and few states have successfully made of themselves both land and sea powers. The Romans managed the feat in the ancient world, the Ottomans in the medieval, and the United States in the modern. But the French failed in their efforts, as did the Soviet Union in the three decades before its collapse. But for the kaiser's Germany, there were no bounds, and a navy and an overseas empire beckoned. Years earlier, the prospect of a powerful seagoing German navy had caught his attention. Might he do for the German navy what his ancestors had done for the army? And within the service's ranks, a navalist officer—Alfred von Tirpitz, one of the foremost proponents of a large, seagoing German navy—also caught the kaiser's attention.

Tirpitz advocated what was termed the "risk theory." He did not advocate the construction of a navy greater than that of Great Britain, but rather one large enough to threaten British command of the sea to the extent that the British would seek to avoid a war with Germany. He believed this challenge was possible with a smaller force because he was convinced that, in the event of war, the British navy would seek to take out the Germans in a direct assault on its bases, much as they had twice struck Denmark's navy at Copenhagen during the French Revolution and Napoleonic Wars. Tirpitz believed that a smaller German fleet could defeat a British assault with the assistance of coastal batteries, minefields, and torpedo boats (later submarines, as well).

There were several problems with Tirpitz's strategic concept. What if the Royal Navy chose not to try to "Copenhagen" the Germans, but instead blockaded Germany at a distance by closing off the English Channel and the North Sea between Scotland and Norway? What could a weaker German fleet do in that case? The answer, as the actual course of the Great War at sea would demonstrate, was very little. Tirpitz's concept also ensured that Germany would have to ride out a window of danger, lasting perhaps a decade or so, during which the kaiser's fleet would be too weak to do much of anything, no matter which strategic posture the British adopted. During this period, Germany itself would be at greater risk, with a navy too weak to deter Great Britain or to contest the North Sea. Moreover, the duration of this period of danger was dependent not solely on the pace of German naval construction, but also on the nature of the British diplomatic and military response. Tirpitz based his strategic conceptions on false assumptions concerning British behavior.

The British did not sit idly by as Germany began to expand its navy from one geared to coast defense to one capable of global blue-water operations. The German effort sparked a British response—the well-known Anglo-German naval race—that further drove Great Britain toward an anti-German alliance. Diplomatically, in the decade or so before the Great War, the British entered into an alliance with Japan and an entente with France, and reconciled with the United States. By removing potential naval challenges in Asian, Mediterranean, and American waters, the British could concentrate the Royal Navy in home waters, poised against Germany.

The Tirpitz plan was a fiasco for Germany in the realms of war and diplomacy. Growing German naval power, far from deterring the British, helped drive them into the arms of the Entente. Nor, in the face of the British refusal to strike at the German navy in its bases in August 1914, was there any contribution the navy could make to the quick campaign that the Germans launched against France. When the fighting settled into the trenches and the quick war became a struggle of attrition, the kaiser's navy sat in port and watched, powerless to break the blockade that slowly starved the German nation. A historian of the German navy, Holger Herwig, would term it a "luxury fleet"—a military commodity that the German nation could not afford and did not need. The Second Reich could have better spent the millions wasted on the navy on further expanding the army. The Second Reich's fleet was a waste fleet.

As the pace of the Anglo-German naval race quickened, other crises strained relations between the two powers. The Anglo-Boer War that began in October 1899 (and lasted until May 1902) helped drive a further wedge between Germany and Britain. During the war, German public opinion was openly pro-Boer. After the British victory, the kaiser was interviewed by the British press and tried to make of himself a great friend of John Bull. Wilhelm claimed that he had rejected an offer from other European powers to take advantage of the British problem in South Africa by striking Britain. He also alleged that he had personally drawn up a military plan to counter the Boers and supplied it to the British, suggesting that the ultimate British strategy that led to victory bore striking similarities to his plan. British opinion reacted harshly to such claims.

German diplomacy also did not do anything to alleviate the fears of the continental powers. In August 1899, the French and Russians extended and deepened their alliance. Then in the fall, the kaiser visited Istanbul, the capital of the Ottoman Empire, in an effort to further development of the Berlin-to-Baghdad railway, but the visit threatened British and Russian interests in the fate of the Ottomans. On his return to Berlin, the kaiser oversaw the passage of a second German naval construction bill.

In the summer of 1900, the world was regaled by more of the kaiser's bombastic rhetoric. German diplomats and soldiers had been trapped, along with other western and Japanese contingents, in the foreign quarter of Beijing (Peking) during the Boxer Rebellion. Germany, which had recently secured a concession at Tianjin (Tientsin), contributed to the international expeditionary force sent to relieve the besieged garrison. As the kaiser bid farewell to a contingent of the soldiers prepared to ship out, he told them:

> When you come upon the enemy, smite him. Pardon will not be given. Prisoners will not be taken. Whoever falls into your hands is forfeit. Once, a thousand years ago, the Huns under their King Attila made a name for themselves, one still potent in legend and tradition. May you in this way make the name German remembered in China for a thousand years so that no Chinaman will ever again dare to *even squint at a German!*

Thus the Germans earned the sobriquet "Huns," which would so haunt them during the Great War.

In February 1904, Russia and Japan went to war. As the conflict in the Far East developed, the situation presented the Germans with an opportunity to separate Russia from the Entente. Britain was an ally of Japan; France was an ally of Russia. In April, the British and French, fearing that they might be dragged into the war on opposite sides, signed a series of agreements generally termed the Entente Cordiale. Russia had its own problems with Britain in the Middle East and south Asia, and while fighting against Japan in Korea and Manchuria, was vulnerable in Europe to a German attack. One can only wonder what Bismarck might have made of the situation, but the Germans totally misplayed their diplomatic hand. They offered the Russians encouragement and a secure western frontier, but they received nothing but temporary goodwill in return. Wilhelm's support for Tsar Nicholas II further antagonized Great Britain, to the point of a mild war scare. In response, the British pulled their capital ships from the Mediterranean, thanks to their new accord with France, and concentrated them in the North Sea against Germany. The list of Germany's potential enemies was growing.

While the Russo-Japanese War was not a European conflict, the European powers nevertheless paid great attention to the struggle in east Asia; all sent observers, and most published multivolume official histories. The true nature of modern, industrialized warfare was there for all to see. There were trenches. Repeating rifles, machine guns, and quick-firing artillery made attacks difficult. Casualties were enormous. The Russians deployed about 500,000 men, of whom half became casualties; the Japanese deployed 800,000 men, of whom over a quarter were casualties.

There were many valuable lessons drawn from both the Russo-Japanese War and the earlier conflict in South Africa between the British and the Boers. Several of the lessons drawn from the Russo-Turkish War were reinforced, including the value of entrenchment tools for every soldier and the changed role of cavalry from a shock force to mobile firepower. The Russo-Japanese War also highlighted the importance of artillery, a lesson not evident in the Russo-Turkish conflict. Drab uniform colors became the rule after 1906, except for the French. The Germans adopted field gray; the British, khaki; and the Russians, tan.

But the primary lesson drawn from the Russo-Japanese conflict reinforced prevailing European assumptions about the nature of modern warfare. Whereas today historians see in the experiences of the Russo-Japanese War a preview of the Great War's Western Front, at the time, observers, lacking the benefit of foresight, saw things very differently. Yes, casualties were atrocious, but in battle after battle, the Japanese defeated the Russians and won the war. All the European observers drew the same conclusions: the Japanese command embraced the offensive, their army possessed superior morale, their soldiers attacked with great spirit and, despite often horrendous casualties, took the positions of the Russians, who remained on the defensive. The keys to victory were offensive operations conducted by well-led and well-motivated troops. Unfortunately, as historian Gary P. Cox wrote of the conflict, "Good history often makes for poor soothsaying."

So with all the major European powers embracing the concept of the offensive, Europe continued along the path toward Armageddon. And the Germans, who under Bismarck had worked so diligently to isolate potential enemies, now worked just as diligently to isolate themselves. The kaiser was not content with antagonizing the British in 1904. In early 1905, when it became clear that the French were intent on establishing a protectorate over Morocco, German diplomats saw an opportunity to drive a wedge between France and England, unaware that the British were already in agreement over the issue with the French. In March 1905, Wilhelm personally visited Morocco and promised his support to the kingdom. But the other powers showed no interest in rallying around Germany, despite the fact that the Russian army was deeply involved in Asia. In early 1906, the major powers gathered at Algeciras, Spain, and the Germans, to their horror, discovered that they, and not the French, were now isolated. Only Austria-Hungary offered the kaiser support. Even Italy, a signatory of the Triple Alliance, supported France. The French occupied Morocco, although it remained nominally independent.

In February 1906, Great Britain launched the first all-big-gun battleship—the HMS *Dreadnought*, which gave the new type of capital ship its name. Technology, especially the problems of range-finding, drove the design. The newly designed vessel made all previous battleships with their mixed armaments—henceforth labeled predreadnoughts—obsolescent, if not obsolete.

The dreadnought revolution presented the Germans with the opportunity to rethink their naval strategy. If the Germans were to continue building their navy, they would have to start all over again. But the British predreadnoughts were also obsolete, and Britain, too, was beginning anew. To Tirpitz, the kaiser, and other navalist proponents, the opportunity was great, and in May 1906, the Reichstag passed its third naval construction bill, further antagonizing and threatening the British.

Thereafter, diplomatic moves seemed to lead inexorably toward a general European war. In August 1907, the French and Russians further strengthened their alliance. In October 1908, the Austrians annexed Bosnia and Herzegovina. Serbia refused to recognize the annexations and turned toward Russia for help. In response, in January 1909, Austrian diplomats reached an agreement with the Ottoman Empire. By March, a war scare had seized central and eastern European capitals. The Germans supported Austria, sending a virtual ultimatum to the Russians. The tsar, his army weakened by defeat and his state torn by popular revolution in 1905, had no choice but to retreat. Serbia, isolated, had little choice but to accept the Austrian move as a fait accompli. But for both Serbia and Russia, the retreat was temporary. In October 1909, the Russians negotiated an accord with Italy concerning the Balkans—another sign that the Germans were losing another of their few allies.

But if the drift toward war was inexorable, it was not inevitable. The tsar worried about the deterioration of relations with Germany. Even when Russia recovered fully from defeat and revolution, the risks of war, both military and political, for Russia were great. The state had nearly collapsed during a war with Japan. What would happen in the event of a conflict against Germany and Austria-Hungary?

In February 1910, the tsar and his entourage traveled to Potsdam, a suburb of Berlin, and with the kaiser and his diplomats, reached agreements on the Balkans, Persia, and the Berlin-to-Baghdad railway. But the Balkan arrangements were soon overtaken, since the Balkan states had minds and interests of their own. In March 1912, Bulgaria and Serbia formed an alliance, with Russian backing, and in May the Greeks, at the instigation of the British, struck their own deal with the Bulgarians. The prospect of a Balkan war setting off a major European crisis loomed. In July, the British, further angered by the March passage of yet another naval-construction bill by the Reichstag, concentrated all British battleships in the North Sea, a move clearly aimed at the Germans. In September, the Balkan League—Bulgaria, Serbia, and Greece—moved, with Russian support, against the Ottoman Empire. The

Albanians, mostly Muslims, took the opportunity to rise up against the Ottomans and declare their own independence.

Amidst the crisis, the Russians mobilized partially in Poland, threatening Austria-Hungary and Germany. But the French refused to support Russia if the tsar initiated a war over the Balkans. The main reason that the crisis did not further deteriorate was that by October the Balkan League had defeated the Turks and the Bulgarian army threatened Adrianople, the gateway to the Ottoman capital. Immediately, the larger powers, especially Russia, moved to contain the situation. The British and French had already agreed that in the event of a major war, the Russians would receive control of Turkey in Europe and the Straits. In November, with the Bulgarians poised to advance, the Russians warned their ally off and ordered an immediate halt in operations. The Serbs, too, had their own agenda, and seized part of the Albanian coast in an effort to secure an outlet to the Adriatic. That move threatened Austrian interests. Nevertheless, under great-power pressure, on 3 December, all parties, except the Greeks, had agreed to an armistice.

Before a final agreement could be reached, a coup swept leaders of the Young Turk faction—nationalist and reforming Turks—into power in Istanbul in early 1913. In February, the war resumed. On 26 March, the Bulgarians took Adrianople. Under heavy Russian pressure, the Bulgarians agreed to another armistice. By May, the Austrians had forced the Serbs away from the coast.

On 30 May, the powers signed the Treaty of London, ending the First Balkan War. Albania became independent. The Bulgarians gained Thrace and the Aegean outlet they had long sought. The Serbs yielded their Albanian gains, but secured part of Kosovo. The Greeks were the least satisfied of the combatants; they lost a slice of ethnic Greek territory in southern Albania and failed to secure Macedonia.

Within a month—on 29 June 1913—the Second Balkan War had begun. The Bulgarians, having only recently freed themselves from the Ottoman Empire, now sought an empire of their own that included Istanbul, the Straits, and territories held by Greece and Serbia. The Russians struggled to maintain a relationship with both Slavic states, Serbia and Bulgaria. Tsar Nicholas offered his personal mediation in an effort to head off another crisis, but the Bulgarians rejected the offer. Despite a clear warning from Russia, the Bulgarian army launched offensives against both the Greeks and the Serbs.

The Bulgarians met defeat and soon found themselves facing the Romanians, Montenegrins, and ultimately the Turks as well. They accepted defeat in the Treaty of Bucharest on 10 August 1913. The Romanians, Serbs, and Greeks all secured additional territory. The Bulgarians lost land, but remained determined to strike again. The Ottomans, who had remained neutral until the endgame, gained little, but for once emerged from a conflict on the winning side and at minimal cost.

Balkan instability remained a problem. In September 1913, the Serbs invaded Albania. Only an Austrian ultimatum in October forced the Serbs to yield. Russia was not prepared to go to war to secure an outlet to the Adriatic for Serbia, but would Russia back down if the existence of Serbia was at stake?

CHAPTER III

The Great War

A S THE WORLD ENTERED A NEW CENTURY, the Industrial Revolution hit full stride in the West. On the whole, Europeans and Americans were becoming wealthier, as their booming industrial sectors provided jobs for the ever-increasing number of young men and women no longer needed to work farms, which, in turn, were witnessing a new phase of the agricultural revolution. Factories produced a wide array of increasingly inexpensive products for the workers to purchase. Scientific advances beckoned, offering solutions to age-old problems, such as the scourge of disease. Overall, infant mortality rates, despite often-harsh urban conditions, improved. Projected life spans increased. Education became available to a broader sector of the population. The inevitability of "progress"—be it political, industrial, scientific, educational, social, or whatever—seemed to ensure a bright and increasingly prosperous future.

But with the progress of the Industrial Revolution came the trials of modernization. Rapid advances associated with industrialization placed heavy burdens on Western states and cultures. Societies that had been rural and agricultural rapidly became urban and industrial. Nor was progress, while marked, even or painless in its application. Industrial development meant jobs, but it also meant overcrowded tenements, unemployment, unsafe and unhealthy working conditions, child labor, the demands of an industrial work schedule, and a variety of new social ills that placed enormous pressures on individuals, societies, and states.

Amidst the turmoil of the Industrial Revolution, Europe witnessed paradoxical developments—namely, the simultaneous rise of an internationally focused socialism alongside often-virulent nationalism. For some Europeans, the strains and stresses of the new order called for international organization and rising class consciousness, if not class struggle. But to others, the chaos of the era demanded not internationalism, but stronger ethnic identification—nationalism—and perhaps struggles not between classes, but between nations. On the eve of the Great War, nationalism was the still-dominant force in the West, and that force was perhaps most evident in the decision of the German Socialists to support the war when it came in 1914.

European militaries reflected the rapidly industrializing societies they served: they were in the grips of both modernization and nationalism. The output of Western military factories soared, although they mostly produced new and improved versions of old weapons. To be sure, there was a new day dawning in warfare. But just as Western states and cultures struggled to cope with the travails of industrial and social modernization, so, too, did their military establishments wrestle with the implications of the modernization of warfare.

Industrialization produced dramatic changes in what might be termed the quantity and quality of the tools of warfare. Increasing industrial productivity ensured an ever-greater supply of weapons, while the continuing agricultural revolution simultaneously freed an ever-larger proportion of the population for other duties, including military service. As a result, modernizing twentieth-century states could field extremely large armies and sustain them in the field for extended periods of time. Moreover, the weapons now in production were more "efficient"; these new mass-produced machines of war generally had higher rates of fire, were more accurate and longer ranged, and discharged more deadly projectiles than had their predecessors.

This greater efficiency created a dilemma on the battlefield, although the scope was not yet fully grasped as the world moved toward war in the summer of 1914. The impact of the increased lethality of the weapons of war on the battlefield suggested the need for troops to disperse and to go to ground—to dig in. Thus, in the face of more lethal weapons, relative mobility decreased. Moreover, the more rapid expenditure of ammunition, caused by greater rates of fire, placed an increasing premium on resupply. The railroads of Europe were ideally suited to move the mountains of materiel needed by the armies to the front. But moving such materiel onto and about the battlefield now became a problem more daunting than ever. No longer could armies survive on their own, foraging for supplies, with enough ammunition at hand for a major battle. The logistical tether on armies grew thicker, heavier, and shorter, further reducing the mobility of European land forces.

The same was true at sea. In the age of fighting sail, warships had been able to cruise for months on end. But the steam-driven dreadnoughts that had replaced the ships of the line measured their operational radii in hours steamed.

Worse yet, on land, at sea, and subsequently in the air, the technology and practice of command and control failed to keep pace with developments on the battlefield. Field commanders during the Great War faced a more complex twentieth-century environment, but did so with early nineteenth-century means. Troops that previously had been arrayed in the open, deployed in close order, and clad in brightly colored uniforms, were now dispersed, often dug into the ground, and dressed in drab-colored clothing meant to mask, not reveal their position. The prospects of a commander being able to control his troops were greatly reduced. He could no longer sit his horse on a prominent hill and watch his army maneuver about the battlefield, relying on aides to carry orders to the units engaged in a timely fashion. The Great

War battlefield was far more chaotic, far more deadly, and far more difficult, though by no means impossible, to manage than the fields of previous conflicts. Nevertheless, amidst the advent of the modern technology of war, the commander still found himself working with methods of command and control literally centuries old.

The increased lethality of forces combined with lessened mobility and more difficult command and control gave to the defensive a great advantage in the coming war. Already existing technology—namely, wireless radio, the development of armored forces, and broad-based motorization—would eventually address some of the problems of both mobility and logistics. But these developments were, for the most part, a decade or more distant in 1914. The commanders of the Great War, although they made some use of these advances toward the end of the conflict, were forced to wage a less-than-mobile war that, in the West, became a bloody and prolonged struggle of attrition.

Nevertheless, too much can, and often is, made of the "inde-cisiveness" of the Great War. Much of our appreciation, or lack thereof, of the Great War is impressionistic—that is, based less on the raw statistics of the struggle than on the horror that people experienced as they faced their first truly modern conflict. The Great War was no less decisive than the Second World War that followed it, nor, for that matter, than the incredibly long war fought against Napoleon in the early nineteenth century. After all, it took more than a decade to defeat Napoleon I. And so it would take four years of bloody and constant struggle to bring the central powers—Imperial Germany, the Austro-Hungarian Empire, and the Ottoman Empire—to their collective knees.

What made the Great War so horrible was not simply the reality of industrialized war; it was the fact that such a war took place at all. As the West entered its new age, its new millennium, such occurrences were supposed to have become a thing of the past. Prosperity, enlightenment, and progress, epitomized by the Progressive movement in the United States—not the slaughter of millions in the trenches of Europe—were supposed to be the hallmarks of the modern world. Such old-fashioned conflicts were supposed to occur in non-Western lands—in Africa or Asia. Europeans were expected to confine their contests to economic competition. Or, if there was a European war, it would have to be short, akin to the wars of German unification. After all, the major European powers had far too much to lose economically to allow themselves to engage in a long and costly internecine war. In the fall and winter of 1914, Europeans and Americans saw their assumptions dashed as they endured, or from the American perspective, watched, a grand struggle that combined the worst aspects of past wars combined with the murderous marvels of modern technology.

The industrial advances made by the Western nations in the decades before the Great War wrought many changes on the battlefield. These had an impact on several aspects of what had become modern war: mobilization, transportation, the lethality of weapons, and communications.

By the twentieth century, modern industrialized nations had developed the ability to raise and to equip—to mobilize—armed forces numbering in the millions. The continued agricultural revolution freed a large percentage of the Western states' population for service in the ever-increasing number of factories, or, in the event of war, in the military establishments. Never before had states been able to raise such substantial forces and to keep them in the field.

A crucial element of the mobilization systems adopted by the major European powers involved well-developed reserve systems. It was unnecessary, prohibitively expensive, and a misuse of badly needed labor resources to maintain all the available young men of military age in uniform. Instead, the major European powers developed military systems through which young men were funneled for a few years to gain military experience before being released back to the civilian sector to work in the factories or on the farms. Once released, these men were assigned to reserve units—second-line military formations that could be called into service in time of war. The process of national military mobilization involved deploying not only the regular units of an army's field forces, but also these reserve units. The movement toward the front of all of these formations involved extensive planning and the development of extremely complex synchronized schedules, most especially those involving the use of a nation's railroad system. This combination of large standing armies backed up by extensive and fully deployable reserve systems allowed the European nations to field incredibly large, well-equipped, and well-trained armies.

The impact of the Industrial Revolution on transportation—primarily the development of extensive railroad nets, but also advances in steam-powered transport on the seas and waterways and motor transport ashore—allowed the major European powers not only to raise these large armies, but also to move them rapidly to the front and to supply them there with the food and the ammunition that they needed to operate. This newfound ability had a profound strategic and operational impact on the course of the war. In the past, nations with powerful navies had been able to move quickly by sea and to strike at any number of coastal positions held by an enemy. Troops could always move more rapidly by sea than an enemy could react moving by land. But the railroad had changed strategic geography. By the early twentieth century, troops could move—that is, react—more quickly on land, by making use of the extensive railroad nets in Europe, than troops moving by sea. Transportation developments had a similar impact on strategic geography ashore. In previous wars, if an army could march its troops around the flank of an enemy army, that enemy would have to shift troops itself by foot to block such a move. But in the industrial age, while the troops of the outflanking force marched on foot, the enemy force reacting to such a move could use rail or motor transport to do so more quickly and efficiently.

As was the case with many other developments, those in transportation usually often favored the defensive. Moreover, such advances had an impact primarily at the strategic and operational levels, but little impact at the tactical. Railroads allowed states to move massive armies to the front and to supply them there. But at the front, those armies faced comparably armed, supplied, and numerous opponents. The means of tactical movement available to the armies of the Great War—namely, the feet of the soldiers and the legs of horses—remained unchanged from the days of the ancients. Until late in the war, only occasionally did motor transport play a tactical role in movement at the front.

In fact, in the absence of tactical mechanization, the large European armies were, in a sense, stranded near their railheads. The large size of these armies, combined with their voracious appetites for ammunition to serve weapons with greater lethality and higher rates of fire, left the armies of the early twentieth century, tactically speaking, less mobile than their predecessors.

Moreover, these slower moving giants also had to traverse a far more lethal battlefield environment. Early twentieth-century artillery had substantial rates of fire, greater accuracy, longer ranges, and more lethal projectiles. If one looks at the preindustrial battlefield as one where artillery, infantry, and cavalry were parts of a combined arms triad, then the increased capability of artillery, which helped drive cavalry from the field and forced infantry to disperse, had upset the old tactical balance. Until the European armies redressed this imbalance by developing armored and mechanized forces that allowed more rapid and protected movement on the battlefield, attacking forces would face a difficult time.

Worse yet for the attackers, infantry support weapons, such as mortars and machine guns, further enhanced the defensive capability of soldiers dug in on the defensive. This ability made it more difficult to attack because it forced dispersion, diluting the attacker's force and exacerbating the problems of battlefield command and control. Small arms—that is, those weapons actually borne by the infantryman—were themselves also enhanced. The infantryman now carried a breech-loading repeating rifle, with a good

Was the First World War Inevitable?

Because the Great War was such a catastrophe for the modern world, historians have long wrestled with its causes. Was the tragedy brought about by some combination of calamitous causes, including imperialism, the arms race, militarism, capitalism, nationalism, and the European alliance system? At the heart of this question is an underlying assumption that the war was somehow unavoidable.

Historians often portray the coming of war in 1914 as an inexorable force, an inevitable conflagration awaiting only the spark that would set off the European powder keg. Imperialists sought expansion. Militarists needed a justification for their efforts and planned to use the force they controlled to expand national territory or to settle myriad problems. The arms race fueled international controversy, most notably the Anglo-German naval race, and ensured that sooner or later a crisis would lead to a broader conflict. The intricate alliance system raised the prospect that even the smallest crisis could easily expand into a continental or global conflagration. Socialists believed that capitalism was beset by "internal contradictions" that would ultimately impel it toward self-destruction. Rampant nationalism likewise set the stage for internecine European warfare. If one accepts the inevitability of the war, the obvious lesson to be learned was that the way to prevent future conflicts was to curtail arms races, eliminate militarism, bring an end to imperialism, avoid entangling alliance systems, replace nationalism with brotherhood, or, perhaps, bring about a socialist utopia.

But many historians consider the First World War not inevitable, but avoidable. The causes of the war were mistakes committed by European leaders—mistakes that could well have been avoided. In the Europe of 1914, socialism was growing stronger, militarism and nationalism weaker. Few imperialists wanted war. Most business leaders believed that a war would be a disaster for Europe, and even arms dealers, the proverbial "merchants of death," were hardly facing peacetime bankruptcy. The growing relative weakness of Germany compared to its neighbors, especially Russia, and not any militaristic imperative, increased the likelihood of war. Similarly, it was not the rigidity of the alliance structure, but the failure to include Great Britain as a formal component of the Entente that undermined its deterrent value. To this latter school of historians, the Great War demonstrated the critical importance of sound policy and good leadership, and the terrible cost of miscalculation.

Which school is correct? The history of the Cold War offers some interesting insights through which we can look back at the Great War. What if, instead of the fall of the Berlin Wall and the collapse of the Warsaw Pact and the Soviet Union, a "hot" Third World War had erupted in the late 1980s? Would historians (assuming mankind survived) have not concluded that the war had been inevitable, caused by (take your pick) imperialism, capitalism, communism, the competing alliance structures (NATO and the Warsaw Pact), militarism, and the arms race? And yet, because of careful decisions made in several capitals, a twilight war that had gone on for nearly a half century came to an abrupt and peaceful end. If, then, one concludes that the Great War was not inevitable, we are left to ponder the tragedy of what may well have been a totally unnecessary struggle, the costs of which remain beyond calculation.

range and rate of fire that could be discharged from a dug-in or prone position.

Military communications had also benefited from the Industrial Revolution. At the strategic and operational levels of warfare, the telegraph gave high-level commanders the ability to communicate rapidly over submarine cables and land lines. Generals in London could communicate instantaneously with senior commanders at the front in France. That commander could likewise communicate by voice telephony, if his army was stationary, with his army, corps, division, and other commanders, down to the battalion level.

Unfortunately, these communication advances were felt primarily at the strategic and operational levels of warfare, and not at the tactical. Once an offensive began, artillery barrages often cut the telegraph and telephone lines linking the battalions at the front with the rear echelons of command. As a result, as the attackers moved forward, they did so without any means to communicate with their leadership, and the overall commander would usually lose control of his force to some extent. Thus, at the lowest levels of combat, despite the modernity of the Great War battlefield, with its rifles, machine guns, poison gas, flamethrowers, and massive artillery barrages, the methods of command and control remained little changed from those of the French Revolution and Napoleonic Wars. Runners now scurried across no-man's-land and through the trenches, playing the role once filled by the nattily uniformed aides of an earlier era.

By 1914, the Industrial Revolution offered a technological answer to the problem of battlefield communications: wireless radio. But at that stage of development, wireless-radio technology was still too primitive and undependable for use on the battlefield. The navies of the era were increasingly equipping themselves with wireless telegraphic sets, referred to as WT. But placing large wireless sets on a warship was one thing; deploying them on a battlefield was another. Another two decades would pass before reliable FM voice radio would revolutionize communications on the battlefield ashore.

In the absence of an effective technological means of commanding and controlling armies on the battlefield, armies adopted a coherent doctrine, supported by thorough training, that would allow the commanders of small units to operate on their own, but within a consistent overall framework. Unfortunately, the European armies had not developed such doctrine in the decades before the Great War. All the major armies remained wedded to the offensive. Commanding generals expected to deploy their troops in proper formations and to maneuver them about the battlefield in ways not unlike armies had been maneuvered a century earlier. There were some experiments with dispersed formations, but in the absence of radios, dispersal only exacerbated the already daunting problems of command and control. The technological changes in battlefield weaponry had been so great in the decades before the Great War that no army had a doctrine that took fully into account the new deadly reality of the battlefield. As a result, European armies would have to develop new and appropriate doctrine during the course of the war through painful, and costly, trial and error.

There thus were a variety of factors that would make the Great War a long and costly struggle, a struggle won ultimately not so much by operational or tactical finesse as by strategy and attrition. The European states had the ability to mobilize themselves for war in a manner that no previous state had possessed. This ability meant not simply more men for the front, but also more of everything those men would need, supported by the simultaneous mobilization of the society to support the war effort.

On 28 June 28 1914, in Sarajevo, a Bosnian town then part of the Austro-Hungarian Empire, Gavrilo Princip assassinated the Archduke Franz Ferdinand of Austria and his wife, Sophie. The authorities captured Princip along with several of his coconspirators. Interrogating the men, the Austrians learned that Princip and company were Serbian terrorists, belonging to the group the Black Hand. As the nature of the conspiracy became evident and suspicion of official Serbian complicity grew, so, too, did the pressure in Vienna, the capital of the dual monarchy, to punish Serbia.

In late July, the Austrians presented the Serbs with an ultimatum: suspend anti–Austro-Hungarian propaganda and accept Austrian police on Serbian soil to help track down the terrorists. The Serbs refused, and the two countries headed for a showdown.

As the crisis deepened, the question became, could the showdown remain isolated if the two countries went to war? Serbia had great protectors—the fellow Slavs of the Russian Empire of Tsar Nicholas II. Austria-Hungary likewise had a great and powerful ally, namely the German Empire of Kaiser Wilhelm II. But if the Russians intervened and the Germans did likewise to defend Austria-Hungary, what of France, Russia's ally, and Britain, France's partner? The First and Second Balkan Wars had remained isolated, but unless the diplomats of the major European powers played their cards carefully, a political assassination in Sarajevo might well plunge all of Europe into war.

Several factors complicated the efforts of European diplomats. First, they had to contend with the interlocking systems of alliances within Europe, a reality that restricted their freedom of action. Second, a powerful sense of nationalism was alive and well in all of the major, and some of the minor, European countries. Extreme nationalism, bordering on chauvinism, propelled these nations toward the brink and did nothing to break the drift toward war. Third, there was the problem of military mobilization. The war plans that had been meticulously prepared before 1914 to mobilize the armed forces of the European powers were extremely detailed and comprehensive, but not particularly flexible. There was no way to call up just a few troops. Austria-Hungary could mobilize against Serbia, Russia, or both countries. Germany could mobilize against Russia, France, or France and Russia. Mobilization was more or less an on-off switch: either one mobilized or one did not. The problem was that if Germany, for example, held back and did not mobilize while either France or Russia did, and war subsequently began, Germany, having mobilized late, would be at a distinct disadvantage in the early and expectedly crucial state of what was anticipated to be a quick war. Conversely, if the Germans mobilized first, they would gain an important advantage in the opening stage of the war. As a result, there was extreme pressure on the leaders, both military and civilian, of all the powers to order mobilization sooner rather than later. Fourth, once any of the states did mobilize and the troop trains began heading toward the front, it was extremely difficult to turn back. The mobilization plans were so complex that it was close to impossible to halt the process or to adjust it. As one contemporary put it, "Mobilization means war."

Unfortunately for the Europeans, the diplomats that summer of 1914 did not play their cards very well. The crisis drifted toward war, and in late July 1914, Austrian naval monitors on the Danube shelled Belgrade as ultimata flew from capital to capital. On 28 July,

Austria-Hungary declared war and mobilized against Serbia, but not Russia. The Russians nevertheless mobilized on 30 July along their entire front. The Austro-Hungarians responded by ordering general mobilization on 31 July to include the armies in Galicia, facing the Russians. The Germans were now all but forced to mobilize themselves, at least in the east. But Berlin was reluctant to turn its back on the French. The Germans demanded a promise of French neutrality from Paris, backed up by hostages—the border fortresses of Toul and Verdun. No government could comply and hope to remain in power in Paris, so the French mobilized on 31 July. That same day the Germans began their own mobilization. Europe was about to descend into the abyss.

As Europe moved toward war in the summer of 1914, the two alliances were well armed with troops, modern weapons, and plans for their deployment. In the initial mobilizations, the Germans fielded 2,000,000 men, the Austro-Hungarians 500,000, the French 1,600,000, and the Russians 1,400,000.

The most powerful and central of the European states during the Great War was Germany. Without German support, the Austrians could not have possibly contemplated war with Serbia and Russia. Germany's decision to back its ally ensured that the French would take the field, most likely with the support of Great Britain.

As a result, the Germans faced a strategic dilemma: a two-front war against France in the west and Russia in the east. The overarching German objective in the war, as was the case with the plans of all of the great powers, was not solely to win the war, but also to win it quickly. The kaiser wanted his troops home before the autumn leaves fell from the trees. But how could the German-led alliance, since known as the Central Powers because of its location in Europe, defeat the Allies quickly?

The Germans based their plan, devised by General Count Alfred Graf von Schlieffen, chief of the general staff, on a number of factors. The French were likely to mobilize quickly, whereas the Russians, who were less industrially advanced, especially in the realm of railroads in an expansive theater of operations, were less likely to do so. There were two ways the Germans could take advantage of the asymmetrical nature of Allied mobilization. Germany could adopt a defensive in the west facing the French and strike the Russians in the east before they could fully mobilize. Conversely, the Germans could take advantage of the slower Russian mobilization and try to knock out the French quickly, and then shift forces to the east, using the advanced German rail system.

Schlieffen viewed Russia as the weak link in the enemy alliance. The Russian standing regular army was smaller than that of France. Moreover, while Russia's population was larger, its reserve system was less developed, and its industrial base remained comparatively small and primitive. The Russian transportation system, principally its railroads, was far less developed. But the fact remained that Russia was vast—too vast to be conquered in a single, quick campaign. Thus, in the event of a two-front war, Schlieffen believed, the Germans should strike a sudden knockout blow against the French, whose army had been defeated in short order in the war of 1870. Schlieffen chose this approach in 1905, and his successors in the years before the Great War, while they tinkered with his original plan, did not alter the basic strategy.

Having decided on a western strategy, the Germans faced another set of problems. The Franco-German frontier was heavily and strongly fortified and too short an area on which to deploy the number of troops the Germans expected to mobilize against France. Schlieffen decided that the best way to solve both problems was simply to march through the Low Countries—neutral Belgium and Holland. This, he understood, would most likely lead Great Britain to join the alliance. But there was little the British could do to influence the course of the war in the short term. In a long war, British sea power might prove troublesome, but Schlieffen and his successors assured themselves and their political masters that marching through the Low Countries would ensure a quick end to the conflict.

Armed with the Schlieffen plan, the Germans expected to knock the French out of the war in about six weeks, overrunning

Belgium and Luxembourg in the process. In the east, German and Austro-Hungarian forces would hold off the Russians until reinforcements could be sent by rail from the west. In subsequent campaigns, the Central Powers could wage a more leisurely war in the east, should the Russians choose to continue a hopeless struggle without their French allies.

But what if the German strategy failed in the west? What if the Germans were unable to attain the quick victory that would enable them to shift their forces east? What if the British intervened, and the war became a prolonged struggle? The Germans had based their strategy, adopted a decade before the start of the Great War, on a crucial miscalculation.

The Germans were not alone in their decision to gamble strategically. The French did the same and also made major miscalculations.

Early in the century, French strategy, as incorporated in Plan XV, was defensive-offensive. Since France would mobilize more slowly than Germany, the French army would adopt the defensive until mobilization was complete and the direction and weight of the German offensive became evident. At that point, the French would counterattack, hopefully in combination with a Russian offensive in the east.

Plan XV ignored ongoing German rail construction near Aachen, well north of the Franco-German border. It also assumed that the Germans would not strike through Belgium, but if they did, that drive could be met by French reserve divisions. The plan contained no detailed provisions for the deployment of British troops. The French concentrated their forces, except those guarding the coast against a possible British assault and others along the Alpine border with Italy, in Lorraine.

Changing circumstances led the French to begin work on a new plan—Plan XVI—in 1907. Additional railroad construction in Lorraine permitted a more rapid mobilization of the army and an earlier transition to the offensive. Diplomatic developments also allowed a greater concentration of effort in Lorraine.

continued on page 80

The Face of Battle in the Great War

Being a soldier in the Great War was not a pleasant experience. Death waited around every corner, in the form of a shell, mortar bomb, strafing aircraft, sniper, machine gun, mine, rifle fire, or disease.

Despite some popular misconceptions, soldiers did not usually spend week after week in the trenches. The high command of all militaries rotated units regularly. Infantry battalions usually spent about a third of their time in the front lines, another third in reserve, and the final third somewhere farther behind the lines, where the men could rest and recuperate, and their units could incorporate replacements before going back into the line.

As was generally the case in wartime, the bulk of a soldier's life was monotony, punctuated periodically by the terror of combat. But soldiers did have leaves at home, they did drink, and they did carouse with their comrades and cement the bonds that would hold a unit together under the strains of combat. These times of psychological release would be the moments that the soldiers who were fortunate enough to survive the conflict would recall, or choose to recall, in the years after the war.

Nevertheless, all soldiers knew that eventually they would return "to the front." Life at the front was often a living hell. The troops "lived" in trenches that were rarely dry. They were dirty, muddy, wet, damp, hot, or cold, depending on the weather. The trenches stank from the smell of urine, feces, and the dead. They were filled with rats and other vermin, most notably the lice that kept the men "lousy." There often was near-constant artillery bombardment, if only harassing fire meant to deny an enemy sleep, and periodic trench raids that forced everyone to remain alert night and day.

When an attack came, soldiers could spend hours or even days in a dust- and smoke-filled dugout under artillery bombardment, wearing cumbersome protective gear to ward off the effects of poison gas. The earth would shudder, and the soldier would wonder if an unlucky direct hit might blow him to bits or, worse yet, bury him alive. If he survived the bombardment, he would rush out of his dugout as soon as it lifted, take his place on the firing steps cut into the side of the trench, man his weapon, and attempt to repulse the enemy assault. As he readied his rifle or machine gun, he would be looking about his own trench, trying to see which of his friends had survived along with him. Amidst the loose soil churned up by the barrage, one could often see human body parts, large and small, scattered about.

To the soldier's front, he would be able to see the enemy advancing through the smoke and clouds of gas. Early in the war, these attacking soldiers might be coming on in well-dressed lines. But later in the struggle, the veterans would know to scurry across no-man's-land, the neutral area between the opposing trench systems, seeking temporary shelter in shell holes or at times behind the bodies of the fallen. Earth would be thrown up as supporting defensive artillery opened up on the attackers. Some men would be blown to bits and add their parts to the unburied mess that was part of no-man's-land. Others would be cut down by the machine guns that had been drug out of the dugouts and set up, and that were now mechanically spitting hot lead at the attackers. As men struggled to get clear of the barbed wire, many would be cut down. Those who followed might use their dead comrades's bodies draped over the wire for a path. Many of the wounded would be screaming, though their voices might not be heard over the din of battle. Those short of breath might rip off their masks, only to succumb to poison gas. But the attackers would press on toward their objectives. As they drew closer, some would stop and fire. Others would hurl grenades. And if there were enough of them, they would soon be jumping into the trenches with the defenders. Most soldiers would flee down one of the many linking communications trenches that ran to the second line of defense, but a few would be trapped and either forced to surrender, if they were lucky, or be beaten or bayoneted to death.

Of course, attacking was an even grimmer fare than defending. On the first day at the Somme, 1 July 1916, the attacking British suffered 60,000 casualties. In ten days in April 1917, the French lost 187,000 men along the Chemin des Dames and barely scratched the German defenses.

Given the casualty rates and the prolonged nature of the war, soldiers did not need to be statisticians to know that, before long, their "number" would be called. That pressure, that realization that "sooner or later," was too much for some men to bear. Minds snapped, nerves frayed, hands shook, and legs would no longer bear the weight of the man as shell shock took another victim.

But most of the men of the armies soldiered on out of a sense of personal or national duty, or, more often, a feeling of loyalty toward comrades. For the soldiers, war was a miserable, unglamorous existence. Gone were the days of the colorful military uniform. Gone were the celebrations that heralded the conclusion of a victorious battle. The tired men soldiered on in their dirty, drab garb, covered by a sweat-caked layer of mud or dust that housed a vermin-infested body that ached and itched. The soldier's ears rang, his eyes burned, and his soul prayed, or hoped, that the damned war would come to an end before his own luck ran out.

The increasingly cordial entente with Britain made the coastal garrisons superfluous. Improving relations with Italy meant that another two corps could be shifted north. French intelligence then warned of a German move through Belgium, but the analysts believed, wrongly, that the Germans would not employ their reserve corps in the initial offensive. Such a limitation would restrict the extent of a German drive in the north to the Belgian Ardennes and Luxembourg, south of the line formed by the Sambre and Meuse rivers.

The new plan retained the old concept of an initial defensive phase followed by a massive offensive effort. But the plan also incorporated to a degree the latest twist in French military thinking—the concept of the *offensive à outrance* ("the offensive to the utmost"). Many French military theorists were convinced that morale in warfare was more important than numbers or equipment. Of course, the only way to exploit an advantage in morale was to attack—hence, the desire in French plans to transition from the defensive to the offensive as quickly as possible. While the history of the development of the principle of the *offensive à outrance* was many fathered, the chief public proponent was Lieutenant Colonel François Loyzeau de Grandmaison. He wrote:

"In order to be the conqueror, one must make the enemy afraid; when one is afraid, he is beaten. The only way to make the enemy afraid is to attack resolutely without worrying about who is the strongest." The implications of the adoption of such an aggressive doctrine were many. French training focused on developing in the troops a sense of *élan*, or zeal. As a result, the French favored the concentration of formations over their dispersal to ensure better command and control. They also equipped their units with fewer machines guns than the Germans—the Germans equipped each infantry regiment with eighteen, the French six—and lacked heavy artillery. Unlike the other combatants, French infantrymen went to war in the summer of 1914 dressed much as they had in 1870: in blue serge kepis, tunics, and greatcoats, over red pantaloons. They would make spectacular and highly visible targets for the Germans.

Early in 1911, General Victor Constant Michel, now serving as the army's generalissimo, began to rethink Plan XVI. Michel, presciently, expected a German invasion of Belgium, but one that would sweep both south and north of the Sambre-Meuse line through the Belgian plain. Michel assumed that the Germans would employ their reserve corps in the initial offensive, and to meet such an extended German thrust, he proposed to employ his own reserve corps at the front. Michel wanted to concentrate almost 700,000 troops—eleven French corps and the British Expeditionary Force (BEF)—along the border with Belgium to block a German sweep north of the Sambre. But Michel's military and political opponents, determined to concentrate as many troops as possible in Lorraine, forced the generalissimo to resign in July 1911.

On 28 July 1911, Joseph Jacques Césaire Joffre became the first to hold the newly created post of chief of the general staff. Joffre was a strong proponent of the *offensive à outrance* and doubted that the Germans would employ their reserve corps in the initial offensive, which meant that they would not have sufficient force to swing north of the Sambre-Meuse line. Nevertheless, he did share some of Michel's concerns about a German strike through Belgium. In Joffre's revision of Plan XVI, he deployed about 350,000 men, half of what Michel had wanted, along with the BEF, to counter a German invasion of Belgium. French reserve corps would be withheld until they joined the Lorraine offensive. Joffre also implored the Russians to launch an offensive against the Germans as early as possible.

In May 1913, the French adopted a new plan—Plan XVII—which they would go to war with in August 1914. The French retained their convictions concerning German reserve units and the extent of any move through Belgium. The main shift evident in Plan XVI compared to XVII was a total embrace of the *offensive à outrance*. There would be no initial defensive phase. As soon as units deployed, they would move forward and assume an offensive posture.

Nevertheless, the probable strength of the French headlong attack had caused doubts among German planners. The new German chief of the general staff, General Helmuth von Moltke, the nephew of the great Moltke of the Franco-Prussian War, tinkered with the Schlieffen scheme, dropping plans to move through southern Holland and shifting more troops to the German left flank opposite the French. Moltke changed the plan not as a defensive measure, but as a move to strengthen the German left flank, allowing it to conduct an offensive of its own and, hopefully, to conduct a classic, Cannae-like double envelopment of the French army.

Germany's ally, Austria-Hungary, faced a similar dilemma with war on two fronts, one in Galicia against the Russians and the other along the Danube against the Serbs. The Austro-Hungarian chief of the general staff, General Franz Conrad von Hötzendorf, commanded six armies and had two options. He could concentrate three armies in Galicia and three against the Serbs, assuming the Russians did not mobilize. Alternatively, Conrad could concentrate his two weakest armies along the Danube and four in Galicia. Early in the crisis, the Austrians chose the former plan and concentrated three armies, including the swing Second Army, against Serbia. But when Russia mobilized, the absence of the Second Army left the Austrian right flank exposed. Unfortunately, given the highly detailed mobilization schedule, Conrad had to allow the transport of the Second Army to the Danube, wait for the initial stage of mobilization to run its course, and then reload the army onto the trains and transfer it to face the Russians. As a result, Conrad faced the prospect of defeat in Galicia and lacked the strength necessary to defeat the Serbians.

The Russians faced their own problems, confronting as they did both Germany and Austria-Hungary along an extended front. Further complicating their strategic problems was the fact that the central point of the Russian rail system in the west was Warsaw, in the Polish salient that jutted deeply into an area flanked on the north by German East Prussia and in the south by Austrian Galicia. While the Russian western front was, technically speaking, a single theater, the realities of geography and the layout of the Russian rail net broke the front into two rather distinct areas of operations. The Russians also had to maintain a third front in the Caucasus mountains where they faced a potential threat from the Ottoman Turks, who would, in fact, ultimately join the Central Powers and enter the war in the fall.

From the end of the Russo-Japanese War in 1906 until 1912, a weakened Russia adopted a cautious strategy. The Russians feared that the German would strike east and that the French, despite the Franco-Russian alliance, might remain neutral. Plans called for the tsar's armies to mobilize behind the frontier, initially to remain on the defensive until mobilization was complete, and then to go over to the offensive, depending on circumstances, against either Germany or Austria-Hungary.

But as Russia recovered from its Far Eastern defeat, and its railway network expanded in the west and, along with it, the speed of mobilization, the Russian planners became more audacious. As the years passed, the French alliance seemed more secure, the growing Anglo-French entente made Great Britain a more likely ally, and the Russians became convinced, correctly, that the Germans would strike not east, but west against the French army. The Russian planners now began to fear that if the Germans beat the French quickly while the Russians sat on the defensive, the empire would be left to face the Germans and Austro-Hungarians alone.

Russian planners reached a consensus that the armies must be deployed farther forward, along the frontier itself, and that they must take full advantage of the initial phase of the war during which the bulk of the German army would be tied down in the France.

But there the consensus ended. One faction within the high command wanted to strike first against Austria-Hungary, which was clearly the weaker of the two major Central Powers and offered the prospect of early and easier victories. But a second faction considered Germany to be the lynchpin of the opposing alliance and argued that to win, the Russians would ultimately have to defeat the German army in battle. Why not take advantage of the German preoccupation with France? Moreover, a Russian offensive against Germany in the east would help the French in the west. In 1912, the Russians resolved the dilemma by compromising: they decided to attack both the Germans and the Austrians simultaneously. Two Russian armies would move against the lone German army defending East Prussia; four Russians armies would drive into Galicia.

In retrospect, the plans of all the major belligerents were fatally flawed. To one degree or another, all of the plans of the major powers were based on false assumptions: the Germans on a slow Russian mobilization, the French on the unwillingness of the Germans to deploy their reserves in the front lines and constrain any swing through Belgium to the Ardennes. The Austrians mobilized their Second Army in the wrong theater, and the Russians launched two separate offensives, both of which lacked the strength to succeed. How the opening and critically important stage of the war unfolded would depend primarily on the ability of commanders at all levels to react quickly to the inadequacies of their plans, to the newly revealed tactical realities of the battlefield, and to events as they developed. As the elder Moltke had warned decades before, no plan survives contact with the enemy.

In the west, both the German and French plans for the campaign failed. Neither the French plan, Plan XVII, nor the German Schlieffen plan yielded the expected victory.

Under Plan XVII, the French embraced the offensive along the entire front in what has been termed the Battle of the Frontiers. French soldiers, still wearing colorful and highly visible uniforms, charged bravely into the German defenses. Machine guns, artillery, and rifle fire cut swathes through the lines and columns of the poor French *poilus* (hairy or shaggy ones). Nevertheless, the French charged on, to almost certain deaths in bold displays of their *élan*—that irresistible, dashing spirit of the offensive— which was supposed to carry France to victory. In a few weeks, the French suffered 300,000 casualties, almost a fifth of their entire army, and found themselves driven back by the victorious Germans, who now went over to an offensive that threatened to destroy the French army.

Worse yet, as the French armies along the frontier recoiled, farther north, the Germans swung through Belgium and drove around the Allied left flank. After heavy siege guns knocked out the Belgian forts near Liege, the two German armies marched west through the Belgian plain while three others struck through the Ardennes.

Two Allied armies lay in the path of the German onslaught through Belgium—the French Fifth Army and the British Expeditionary Force—four infantry and one cavalry division. Rather than attempt to maneuver around the Allies, the two German armies—the First under General Alexander von Kluck and the Second under General Count Friedrich Wilhelm von Bülow—drove head long into the enemy. The French Fifth Army fell back under German pressure. But the British, near Mons on 23 August, in a somewhat exposed position on the extreme left of the Allied line, demonstrated that German tactics had not fully incorporated the realities of modern warfare.

continued on page 90

The "Typical" Battle

It is difficult to define a "typical" battle during the Great War. Despite popular impressions of trench warfare, the nature of combat differed greatly over the course of the four years and from theater to theater. On the eastern front, the density of troops per kilometer of front was never anything akin to what it was in the west. As a result, combat on the eastern front remained more mobile. Even cavalries played an important role at times. Following the entry of Italy into the war in May 1915, the Italians and the Austrians engaged in mountain warfare along the Alpine front. The same was true in the mountains of eastern Anatolia, where the Russians and Turks fought. In the Middle East, or Turkish theater, combat was very different. The Turks and the British fought in desert or near-desert conditions in Mesopotamia and Palestine. The fighting in the Gallipoli peninsula resembled that of the western front, although the terrain was more rugged and the Commonwealth forces had their backs to the sea.

But it is the western front that people usually think of when they consider the Great War. And the nature of combat there was very different over the course of the four years of war.

In the initial, mobile stages of the war, both sides fought much as they had during the wars of the 1860s and 1870s. Formations of infantry and cavalry maneuvered about the battlefield. Troops brought firepower to bear on their opponents, sought cover where they found it, and called up their artillery howitzers in direct support. Eventually, one side was forced to retreat, and the victor moved forward.

The costs of such assaults, in the face of defensive rifle and machine-gun fire and artillery, were high. Casualties were usually heavy for both victor and vanquished. Moreover, defenders soon learned that it was best to entrench, to generate one's own cover, in order to avoid the firepower of the attacker. A successful stand by an entrenched defender led to attempts by an attacker to turn a flank. As those attempts were met, in turn, by more entrenched defenders, these temporary positions became increasingly permanent. Trench systems grew as the troops dug in and spread obstacles, such as barbed wire, in front of their positions.

Driving an entrenched enemy from the field became increasingly difficult. The flat-trajectory field howitzers that dominated early artillery arms were not much use against an entrenched enemy. Infantrymen were forced to carry the defender's positions alone, and that drove up the costs of the attack. Eventually, those costs became prohibitive, and the armies entrenched while they waited for more reinforcements, new weapons, and new forms of artillery, such as mortars and long-range guns that fired their shells in a higher trajectory.

The new battles on the western front became what the Germans called *Materialschlact*—battles of materiel. In an effort to overwhelm a defender, the attacker would concentrate masses of troops and guns along a narrow sector of front, pulverize the enemy lines with a massive artillery barrage that might last for days, and then send the attacking battalions forward.

Defenders soon learned to adjust to these tactics. The lengthy preparatory barrages revealed an enemy's intentions and allowed the defender to mass reserves to repel the coming offensive. The trench systems themselves became ever-more elaborate. Men dug deeper, building wood-, concrete-, and steel-reinforced trenches and deep, often spacious dugouts where the men could ride out the artillery barrage. The depth of systems grew as the defenders added additional lines of trenches. Rear lines housed reserves that would counterattack the assaulting force while it was still weak, disorganized, and confused, generally regaining the front line. The inability of a successful attacking force to survive a powerful counterattack by the defender's reserve was the principal reason that the position of the trench line in Flanders so rarely moved. Over the course of the war, defenders learned to cheat—to thin out the forwardmost trench lines, the ones likely to be pulverized in the opening barrage. These trenches now became mere outposts meant to break up an enemy attack, not to stop it, and prepare the stage for the inevitable counterattack.

Amidst all of these changes, both sides began using poison gas. Early on, gas was deadly against troops who had no defense, other than to collapse in place or run toward the rear. But as the war progressed, all the armies began to issue gear that, if used properly, did protect soldiers from the gas and allow them to keep fighting. Nevertheless, with both armies wearing gas masks and other cumbersome gear, the tempo of the battlefield slowed down, a factor that could work for or against an attacker, depending on the circumstances, but that added an extra measure of horror to the Great War battlefield.

In the final stages of the war, during 1917 and 1918, both the Germans and the Allies developed new, though very different, tactical methods. Both sides realized that massive preparatory barrages did not work and surrendered the element of surprise. The Allies, especially the British, developed the "rolling" or "creeping" barrage. The artillery concentrated to support the attack would hit the front sectors for a short barrage and would then lift and move forward along preregistered lines ever more deeply into the enemy rear. The infantry would advance according to a set timetable that would bring them to a given position on the trailing edge of the barrage, so that they could assault the enemy position before the Germans could fully recover, dig themselves out of their dugouts, and set up their machine guns. It was said of the best British rolling barrages of the war that an advancing soldier would be so close to the fire that he could "light his pipe" with it.

Another British innovation, soon adopted by the French and the Americans, involved the use of tanks. These tracked armored vehicles, mounting cannon and/or machine guns, could cross the devastation of no-man's-land, drive over obstacles such as barbed wire, brave the fire of rifles and machine guns, and provide both cover and fire support for the attacking infantry.

While such developments marked major tactical advances, they nevertheless were not the entire answer to the problems facing the Allies. Tanks tended to break down on the battlefield and could not always be depended upon to support the advance beyond the initial lines of defense. The rolling barrage worked well during the initial assault, but as the first wave of attacking battalions went forward, an increasing number would inevitably fall behind schedule as their artillery support mindlessly moved on without them. Battlefield communications remained so primitive that it was difficult, and often impossible, to make the necessary adjustments.

As a result, while Allied attacks late in the war were more successful and not as prohibitively costly as they had been earlier, they were still not cheap. Nor were they able to break through the entirety of the German defensive system until the very end, when the German army began to collapse from exhaustion and loss of hope for the possibility of victory.

Toward the end of the war, the Germans worked out their own set of tactics known as *stoss* ("shock"), or infiltration tactics (and occasionally and incorrectly as Hutier tactics). The Germans developed their new tactics through experience gained on all fronts and employed them first on the eastern front at Riga in September 1917, then in Italy at Caporetto in October 1917.

The keys to the new German tactics were surprise, speed, and initiative. Attacking units at the front moved only at night. Specially prepared shelters hid the new units from enemy eyes. The Germans employed a short but sharp preparatory artillery barrage using explosives and gas, followed by a rolling barrage. There was thus no need to stockpile mounds of shells that were certain to be seen by enemy reconnaissance aircraft.

Immediately behind the barrage came not masses of infantry, but small *Stosstruppen*. These were specially trained, organized, and equipped units. The basic unit was not the battalion, but the squad of about a dozen and a half men. Each squad included teams of men carrying light machine guns or automatic rifles and small mortars. These units were trained not to assault the entirety of the forward enemy trench line, but to search out the weak spots, bypass the strong points, and to move into the enemy rear. There they would dislocate defenses, disrupt communications lines, prevent the movement of reserves to the front, and, if all went well, achieve a breakthrough. Subsequent waves of additional *Stosstruppen* would be fed into the discovered gaps in the enemy defenses, while regular infantry units moved forward to mop up strong points bypassed by the *Stosstruppen*. The leaders of *Stosstruppen* units were expected make decisions on their own initiative, without receiving orders from the rear. They would, using flares and runners, identify for subsequent waves the weak spots they had found and keep moving through the enemy defenses.

The Germans unleashed their new tactics along the western front in 1918 and in a series of offensives between March and May that shattered the Allied lines, nearly breaking the British front and driving through the French toward Paris. For the first time in years, the opposing armies found themselves fighting in open terrain, areas such as Belleau Wood, where the American Marine Brigade checked the German advance toward the Marne.

But even the German tactics, while a major advance, were not the complete answer to the tactical conundrum facing Great War commanders. As the German advance progressed, the *Stosstruppen* eventually outran their supplies and artillery support and collapsed, exhausted. Moving supplies, guns, and reinforcements forward over the battlefield remained an unsolved problem. Poor communications bedeviled the advance. There was now more mobility on the battlefield, but not enough to bring about a decisive result. The war continued to be a contest of attrition, and one that the Germans could not win.

Nevertheless, the outlines of future warfare were becoming apparent. The marriage of German tactics, Allied armored developments, the motorization of logistic and artillery elements, wireless voice radio, and the use of aircraft in direct ground support would form the core of what in 1939 would be termed *Blitzkrieg*—"lightning war!"

The Germans attacked as they had elsewhere: they strengthened their firing line of infantry, brought up howitzers in support, waited for the enemy to waiver, and then sent in a massed infantry charge. But at Mons, the British displayed the steadfastness and fire discipline that had long been associated with their infantry. They did not waiver, and when the impatient Germans charged, the attackers were slaughtered. While the British held their ground and checked the German advance, they had themselves suffered heavy casualties, and when the BEF's commander, General Sir John French, learned of the retreat of the French Fifth Army, he ordered the BEF to fall back as well.

August 24, 1914, found all of the Allied armies in full retreat. The French commander-in-chief, General Joffre, at last recognized the total failure of his strategy. The question now became, where would the retreat end?

In late August, the French line slowly began to stabilize in the south as the troops went over to the defensive along the well-fortified border. Gradually the Germans, themselves suffering heavy casualties, slowed their attacks, and the French line held. But on the Allied left, the Germans continued to advance. The Germans swung their First and Second Armies around the flank. This change in axis, however, brought the German line of march inside Paris. Joffre, already stung by the French defeats, was in no mood to yield the capital without a fight. Instead he decided to use the French railway system to concentrate a new army in Paris, both to defend the city and to threaten the flank of the Germans as they advanced past the capital. As the *poilus* detrained in Paris, the city's taxis doubled as motor transport and carried the troops out to the front.

This sudden French concentration of force on the flank of the German First Army forced Kluck to shift divisions from his left to his right. As the First Army gradually turned toward the west, and Bülow's Second Army advanced to the south toward the Marne River, a gap yawned between the two German armies.

Between 5 and 9 September the French, British, and Germans fought what became known as the Battle of the Marne. The French attacked along the entire line, pinning the Germans, while the BEF advanced slowly but steadily into the gap between the two German armies. At the German headquarters in Luxembourg, the situation at the front appeared confused. Communications between Moltke and his forward armies while they were still advancing were conducted as they had been a century earlier, by staff officers (although the modern staff officers rode in cars and not on horses). Moltke, ill and exhausted, sent one of his general staff aides—Lieutenant Colonel Richard Hentsch—to the front to survey the situation and fully empowered him to take any necessary actions.

Hentsch's mind was filled with bad news as he drove west toward the headquarters of the Kluck and Bülow. The German armies further south were stalled. The British had landed an amphibious force at Antwerp in the German rear. The Germans had won a great victory in the east at Tannenberg, but the pair of corps Moltke two weeks earlier had stripped from the German right wing to reinforce the eastern front were to remain in East Prussia. To Hentsch, the situation along the front of the two German armies appeared confused at best and disastrous at worst. The German infantry appeared dirty and exhausted. The proper and safe course to prevent a disaster was to order a withdrawal to restore contact between the two German armies. Thus began the retreat to the Aisne River.

Historians will long debate Hentsch's decision and the viability of the Schlieffen plan itself. There can be no doubt that the Germans had landed themselves in a predicament. No one will ever know if they could have wrested victory from defeat along the Marne. Nor can we know what the impact of such a victory might have been. Perhaps the German plan was doomed to failure from the start, its unrealistic assumptions about modern war evident in the rapid French concentration of force by rail around Paris. Or perhaps it was Moltke who, through his tinkering with the original plan and hesitancy in its execution, ensured its failure. Whatever the truth, the fact remains that the Germans did withdraw, and the fighting around Paris became, both in military and psychological terms, a great Allied victory—the Miracle of the Marne.

In the weeks after the Marne battle, both sides hustled north in an effort to outflank the other and to regain the initiative. But by early October, the "Race to the Sea" had ended in a draw when the armies of the two alliances reached the coast. A continuous and increasingly entrenched front now wound for about six hundred miles from the English Channel to the Swiss border.

Looking at the campaign as a whole, the Germans had performed better than the French had. Unlike Schlieffen's scheme for destroying France, Plan XVII had not even come close to success. The German armies stood deep in French territory. Nevertheless, the German strategy had failed. The Germans had gambled on defeating the French in a single campaign and had lost. The cost of that miscalculation would be substantial, for both Germany and for the world.

The war in the east opened with the Austro-Hungarian invasion of Serbia. The Serbs fielded three armies totaling about 200,000 men commanded by Field Marshal Radomir Putnik. The Serbs were the least well equipped of any of the European armies taking the field. Putnik himself was a near invalid who commanded from a cart. But the Serbs were tough, battle-hardened veterans of the Balkan wars, and Putnik was a more experienced and wily commander than his Austrian counterpart, General Oskar Potiorek.

In August 1914, the Serbs crushed the initial Austrian assault and drove the invaders back across the border. Potiorek stabilized the situation, but only by convincing Conrad to commit one of the two corps of the Second Army, meant for Galicia, to the Danube front. In September, the Serbs defeated a second invasion, although the Austrians did gain a few bridgeheads over the Drina River. These served as jumping off points for a winter offensive that gained Belgrade, the capital, and drove deep into Serbia. But Putnik struck again, drove the Austrians back, and recaptured Belgrade. The Austro-Hungarian invasions had not only failed, but through their failure had also compromised plans for the campaign against Russia in Galicia, where the outnumbered Austro-Hungarians faced four Russian armies.

The opening battles in Galicia were meeting engagements fought as the armies marched toward one another from their respective railheads. Between 22 August and 1 September, two of Conrad's armies drove into Russian Poland and defeated a pair of Russian armies at the battles of Krasnik and Komarov. Unfortunately for Conrad, at the battle of the Gnila Lipa, from 26 to 30 August, two other Russian armies drove back the Austro-Hungarian Third Army, unsupported on its right wing because of the redirection of the Second Army to the Serb front and elements of which were only beginning to arrive from the Danube. The advancing Russians captured the important Galician rail junction of Lemberg. There followed roughly two weeks of bitter seesaw fighting, at the end of which the Austro-Hungarian front collapsed and the Russians drove to the foothills of the Carpathian Mountains. But while the Russians were winning their string of victories in Galicia, their armies farther north were suffering a stunning defeat in East Prussia.

Geography shaped the Russian invasion of East Prussia. The Russian First Army, commanded by General Paul Rennenkampf, advanced west from its base in Lithuania. General Alexander Samsonov's Second Army advanced northward from Poland. An area of East Prussian swamps and forest formed a natural barrier between these two advances and made communication and coordination of the Russian invasion difficult. So, too, did the personal animosity of the two Russian commanders, rooted in a dispute that had occurred during the Russo-Japanese War.

A single German army, the Eighth, commanded by General Max von Prittwitz, stood between the two Russian armies. The German plan was to fall on Rennenkampf's First Army, defeat it quickly, and then race back west to meet Samsonov's army and defeat it. Unfortunately for Prittwitz, in the opening battles of Stalluponen and Gumbinnen (17 to 20 August), the Germans failed to do more than temporarily check the Russian advance. Prittwitz panicked, telephoned Moltke, and talked of retreat to the Vistula River, surrendering all of East Prussia. Moltke promptly sacked Prittwitz and replaced him with General Paul von Hindenburg, aided by a talented chief of staff, Erich Ludendorff, and he stripped two corps from the right wing of the German advance in France and shipped them east.

The situation was not as bleak as Prittwitz believed. By the time Hindenburg arrived at Eighth Army headquarters, the able Lieutenant Colonel Max Hoffman had devised an alternative plan. Leaving a screen to slow the advance of the Russian First Army, which was moving westward slowly, the Germans would use the ample rail net in East Prussia to concentrate their forces against both flanks of the Second Army as it advanced northward from Poland.

Hindenburg and Ludendorff approved the plan. Between 26 and 30 August, the Germans closed in on Samsonov's army and virtually destroyed it in a classic double-envelopment near Tannenberg, capturing 125,000 men and 500 guns. Samsonov committed suicide. The Eighth Army, now reinforced by the troops from the west, next turned its attention to the Russian First Army and drove it back, but was unable to destroy Rennenkampf's force.

Over the next several months, both sides extended their front into Poland, as the Germans and Austro-Hungarians attempted to establish contact between their armies. The Central Powers launched offensives in the fall and winter in an effort to capture Warsaw, an important rail center in the Polish salient. Both the Austrians and Germans made headway, only to retire in the face of spirited Russian counterattacks. There was particularly bitter fighting in November near Lodz, in which an entire German corps was almost cut off and annihilated. But neither side could achieve a decisive result. When the fighting finally stopped for the winter, the line had stabilized. The Austrians had lost territory in Galicia, the Russians in Poland. All the armies were exhausted.

As 1914 ended, the European powers faced difficult choices. Their plans for a quick, victorious war had failed to produce the expected results. The Austro-Hungarians had even failed to knock Serbia out of the war. All the armies had suffered horrific casualties. Stocks of weapons and ammunition, especially artillery shells, were low. What was now to be done?

The forces that had helped to propel Europe toward war—nationalism, large military establishments, miscalculation, and pride—were no less present in January 1915 than they had been in August 1914. In fact, as the realities of the huge national—human and materiel—commitments already made during the opening stage of the war became clear, the likelihood of a diplomatic settlement receded as war aims began to expand, rather than contract.

continued on page 99

The War in the Air

The airplane was in its infancy when the Great War began in August 1914. The major powers possessed small air arms whose principal mission was reconnaissance. Aircraft played an important role early in the war, supplying information, most notably during the mobile stage of operations in the west.

As the war settled into a stalemate, reconnaissance remained important. Aircraft began to carry cameras to photograph the development of enemy trench systems and to document the buildups of troops and supplies that heralded the start of any new offensive—a big push. Aircraft also were useful spotting the fall of artillery rounds, now fired mostly at distances beyond the line of sight of the gunner. Aircraft using visual signals or, later, wireless telegraphy could indicate whether rounds fell short, long, left, right, or on target. Airmen also started carrying primitive bombs that they dropped on enemy targets. Although these raids were hardly deadly, they were annoying.

As the importance of aircraft increased, so, too, did the desire of the respective forces to eliminate their enemies' airborne pests and spies. But how? Early in the war, aircraft were unarmed. Some pilots took to the air with rifles or grenades, but the odds of hitting an enemy flying machine were long. A few pilots used their own propellers to chop off parts of an opponent's plane. This maneuver was, of course, risky.

The machine gun, so effective on the ground, was the obvious answer to the question of how aircraft could be armed to bring down other aircraft. But how could one mount such a device on an aircraft? Two-seater reconnaissance aircraft mounted a machine gun for the use of the observer, but employing the weapon offensively from such a position was difficult. In February 1915, the British began to deploy the Vickers F.B. 5 "Gunbus," a two-seater pusher fighter with a light Lewis machine gun mounted forward for the gunner.

The more efficient planes, however, were tractor types—that is, those with the engine and the propeller situated ahead of, rather than behind, the pilot. Attempts to fire machine guns through the revolving propeller destroyed the blades. In March 1915, a French pilot, Roland Garros, devised a partial solution to this problem when he affixed steel deflectors to the propeller of his Morane monoplane to deflect the bullets that might otherwise strike the blades. This was dangerous, since the ricocheting bullets could go in any number of directions. Nevertheless, Garros had a string of victories—five kills in three weeks—before he force-landed behind German lines. Roland Garros had become the Great War's first air ace.

Initially the Germans tried to copy Garros's deflector system. But then engineers employed by the Dutch aircraft designer Anthony Fokker developed a synchronized gear system that timed the firing of the machine gun to the rotation of the propeller. The first German planes to mount a synchronized Spandau machine gun were single-wing Fokker Eindeckers, which took to the air in June 1915. By the late summer, as the numbers of Eindeckers grew, the Germans shot down more and more Allied planes in what became known as the Fokker Scourge.

The Allies rushed new biplane designs to the front. In February 1916, the British sent the first single-seat fighter squadron, No. 24, to France, armed with the Airco D.H. 2 pusher and mounting a Lewis gun in front for the pilot. In March, the French began to employ their Nieuport 11 "Bebe," which had a Lewis gun mounted on the upper wing where it could fire over the propeller. While the Fokker's Spandau was more effective than the Lewis, the D.H. 2 and Nieuport 11 were more powerful and maneuverable aircraft that quickly brought an end to the Fokker's dominance of the sky.

In the late summer of 1916, the Germans responded to the Allied challenge and formed their own all-fighter squadrons, termed *Jagdstaffeln* (*Jastas*), and equipped them with powerful biplanes, most notably the early Albatross series (D I and DII), which mounted synchronized twin-Spandau machine guns. The Germans quickly regained superiority in air-to-air fighting. Nevertheless, the pattern of shifting air dominance between the Allies and Germans continued as one side and then the other introduced new and more powerful aircraft designs at the front.

But the Germans did more than unveil new aircraft in the late summer of 1916. The commander of Jasta 2, Captain Oswald Boelcke, developed a set of rules, since known as the *Dicta Boelcke*, that represented the first set of tactical doctrines for air-to-air fighting. Boelcke's work and the example he set in training his pupils—among them the famous aces Werner Voss and Manfred von Richthofen (the Red Baron, whose eighty kills made him the top-scoring ace of the Great War)—inspires air warriors to this day.

Focus on the technological side of the air war too often hides more important developments in strategy, operational concepts, and doctrine taking place during the war. While the Germans often had the more technologically superior aircraft and fielded some of the best pilots, the Allied air forces, especially that of Great Britain, were at the forefront of overall doctrinal developments.

The Allies, despite their inferiority in plane-to-plane combat during major portions of the war, developed an aggressive strategy for the employment of their air arms. While the Germans usually employed their fighters defensively over or behind their lines, the British generally employed their aircraft offensively, as part of a strategic concept to fight the air war over enemy lines. This strategy resulted in heavy losses for the British, but it kept the Germans on the defensive and away from Allied lines as much as possible. It also kept unremitting pressure on the German pilots. Given the ability of the British and French aircraft industries to produce more planes than the Germans, the Allied strategy eventually wore down German strength in the air. As was true of the war in the trenches, the fighting in the skies became a war of attrition. While the old hands, the veteran pilots who managed to survive their initial combat experiences, often ran up substantial scores, the typical new pilot had an average life expectancy at the front of about two weeks.

British offensive strategic and operational concepts, however costly, represented the development of what could be termed air strategy. It was no coincidence that the British were the first of the great powers to form an independent air force, the Royal Air Force (RAF), in April 1918. By the end of the war, Allied air power theorists such as Briton Hugh Trenchard, American William "Billy" Mitchell, and Italian Giulio Douhet envisioned air power as a means of bypassing war in the trenches and unleashing a bombing campaign directly against an enemy country. In 1918, such men were little more than visionaries. The technology necessary to wage such a campaign remained to be developed. A generation would pass before an air force possessed the means to undertake a meaningful onslaught from the air. Not until the advent of atomic weapons and "smart" technology would the dream of such men be fully realized. Nevertheless, the air combat of the Great War marked the beginning of a new era of conflict.

After all, if such a war had to be fought, then the benefits ought to be substantial. And such a result required a military victory.

There had, in fact, been great victories on the battlefield. The Russians had struck a heavy blow against the Austro-Hungarian Empire. The Germans had won a great victory at Tannenberg. The French had suffered crushing defeats in Alsace and Lorraine, but had thrown back the Germans along the Marne.

Despite these victories and defeats, costly as they were, not one of the great powers was on the verge of collapse. The resources—human and materiel—of the modern state were so vast that no single set of victories was likely to bring about defeat. The reserve systems and the ability of industry to respond rapidly to the materiel demands of the war all but ensured that there would be a steady supply of men and weapons to send to the front. Moreover, the wealth of the modern industrialized states was so great that they could sustain such efforts for the immediate future. And so the war continued in a state of stalemate—a European conflict that was already spreading and becoming a world war, a conflict that would end only when a prolonged and bloody struggle exhausted one alliance or the other.

In 1915, neither alliance possessed either the tools of war or the overwhelming advantage of numbers that would enable its side to break the stalemate along the western front, the premier arena of the Great War. The Germans and the Allies faced each other along a continuous line of entrenched positions stretching for over 600 miles from the Swiss border to the English Channel. Both armies were dug in and continued to dig deeper and to develop ever more elaborate "trench systems" as the war progressed (see "The 'Typical' Battle").

Faced with this tactical stalemate, the least imaginary military leaders asked for more—more men and more materiel, especially artillery—in an effort to wage and win a war of attrition. If enough guns could be brought to bear on a given sector, ought not it be possible to level the ground and obliterate the defenses that stood in the path of an attacking force? If the attacking force were large enough, would it not be able to bull its way through such a position? The answer, unfortunately, turned out to be no.

More imaginative minds sought alternative techniques to finesse one's way through the front lines. Inventive minds were already working on ways to use new technologies—motor vehicles, armor, wireless radios, and aircraft—to break the deadlock, although these efforts would not fully bear fruit for another generation. But other technological advances offered new methods to kill or incapacitate an enemy. Armies rushed to the front new weapons designed for use against an entrenched enemy. Among these were high-trajectory trench mortars, which were useful for dropping rounds into a narrow trench. Armies now began to field lightweight automatic weapons that could be carried by infantrymen. The Germans also initiated the use of flamethrowers, a much-feared device.

But the most dreaded and infamous of the new weapons of the Great War were chemical weapons. The Germans first used poison gas against the Russians in January 1915, but the subzero weather limited the effectiveness of the chemicals. In April 1915, the Germans used gas cylinders to unleash a cloud of chlorine gas against French colonial troops during the battle of Ypres. The yellow-green cloud enveloped the French soldiers, who choked and panicked, but the German command had not prepared to exploit the resultant gap in the lines. The Germans troops who did advance were less than eager to move too quickly in the wake of the cloud, only to find themselves gassed.

Soon all the armies were using chemical weapons, and as the war progressed, soldiers had to contend with new gases—phosgene and mustard being the most notable—delivered by artillery shell, which enabled even rear areas to be gassed. Armies issued specially designed protective gear, and soldiers added gas drills to their training.

Despite the widespread use of gas, it never proved to be a decisive weapon. The novelty and impact of the new weapon quickly decreased. That is not to suggest that the soldiers lost their fear of being gassed. The chemical remained a dreaded method of warfare, one outlawed after the Great War. But soldiers learned to exist with this new horror, another fruit of the industrial age applied to the battlefield.

But if there were not some way to get through the ever more elaborate trench systems of the western front, was there not some way around them? As European military leaders searched, in vain, for possible technological solutions to the problems they faced, they simultaneously looked for alternative strategic approaches that might lead to victory.

The Western Allies turned their attention eastward toward the weak link in the Central Powers alliance—namely, the Ottoman Empire, long considered the "sick man of Europe." When the Ottomans joined the Central Powers in November 1914, new theaters for potential action opened in the Middle East. Ottoman troops in Palestine threatened British control of the Suez Canal, while other troops in the valley of the Tigris and Euphrates rivers posed a threat to the British positions in Persia and the Persian Gulf. The British responded to these threats with operations of their own.

Allied sea power offered a more direct route to the Ottoman capital, Istanbul. If the Allies could force a naval squadron through the narrow Dardanelles and the ancient Hellespont and shell Istanbul, they might with a single stroke safeguard Persia and Suez, relieve pressure on the Russian Caucasus front, open a more direct sea route to the Russians, and perhaps even topple one of Germany's allies.

Unfortunately for the Allies, the promise of a quick victory in the Middle East never materialized. In February 1915, the

Turkish minefields and shore batteries proved strong enough to repulse the purely naval attempt to force the Dardanelles. In late April, a British and Commonwealth force landed on the Gallipoli peninsula, but were slow to exploit initial success. The Ottomans rushed a force, under the command of Mustafa Kemal (later known as Atatürk) to secure the peninsula. Despite repeated efforts to break out, the Allies found themselves fighting a new trench war in an inhospitable corner of the Balkans. They withdrew at the end of the year.

The Allied forces' focus on the Dardanelles cost them elsewhere in the Middle East. British troops in Egypt easily repulsed an Ottoman attack across the Sinai Peninsula toward the Suez Canal, but a British invasion of Mesopotamia (modern Iraq) failed to reach Baghdad. Turkish troops encircled the British at Kut-al-Amara and in April 1916 forced them to surrender after a prolonged siege.

Nevertheless, the British and their Arab allies, who were eager to drive the Turks from the region, eventually brought about the collapse of the Turkish empire. In March 1917, British troops finally captured Baghdad. In November 1917, another British army, commanded by General Sir Edmund Allenby, took Gaza, the gateway to Palestine. In December 1917, Allenby captured Jerusalem. The following summer, he advanced again and in a series of battles, aided by Arabs operating on the open Turkish desert flank, took Damascus and reached Aleppo in late October 1918, shattering the Turkish army in the process. While the Allies had finally achieved their long-sought goal of toppling the Ottoman Empire, the costly effort had borne fruit far too late to have an impact on the course of the war elsewhere.

Like the Allies, the Germans also looked east in 1915. There seemed to be no quick way to knock the French or British from the war along the western front. Accordingly, the Germans decided to shift primarily to the defensive in the west and to move more of their forces, and their effort, to the east. The eastern front was too long and the number of forces there too small to solidify as had the front lines in the west. As a result, the fighting in the east retained a far greater degree of mobility than had the fighting in the west.

That being the case, the Germans believed that they could profitably launch a successful offensive campaign against the Russians. In May 1915, the combined Austro-German Gorlice-Tarnow offensive ruptured the Russian front line. The Central Powers' forces advanced deeply into Russia, in some places as much as 250 miles, inflicting more than two million casualties on the defenders. A comparable drive in France would have been decisive, but Russia, while gravely wounded, refused to collapse. As the Germans drove eastward, the front lengthened, and they found themselves operating farther and farther from their bases of supply, in an area without the multiple rail lines that crisscrossed the western front. By the late fall, the advance had ground to a halt.

In early October, the Central Powers launched another combined Austro-German offensive, this time against the stubborn Serbs. Finally, the Austrians, aided by the Germans and the Bulgarians, who had also entered the war, quickly overran Serbia and advanced to the Greek frontier, where in the late fall, they were checked by an Allied force deployed to screen the Greek port of Thessaloniki. For the rest of the war, the two armies watched each other along a desolate, disease ridden, and inactive front.

Despite these substantive victories in the east, as 1915 drew to a close, German attention began to shift back toward the west. There, the Germans believed, was where the course of the war would ultimately be decided.

Attrition was the watchword of 1916. The Germans launched their major offensive around Verdun. The British launched a "big push" of their own farther north along the Somme. Despite the fact that the contending German, British, and French armies each suffered hundreds of thousands of casualties, gains were measured in yards and meters.

Perhaps no battle of the Great War so epitomizes the attritional nature of the struggle as does the battle for Verdun. Between

February and December 1916, the German and French armies fought a bloody campaign for control of this historic fortress town along the Meuse River. General Erich von Falkenhayn, Moltke's successor as chief of staff of the German army, planned not to break through the French line nor to regain mobility on the battlefield. Falkenhayn chose Verdun as his point of attack not because he wished to capture it, but because he knew the French would defend it—and to the death. The Germans, in a plan codenamed *Gericht* ("Judgment"), hoped to draw the French army into a sausage grinder that would ultimately bleed France to death.

The battle began on 21 February with a massive two-day bombardment. Two million shells—high explosives, shrapnel, armor-piercing rounds (to destroy concrete forts), and phosgene gas—fell along a six-mile sector of front at a rate of 100,000 per hour. Despite the impact of the bombardment, many French soldiers survived and resisted the German assault. The French high command reacted promptly and rushed reinforcements to plug the gaps. A ten-month-long battle of attrition began as both sides fed ever more men into the cauldron.

In February and March, the Germans made their most dramatic gains. They advanced little more than a mile, but they stormed several important forts, most notably Douaumont. In early June, the Germans took Fort Vaux. But the French resistance stiffened under the command of General Henri Philippe Pétain and the seesaw fighting continued at great cost to both sides. The exhausted Germans, facing a British offensive along the Somme, ended the attacks against Verdun. But now the French took up the challenge and sought to maintain the momentum they had gained. Between October and December, the French retook most of the ground they had lost, including Forts Douaumont and Vaux.

Both armies suffered heavily at Verdun. The French incurred about a half million casualties, and the Germans about 400,000. Falkenhayn's failure led to his replacement as chief of staff. He had bled his own army as much as he had bled the French. Moreover, the successful French defense of Verdun had given them a victory, and a new set of heroes, Pétain among them.

But there were other indirect results of the Verdun campaign. The German army's inability to bring the war to an end in 1916 led to searches for new ways to conclude the war successfully. Early in 1917, the Germans turned to one of their newer weapons—the U-boat—as the key to victory (see "The War at Sea"). That fatal German decision brought the United States into the war and all but sealed Germany's fate.

Verdun would emerge from the First World War as the symbol of the Great War. Ever since, the very word *Verdun* has remained sufficient to call to mind the horrors and futility of modern warfare.

As had been the case in 1915, the more "decisive" campaigns were those fought in the east. There were two: the first along the southern sector of the Russian front, and the second in the Balkans when Romania joined the Allies in the late summer of 1916.

In early June 1916, Russian general Alexei A. Brusilov undertook a massive offensive along the southern half of the eastern front. Brusilov's plan embraced concepts akin to those developed by the Germans later in the war (see "The 'Typical' Battle"). He eschewed the narrow attacks and long preparatory bombardments so prevalent at that stage of the Great War. Instead, he launched his assault following a short preparatory bombardment along a broad, 250-mile-long front manned entirely by Austro-Hungarian troops. "Brusilov's Offensive" surprised and shattered the opposing armies, and the Russians penetrated as much as fifty miles in some sectors. Nevertheless, there the offensive came to a halt as Austrian and German reinforcements arrived. Brusilov attempted to keep his armies moving, but the ill-equipped Russians could advance no further, and despite the promising start of the battle, the campaign became yet another struggle of attrition.

Once the Central Powers were assured that they had checked the Russian advance, they turned their attention back to the Balkans. In yet another successful combined Austro-German

continued on page 111

The War at Sea

While there were few major naval battles of note fought during the Great War, sea power nevertheless played an important role. Naval operations helped to give final shape to the contending alliances and, in the form of the Allied blockade, had a debilitating effect on the German economy and society.

When the war began in 1914, the Allies possessed a substantial superiority in naval power. The German High Seas Fleet was well trained and equipped and, perhaps, qualitatively—that is, ship-for-ship—superior to its British counterpart. But numbers and geography worked against the Germans. Great Britain's Royal Navy was the world's largest and most powerful, and the British Grand Fleet dominated the North Sea from its bases in Scotland. The Germans did possess a number of fast raiding cruisers that could, and would, wreak havoc on British shipping in the opening stage of the war. The German navy also possessed a fleet of excellent submarines—U-boats—but, in keeping with German plans for a short war, initially deployed these assets in support of the main fleet, and not in the commerce-raiding role that they would later dominate.

German prewar planning also posed a handicap. The Germans had invested heavily in their battle fleet in the decades before the war, but without ever defining exactly how they would employ that fleet in wartime. With the initiation of hostilities, the Germans expected—or, more accurately, hoped— that the British, in the style of Horatio Nelson, would strike directly at the High Seas Fleet in its anchorage in an attempt to destroy it. The Germans expected their defensive minefields and submarines to weaken the British to the point that the qualitatively superior High Seas Fleet would be able to meet and defeat what remained of Great Britain's Grand Fleet. This was a chancy strategy, one that has caused some historians to assign the sobriquet "risk fleet" to the German battleships. But, at least, it promised some hope of success.

The British, however, had no intention of undertaking such an offensive. Given the short steaming radius of coal-burning battleships, they knew that the powerful, but short-legged German High Seas Fleet could barely exit the North Sea. In effect, the British began the war with control of the sea and left it to the Germans to figure out how to challenge that control. By the fall of 1914, the German navy discovered that it actually had constructed what some historians have termed a "luxury" fleet—namely, a force that actually did not have much of a role to play in time of war.

Nevertheless, things did not go well everywhere for the British and their allies. The German battle cruiser *Göben*, at sea in the Mediterranean at the start of the war, evaded Allied pursuers and escaped to Istanbul. This proved to be not only an embarrassment for the British, but a diplomatic coup for the Germans, who turned the trapped ship over to the Turks and helped to bring the Ottoman Empire into the war on the side of the Central Powers in November 1914. Elsewhere on the high seas, German raiders and cruisers sank dozens of Allied merchant ships. Not until the end of 1914 were the German craft hunted down and destroyed.

As the war settled into a stalemate ashore, a new pattern of warfare emerged at sea. Faced with a protracted struggle, the Germans sought new methods to employ their sea power against the British. Elements of the High Seas Fleet raided and shelled the British coast, hoping to prompt a reaction and to catch a weaker segment of the Grand Fleet at sea. In January 1915, the British battle-cruiser squadron caught a weaker German force off Dogger Bank, sinking a cruiser and badly damaging two German battle cruisers. Stung by the defeat, the Germans decided to employ their U-boats as commerce raiders, enforcing a naval blockade of the British Isles.

As the Great War drug on, the attitude of the United States, still a neutral power, became an increasingly important consideration. Despite its military weakness, the United States was financially the richest and industrially the most powerful nation in the world. Even as a neutral country, the contributions of its markets and resources could prove to be decisive, especially as the war grew longer.

The war at sea posed challenges to Americans, who traditionally had valued their concepts of free trade and neutral rights. During the course of the Great War, both the British and the Germans tested American neutrality. Unfortunately for the Germans, geography and the nature of German naval power ensured that this test was asymmetrical in character and worked to the advantage of Great Britain.

The ships of the Royal Navy, in their enforcement of the blockade of Germany, operating from bases fronting the Atlantic Ocean, could easily stop American vessels. Once stopped, the ships could be searched for illegal cargoes bound for Germany, seized, and taken into a British port, where the case would be adjudicated in a court. In the event of a condemnation, the British could minimize American reaction by purchasing the seized cargo and releasing the ship and crew. While American "rights" had been violated, no lives or property were lost.

The Germans, operating submarines from bases in the North Sea, could not employ comparable methods. U-boats risked damage if, while surfaced, they challenged merchant ships, many of which were armed. U-boat commanders could not spare the men to staff prize crews to steam a captured ship back to port for adjudication. The most efficient way for a U-boat to operate was to sink the ship in question in a torpedo or gun attack. While the German navy directed its captains to restrict their attacks to British or other Allied merchant ships, inevitably mistakes were made. Such errors would most likely result in the loss of lives and property and, if Americans were involved, lead to protests from the United States.

During the course of 1915 and 1916, the Germans periodically unleashed their U-boats in new offensives. But each time, mistaken attacks, especially the sinking of liners carrying hundreds of passengers, outraged Americans. The sinking of the *Lusitania* in May 1915 cost the lives of 1,198 people, including 128 Americans. That sinking, plus others in 1916 against smaller liners, prompted American protests, German apologies, and restrictions on the operations of the U-boats.

As the stalemate deepened on land in 1916, the pressure on the German armed forces, including the navy, to find a way to end the conflict began to build. In response, the commander of the German High Seas Fleet, Vice Admiral Reinhard Scheer, devised a plan to lure elements of the British Grand Fleet, which was too large to be kept at a single base, into an ambush.

Scheer's plan had several elements. First, he would position U-boats off the Grand Fleet's major bases. Second, zeppelins—rigid airships filled with hydrogen and equipped with wireless telegraph transmitters—would crisscross the North Sea. Third, the High Seas Fleet would sortie from its own anchorage, steam north, and show itself off the Danish coast along the Jutland peninsula. This, Scheer expected, would lead the British fleet, commanded by Admiral John

Rushworth Jellicoe, to sortie from his three main Scottish bases. Submarines would report these moves to Scheer and attack the British squadrons as they left their anchorages. Zeppelins would monitor British moves. Meanwhile, Scheer, with his fleet concentrated, would steam across the North Sea and position himself to bring the full weight of his entire fleet against one of the elements of Jellicoe's still unconcentrated British force. If the Germans could overwhelm one of the elements of the Grand Fleet, the High Seas Fleet would then possess numerical parity and be in a position to continue the destruction of the British fleet in detail.

Unfortunately for Scheer, little went according to plan. The weather was too poor for the zeppelins to play their assigned role. British code breakers intercepted and read the German wireless messages and alerted Jellicoe, who ordered his fleet to sea before the Germans had even sailed. As a result, the U-boats positioned to ambush the British and report their sailing arrived on station too late, and Scheer had no idea that the British were already at sea as he steamed north.

In the mid-afternoon of 31 May, the British battle-cruiser squadron, commanded by Vice Admiral Sir David Beatty, collided with the German battle cruisers, commanded by Vice Admiral Franz Hipper, and began a confused engagement known as the Battle of Jutland. Hipper led Beatty toward Scheer's fleet, pounding the British on the way and sinking several British battle cruisers. Beatty pursued until he realized he was being led into a trap, at which point he led Hipper and Scheer back north toward the Grand Fleet, now deployed by Jellicoe in a line stretching across the path of the German battle fleet. Scheer, well aware of the tactical situation, ordered his destroyers to conduct a torpedo attack while the High Seas Fleet executed a *gefechtskehrtwendung*, a "battle about-turn" or "battle turnaway"—a sixteen-point, 180-degree turn to the right, beginning with the rear ship in the line. There followed a series of maneuvers during the rest of that day and into the next with which Jellicoe attempted to get between the Germans and their base. Despite several close calls, Scheer escaped in the darkness and returned home.

Tactically, the Battle of Jutland was a German success. The British lost more ships and men in the engagement. But strategically, the British won. Scheer failed to catch and defeat a major portion of the British fleet. The British retained their command of the sea approaches to Germany and could continue their blockade unhindered. The German fleet, despite its success, did not sortie again.

After Jutland, the leadership of the German navy was left to find some way for the service, with its huge and costly establishment, to contribute to the war effort. In the winter of 1916, the situation looked grim for the Germans, and many were desperately seeking some means to bring the conflict to a victorious conclusion. Based on statistics extrapolated from past experience, the German navy proposed that if the government would permit the unrestricted employment of the navy's steadily growing force of U-boats against shipping heading to and from the British Isles, Great Britain could be brought to its knees in six months. All the parties involved understood that such a decision would in all probability lead to American intervention. Nevertheless, the Germans concluded, correctly, that it would take at least a year before the Americans could deploy substantial ground forces to Europe. Assuming the war was brought to a successful conclusion in six months, American intervention would be irrelevant.

But the Germans had miscalculated once again. The war was not brought to an end in six months. German planners had mistakenly assumed that the Allies, facing a marked increase in the scale of U-boat operations, would alter neither their tactics nor their procedures, nor would they deploy new technologies in the face of a determined German unrestricted submarine offensive at sea.

As expected, the German declaration of unrestricted submarine warfare in February 1917 brought an American protest. When the British turned over copies of intercepted telegrams indicating that the Germans were attempting to bring Mexico into the war against the United States, President Woodrow Wilson in April asked for, and received, such a declaration of war from the U.S. Congress.

While the U-boats achieved successes, the Allies, albeit slowly, adopted more effective countermeasures, such as the time-tested use of convoys. Gradually, Allied shipping losses declined and German U-boat losses rose, and the German naval campaign, so costly in the diplomatic realm, did not prove decisive.

Unlike the Germans, the Allies never expected sea power to deliver a quick victory, and they persevered in their employment of a maritime blockade.

It is easy to attribute too much to the Allied blockade. It was probably not truly decisive in its influence. But the blockade was effective, and it hurt the Germans in more ways than one. For more than four years, Allied naval power gradually strangled the Germans, cutting them off from their colonies, all of which were lost, and their trade. The frustration of the Germans, who had invested so heavily in their navy, led them to a miscalculation that brought the United States into the war. That intervention, coming as it did at a critical time, may well have been decisive.

campaign, between late August 1916 and early January 1917, the Central Powers totally overran Romania, despite promises of Allied assistance.

For the Central Powers, 1917 was a difficult year. General Paul von Hindenburg, the victor of many battles along the eastern front, replaced Falkenhayn, the architect of Verdun, as chief of the German general staff. Erich Ludendorff, another general from the east, became quartermaster general and the effective power behind both the political and military thrones. At sea, the German navy unleashed its unrestricted submarine offensive in an attempt to bring Great Britain, viewed from Berlin as the lynchpin of the opposing alliance, to its knees. Ashore, Hindenburg, and Ludendorff accepted a defensive posture intended to allow the French and British to exhaust themselves in fruitless attacks against well-defended and prepared positions.

In February along the western front, the Germans fell back to a prepared position, the Siegfried Line, often dubbed the Hindenburg Line. This planned withdrawal straightened and shortened the most vulnerable sector of the line and allowed the Germans to accumulate much-needed reserves in preparation for the expected Allied offensive.

This ensuing attack was masterminded by General Robert Nivelle, one of the French heroes of Verdun. Nivelle's plan envisioned a series of Franco-British offensives that would draw in the German reserves, exhaust the defenders, and ultimately break through their defenses. Despite the fact that the German withdrawal eliminated the salient Nivelle had planned to strike with his major blow, he nevertheless persisted in his plans for an offensive against the new, and much tougher, German line.

As part of the overall Allied plan, the British, under the command of General Sir Douglas Haig, opened the campaigning season with an offensive in the north in the Arras sector, designed to draw German reserves away from the intended main French assault farther south. The British advanced in April and made some initial progress in their drive toward Vimy Ridge, but, as usual, at prohibitive cost. Nevertheless, the British continued their offensive and later extended it northward to include another attack toward Ypres. This drive also made some gains, but eventually stalled.

Nivelle launched his own offensive toward the Chemin des Dames on 16 April after eleven days of preparatory artillery bombardment. By mid-May, the French had advanced little more than three miles, but at an exceptionally high cost as Nivelle stubbornly refused to acknowledge his defeat. Some French units grew mutinous and refused to return to the front; others "baa-ed" like sheep as they marched into the trenches. Shaken, the French government replaced Nivelle with Pétain.

While Pétain worked to restore the morale and effectiveness of his army, Haig did his best to tie down the Germans, lest they launch an offensive of their own against the weakened French. Haig launched the first two of three major offensives: the first at Ypres in June, and the second farther north at Passchendaele in July. While the battle for Ypres was brief, less than a month, the fighting along the Passchendaele front lasted into the winter. In November, Haig launched his third offensive farther south near Arras. On 20 November, the British struck without the usual lengthy preliminary bombardment. Behind a "creeping barrage," British infantry moved forward, supported by two hundred tanks. The attackers broke through the surprised German defenders. But the attack soon lost momentum. Many of the tanks broke down in the difficult terrain, and the British, surprised by their own success, failed to fully exploit their initial breakthrough. Prompt German counterattacks soon erased all the British gains. Nevertheless, the impact of massed tanks on the offensive suggested at least one possible answer to the stalemate that gripped the western front.

While the Germans defeated all of the Allied offensives of 1917, their own losses, while lighter than those suffered by the British and French, were nonetheless heavy. Moreover, given the critical state of the French army in the second half of the year, the Germans were unable to undertake any offensives of their own. German reserves were too few, given the steady pressure of the Allied offensives.

In the east, however, the Central Powers were able to undertake offensive operations. In March 1917, revolution broke out in Russia, the tsar abdicated, and a provisional government took power. As the Germans and Austrians observed, Russia began to disintegrate politically, economically, and militarily. In August, Alexander Kerensky, the new Russian leader, directed General Brusilov to undertake another offensive against the Austrians. The Russian attack achieved initial success; however, the Austro-German counterattack not only regained the lines, but also drove the Russians back in some sectors as much as sixty miles.

In September the Germans struck at Riga, in Lithuania, in an operation meant to open the door to a further advance against the Russian capital of St. Petersburg—now renamed Petrograd. The Germans hoped that this threat would force the clearly weakening Russians to negotiate and lead to an armistice in the east. It was at Riga that the Germans unveiled their new attack methods using Stosstruppen ("storm troops") and infiltration tactics.

In October, the Bolsheviks seized power in the Russian capital and unilaterally quit the war. Still trying to force an official armistice, the Germans advanced, occupying Latvia, Estonia, and most of the Ukraine. In March 1918, at Brest Litovsk, the

Germans and Bolsheviks signed a treaty of peace in which the latter signed away those areas of the former Russian empire then in Germans hands.

The Russian collapse in the winter of 1917–1918 literally freed a million German troops for service in the west. These were men who had tasted victory in the east. Many were schooled in the new methods of warfare demonstrated so effectively at Riga.

The Germans deployed one of the first contingents from Russia to the Italian front in the fall of 1917. Since Italian entry into the war in May 1915, not alongside its German and Austrian allies, but as a member of the Entente, the Italians and Austrians had faced each other along their respective borders with neither side making much progress. But on 24 October, seven veteran German divisions from the east spearheaded an Austro-Hungarian offensive near Caporetto. The Italian front collapsed like a house of cards, and the Germans advanced over seventy miles before Italian reserves, backed by French and British troops rushed from France, halted the drive.

As 1917 came to a close, Germany looked eagerly to the start of the 1918 campaigning season despite the failure of the U-boat offensive and the entry of the United States into the war. For the first time since 1914, the Germans were able to concentrate their power in the west in France and Flanders. A million fresh troops from the east would ultimately reach the front, many of them trained to employ the new tactics that had worked so well at Riga and Caporetto. Surely, 1918 would be the year of decision.

While the Germans hoped to win the war in the west in 1918, the Allies simply hoped to stave off defeat. They expected the war to continue for at least an additional year, perhaps into 1920, by which time the Americans would have fully mobilized and shipped millions of men to the western front. As of March 1918, there were still only a half dozen partially trained American divisions in France, though they were fresher and larger than the corresponding European divisions.

General Ludendorff realized that if Germany were to win, he had to strike quickly and knock the British and French out of the war before more Americans arrived. Ludendorff believed that the methods that had worked in the east would work as well in the west. He planned to unleash a sequence of four offensives, three against the British and one against the French, and tear a series of holes into the Allied line. Events and the degree of German success would determine what course Ludendorff would then follow.

Ludendorff miscalculated. Despite the Germans' display of tactical and operational brilliance in the east, the Russians had withdrawn from the war not because of any German military victory, but because of a loss of will—or, more accurately, desire—to continue the struggle. Russians were still fighting after Brest Litovsk; they simply were fighting each other. In deciding where to conduct his offensives, Ludendorff picked sectors where Allied dispositions and the terrain would offer the least resistance—that is, where the holes he planned to punch would be the biggest. As a result, Ludendorff's offensives were sure to gain ground and to inflict losses on the Allies. But the question remained: would they gain strategically significant ground and inflict enough losses on the Allies to ensure victory?

By the spring, all was ready for the final German offensives. The first of Ludendorff's hammer blows, Operation Michael, opened on 21 March along the Somme. Behind a short barrage of explosives and gas, *Stosstruppen* teams pinpointed the British weak points and kept moving deeply into the British defenses, bypassing centers of resistance and leaving them to be mopped up by follow-up forces. Confronted with the new tactics for the first time, the British front promptly collapsed, and the *Stosstruppen* drove as much as thirty miles into British territory before the offensive ran its course. In April, Ludendorff struck again, along the Lys River, driving a second salient ten miles into the British lines.

On 27 May, Ludendorff launched his third offensive, this time against the French along the Aisne. On the first day, the

Stosstruppen advanced thirteen miles, the greatest single day's advance in the west since 1914! In a few days, the Germans were through the French trench system and at the point of the salient about thirty miles from their start line, heading, once again, for the Marne. But the Germans had outrun their supplies. Allied reserves, among them the American 3rd and 2nd Infantry Divisions, the latter of which included a brigade of U.S. Marines, counterattacked and halted the German advance.

Ludendorff next attempted to exploit his gains, primarily along the Somme and Aisne rivers. But the renewed German offensives gained little ground. Casualties among the *Stosstruppen* had been heavy, and the subsequent German offensives lacked the zest of the earlier drives. Moreover, the Allies had quickly adjusted their dispositions and tactics to meet the new German methods. And unlike the Germans, the Allies had ample reserves. More than a year had passed since American entry into the war, and a steady flow of American divisions were now reaching France. Ludendorff had spent his irreplaceable reserves and failed to achieve the decisive results he had sought.

It was now the turn of the Allies to launch a series of offensives designed to eliminate the German salients. The French, with American support, struck first along the Aisne in a July offensive. In August, the British attacked near Amiens. Everywhere, Allied troops advanced. Once impenetrable, German defenses began to fall. Substantial numbers of German soldiers began to surrender. Ludendorff termed 8 August "a black day," less for his men, perhaps, than for its commander. Ludendorff was close to a nervous breakdown, for he sensed that his army was beginning to break and that his offensives, planned with such hope and expectation, had failed. On 11 and 13 August, Hindenburg and Ludendorff met with the kaiser and advised negotiation. Military victory was no longer possible.

As the world slowly moved toward peace, a new series of Allied offensives drove the Germans back toward their borders.

In September, the Americans, now organized into their own First Army, eliminated the St. Mihiel salient near Verdun, while farther north, the French and British struck along much of the front. In October, a second American army joined the offensive and drove through the Argonne Forest. Unrelenting Allied pressure forced the Germans back.

The pace now quickened. Bulgaria had already surrendered. On 30 October, Turkey quit. The Austro-Hungarian Empire was imploding, its subject peoples in revolt. On 3 November, in desperation, Admiral Reinhard Scheer ordered the German High Seas Fleet to sortie, but the sailors mutinied. On 7 November, the kaiser, faced with the possibility of revolution in Germany, abdicated and fled with his family to neutral Holland. The Socialists took over the German government. On 8 November, in a railway passenger car parked on a siding in the forest of Compiegne, the Germans accepted sweeping armistice terms. Finally, on the eleventh hour, of the eleventh day, of the eleventh month, the guns fell silent along the western front.

The Great War witnessed the advent of new military technologies: wireless radio, chemical weapons, submarines, aircraft and aircraft carriers, and tanks, as well as new concepts and doctrine for their employment. By the end of the war, marriages of tactics and technology existed to break the stalemate of the trenches. But that technology, despite the hopes of some military thinkers, would not make war either cheap or quick if major powers once again drew their swords against one another. The Great War was a costly war of attrition. So, too, would be the war that followed.

But the results of the Great War are far more important than the purely military "lessons." Despite the seeming futility of the struggle, it was one of the most decisive events in the history of the twentieth century.

The realities of the Great War gave conflict a new face. As Lewis Mumford wrote in 1934, "War is the supreme drama of a completely mechanized society." The men who mobilized to fight the war faced a frightful life in the trenches and slaughter on barbed-wire-strewn battlefields dominated by machine guns, poison gas, flamethrowers, aerial bombing, and week-long artillery barrages. Citizen soldiers became statistics: 65 million mobilized, 37 million casualties, including 8.5 million dead.

Nor were the costs of modern war restricted to the battlefield. The struggle caused, directly or indirectly, the death of as many as 10 million civilians. Another 20 million died worldwide in the influenza epidemic of 1918, a plague often linked to the war. The conflict changed the very demography of Europe, killing off a generation in the trenches. The Allied naval blockade brought the war into the very homes of the German people, in the form of privation and outright starvation. The war on the western front, fought mostly in France, literally transformed the geography of the area, which remains scarred to this day. War had become a clash of peoples rather than a clash of armies. Europeans discovered that the modern nation-state could not easily be defeated on the battlefield, but had to be driven to exhaustion through a long and costly war of attrition.

The Great War had a tremendous impact on the minds of Europeans, especially those in the West. States drew so heavily and broadly on their populations to fill the ranks that few families escaped the direct and often bitter impact of the struggle. Governments conscripted farmers, laborers, workers, poets, authors, and artists alike and sent them to the trenches. Those who survived returned to their homes, tutored in the realities of modern war. Photographs and newsreels from the front, shot and filmed in drab monochrome, contrasted sharply with the colorful paintings that had captured the supposed glories of previous wars. Those survivors imbued with artistic talent gave touching testimony, often mute, to the horrors of war. Never again would Europeans march off to war with the enthusiasm of 1914. Even the streets of Nazi Berlin were subdued and quiet in September 1939 when the German people sent their sons off to yet another world war.

But if the Great War changed forever the way people perceived conflict, the degree and depth of change was by no means universal. The Great War was notable not just for its horrors, but also for the dramatic changes it wrought. The 1914–1918 war gave strength to pacifists and internationalists alike, all of whom sought to prevent a future conflict. But the Great War did little to stifle the nationalism that had helped to spark the struggle. In fact, the war played midwife to nascent nationalities as the multinational empires—Hapsburg, Romanov, and Ottoman—collapsed. In Europe, the Finns, Lithuanians, Estonians, Latvians, Poles, Czechs, Slovaks, Slovenes, Bosnians, and Croatians, and in the Middle East, assorted Arabs (in Iraq, Jordan, Syria, Lebanon, and Palestine), gained their limited or complete independence.

The Great War, as was the case with most twentieth-century wars, was also the handmaiden of governmental and bureaucratic growth. To fight and to win wars, governments had to take unto themselves sufficient powers to draft their citizens, to mobilize their industrial infrastructure, to ration resources, to control information (propaganda), and to raise the revenues necessary to wage modern conflicts. The Great War had changed everything.

CHAPTER IV

The Interwar Years, 1918–1937

THE INTERWAR YEARS—the roughly two decades from the end of the First World War to the beginning of the second— marked an era of significant change in military technology. During these years, many of the nascent technologies available during the Great War—wireless radio, the airplane, and mechanization— developed more fully. The integration of these technologies into military forces proved no easy task. Some of the major powers did better than others, but much remained to be learned in the crucible of war.

The growth of antiwar and antimilitary (if not outright pacifist) sentiments following the Great War hamstrung interwar military developments. This mood was strongest in the countries that had won the war (France, Great Britain, and the United States) and weaker among those that had lost (Germany and Russia). The war had been a tragedy, but efforts to link the conflict to the pre-1914 arms race, militarism (especially German militarism), and alliance systems were simplistic. Nevertheless, the logic of such views dictated polices that sought to reduce arms, weaken the military, and make broad international agreements in lieu of military alliances. While well intentioned, such approaches ultimately allowed nations willing to risk another war to hold hostage those who were not. In an effort to escape another march to Verdun, the Europeans chose the road to Auschwitz.

There were many in Europe, and elsewhere, who considered war as a necessary, if costly, catalyst for change—for national independence, expansion, or world revolution. The Bolsheviks proclaimed their desire for peace in 1917, but they fought another half decade to reestablish the Russian empire and Vladimir Lenin proved to be Clausewitzian in his view of war as an extension of state policy. Nor were all defeated Germans or dissatisfied Italians overcome with antiwar sentiments. In Rome and Berlin, hybrid nationalist and socialist regimes clamored for another war, albeit one more limited in chronology and scope. "Struggle is the father of all things," Adolf Hitler proclaimed in a speech in 1928, the same year most nations signed the Kellogg-Briand Pact outlawing war. "It is not by the principles of humanity that man lives or is able to preserve himself above the animal world, but solely by means of the most brutal struggle." Four years later, Benito Mussolini wrote in the *Enciclopedia Italiana*, "War alone brings up to their highest tension all human energies and imposes the stamp of nobility upon the peoples who have the courage to make it."

Nevertheless, throughout the 1920s, the international political mood was hardly conducive to things military. Political factors limited military development in the United States, Great Britain, and France. The Versailles treaty did the same in Germany. It is no accident that in the mid-1930s, the Soviet Union—a state unfettered by treaty strictures and least affected by antiwar sentiment—had arguably developed the most comprehensive and coherent military doctrine in the world.

Despite the fact that time passes in a seamless fashion, historians prefer to chop history into separate pieces. When the Great War ended, the major powers continued along the same lines of development that had appeared most promising during the final stages of the conflict. Since the various powers had adopted somewhat divergent approaches to the strategic, operational, and tactical problems they confronted during the war, they embarked upon correspondingly different patterns of development in the two decades that followed.

Among the most pressing and difficult issues facing interwar military thinkers were questions related to mechanization, especially the use of tanks. Few doubted that mechanization was part of the future of warfare. Nevertheless, several interrelated issues remained to be resolved. To what extent should tanks and other motorized vehicles replace the horse? Could a state afford to mechanize its entire army? If not, should that limited capability be spread throughout the force or concentrated in an elite corps? And should tanks be employed tactically as a distinct element or in combination with the other arms—infantry, cavalry, and artillery?

A desire to spread mechanization throughout an army was not evidence of troglodytic beliefs—quite the opposite. By the 1960s, mechanization had become the norm, not solely for a handful of tank divisions, but for all arms—armor, infantry, artillery, and supporting elements. In the absence of uniform mechanization, something no nation could as yet afford, how tanks, marching infantry, and truck- or horse-drawn guns could effectively combine their efforts on a mobile battlefield remained a question. One solution was to not attempt such a feat; another was to prevent the battlefield from becoming mobile.

All the major powers struggled with these questions during the interwar period. There is a tendency to view this debate as a divide between sets of reformers who saw the future and the more powerful conservative forces that refused to recognize the new realities of warfare. But such a starkly drawn dichotomy does a disservice to the "conservatives" while simultaneously according the "reformers" more credit than they deserve.

When the interwar period is examined, there is a tendency to fault the military leadership of a given country for failing to foresee some aspect of the war that began in September 1939. But military leaders operated within international and national contexts that shaped their priorities.

For Americans, in 1919, the prospects of fighting another major ground war in Europe seemed rather remote. The most likely arena of conflict was the Pacific, and the most probable enemy, Imperial Japan. A Pacific war would be primarily a naval and, to a lesser extent, an air war. Not surprisingly, during the interwar period, Americans considered the U.S. Navy their first line of defense. The service worked to develop doctrine for war in three dimensions while the U.S. Marine Corps strove to design the requisite amphibious capabilities and doctrine. The American Army Air Corps did the same, but with a focus on strategic air warfare. In relative terms, the U.S. Army ground forces were the stepchild of the American defense establishment.

To further complicate matters, the army had never digested the realities of trench warfare. The commander of the American Expeditionary Force, General John Pershing, had insisted on training American soldiers for open-field combat, despite the fact that they were bound for the trenches. Because they were short on much of the paraphernalia needed to wage modern war, Americans adopted both French and British equipment and tactics, depending on where a given unit served. The result was a degree of doctrinal confusion.

The Americans did embrace armor, although here, too, there was confusion as they adopted both British heavy tanks and French light tanks. By January 1918, the Americans had established a tank corps that included fifteen tank brigades, each containing one heavy and two light battalions. The American army could easily have continued the development of an armored force after the war. The United States possessed the requisite industrial base. But the army abolished the tank corps and assigned the individual battalions to the infantry divisions.

While this pattern followed the French model in appearances, there was a critical difference: the American tactical concept was more offensive in its orientation. The prospects of the army fighting a defensive war in North America were slim. If the army fought, it would most likely do so overseas. As a result, while tanks were relegated to an infantry-support role, the aim was to break the enemy line and force the open-field offensive combat for which the American infantry still trained.

Accordingly, the Americans chose to design and to build tanks, preferably from a single design of medium weight, which could answer all their requirements. In 1928, J. Walter Christie presented the army with an innovative design for a medium tank that was maneuverable, thanks to a high horsepower-to-weight ratio, had independent suspension, and had a dual-drive system that allowed it to move cross-country on tracks or, when on a road, on its "road wheels." Christie sold prototypes of his tank to both the U.S. Army and the Russians, but there were complications with the dual-drive system. The Soviets continued to work out the bugs and ultimately developed their successful BT models. In 1936, the Americans gave up on Christie's tanks and sought to develop an alternative all-purpose tank. The pressures of the Great Depression ensured that the tank chosen would be a lighter and cheaper tank.

The light tank fit well into the organization of the small but growing American armored force. In 1928, the U.S. Army, following the lead of the British, established an experimental mechanized force. Speed was the goal for a unit designed to scout and exploit gaps in an enemy line. The conversion of American cavalry regiments from horse to mechanization, beginning with the 1st Cavalry Regiment in 1933, proceeded slowly and reinforced the need for light, fast tanks, since the roles of cavalry units were primarily to scout and to screen. On the eve of the Second World War, the United States possessed only a single mechanized cavalry brigade equipped mostly with light tanks.

Nevertheless, the American failure to develop a coherent doctrine that incorporated armored forces was not the disaster that it might seem. The Americans never adopted the defensive-mindedness of their former French allies. The focus on infantry combat ensured that the American soldier was well equipped, armed with the only semiautomatic rifle, the M-1 Garand, in general use when the war began, and the Browning automatic rifle (BAR). The combination of these two weapons made the firepower of the basic American infantry platoon second only to that of the German infantry. The American artillery, shaped to support the infantry in the attack, was superb. American artillerymen could coordinate fire from multiple batteries in a manner that no other army could match. Moreover, a huge industrial base supplied the trucks that allowed the United States to motorize, if not mechanize, virtually the entire army—something no other nation could afford to do. As a result, despite its shortcomings, the small American army (smaller in 1932 than the Yugoslav army) was structurally designed and intellectually flexible enough to expand and to incorporate quickly many of the lessons learned, and taught, between 1939 and 1942.

The British, much like the Americans, did not envision themselves fighting another major campaign on the Continent. Nor was the postwar political situation in Britain conducive to military development. Whereas the French knew that they had fought to drive an invader from their country, across the Channel, there were many unanswered questions concerning British intervention, or at least the decision to send a large expeditionary force to France.

In August 1919, the British government adopted the infamous Ten Year Rule, which assumed that there would be no war and no need to send a force to the Continent for at least a decade. This estimate was revised and extended every year until 1932—unfortunately, only seven and not ten years before war began in 1939. Until 1932, British defense policy focused on policing the empire.

Such a focus hindered, but did not stop, other developments. The British had been the first to field tanks. Armor played a major role in the British advances in the summer and fall of 1918. Nevertheless, British casualties were higher during the successful offensives of 1918 than they had been in 1916 and 1917, although the high command measured success not in lower casualty rates, but in miles advanced.

At the end of the Great War, the British had yet to develop a coherent doctrine to employ their tanks. J. F. C. Fuller, a young British tank officer, devised Plan 1919, a scheme for a massive armored offensive overtaken by events—namely, the war's end. But that plan was more notable for its mass of tanks than its use of them. Not until 1932 did the British make a concerted effort to identify the lessons of the 1914–1918 war, but there was little effort in high places to accept, let alone digest, those lessons.

Nevertheless, the British had tanks, industry kept developing better models, and there existed in the British army a handful of individuals who sought new methods to employ armor. The army experimented with mixed tank-infantry battalions in 1922. The following year, the British established the Royal Tank Corps, although the largest armored unit remained the battalion. During the 1926 maneuvers, the armored force demonstrated its capabilities, but its success prompted debate. Armored advocates wanted the tanks concentrated in the new corps, whereas others wished to see the benefits of mechanization spread throughout the army. In May 1927, the British formed an experimental mechanized force that consisted of light and medium tanks, a machine-gun battalion, and a motorized artillery regiment. Despite this victory, none of the armored advocates—officers such as Fuller, Percy Hobart, and others—rose into senior positions of leadership within the army (either before or during the course of the Second World War). In 1928, the army disbanded this still tank-heavy, but nevertheless combined-arms, force.

The combining of armored, infantry, and artillery elements into an effective whole did pose daunting organizational, tactical, and doctrinal problems. Fuller's flawed answer to the problem was to form all-tank units, a view that influenced subsequent development. When the army formed the 1st Tank Brigade in 1931, the unit was an all-tank organization, well suited to speedy maneuvering at the strategic and operational levels, but inadequate for the actual demands of combat at the tactical level. In 1934, with the infantry demanding support of some kind, the army, unable

continued on page 131

Conflict in the Interwar Period: The Spanish Civil War

The most important interwar conflict was the Spanish Civil War (1936–1939). Spain in the 1930s was a politically divided republic, torn by the pressures of modernization—pressures only exacerbated by the impact of the Great Depression—and confused by foreign political ideologies, namely communism and fascism. After years of electorally driven power shifts between the right and the left, on 17 July 1936, the Spanish army rose in revolt against the left-dominated republic. The resultant civil war ended in March 1939 with the surrender of Madrid to the Nationalists. At war's end, the Fascist general Francisco Franco ruled as *caudillo*, and his regime survived until his death in 1975. The toll of war was heavy: over 400,000 Spaniards, and assorted foreigners, died from war-related causes—combat, political execution, starvation, or disease. Perhaps half as many fled the country to escape political persecution.

One of the most notable aspects of the Spanish Civil War was the involvement of foreign "volunteers." Some were individuals who, generally for ideological reasons, traveled to Spain, usually, though not exclusively, to fight for the Republican side. Other states secretly sent entire military contingents: the Germans and Italians to aid the Nationalists and the Soviets the Republicans.

Economic and military assistance to the warring factions was fairly balanced, and a slight advantage went to the Nationalists. Officially, only 557 Soviet personnel served in Spain, although the unofficial number was most likely in the thousands. In addition, the Communist International (Commintern) formed about a half dozen "international brigades" whose total strength reached 18,000, and approximately 40,000 foreigners of assorted nationality served in these brigades at one time or another. The German "volunteer" contingent, known as the Condor Legion, reached a strength of 10,000, and 16,000 Germans cycled through Spain during the course of the war. By far the largest foreign contingent was that sent from Fascist Italy. The *Commando Truppe Volontarie* (CTV) reached a strength of nearly 50,000. The German, Italian, and Russian contingents included infantry, artillery, armor, fighters and bombers and their pilots, and other assorted specialists, such as medical personnel.

Historians have long debated the impact of foreign assistance. Ultimately, the Nationalists won because their leadership forged a more united front than that of the Republicans, who often spent as much time arguing with each other as they did fighting the Nationalists. Foreign intervention played a crucial role at various points during the war. German transport aircraft ferried Franco's troops from Morocco to the Spanish mainland. During the following years, when one side or the other seemed on the point of collapse, an influx of foreign assistance provided the means to continue the struggle.

After the Munich accord of September 1938, Hitler, no longer concerned about the possibility of the Spanish conflict spreading to the rest of Europe, began a massive infusion of aid to the Nationalists. Unfortunately for the Republicans, Munich also convinced Stalin of the fecklessness of the western democracies, and he took the first of a series of moves designed to avoid war with Nazi Germany. One of those moves was to disengage from Spain. In the months after Munich, the Soviets cut back on anti-Fascist propaganda, reduced levels of aid to the Republic, and dismantled the international brigades. The following spring, the Republic surrendered.

Historians have also written widely of the extent to which the Spanish Civil War was a testing ground or laboratory for the European powers, especially Nazi Germany. This was true to a degree, although the results of these tests were often exaggerated and are far more apparent in hindsight than they were at the time.

Strategically and operationally, the Spanish Civil War was an attritional struggle that lasted just short of three years. For much of the conflict, the Nationalists and Republicans faced each other along fortified lines, where positions were broken occasionally, but not with any degree of regularity, by offensive actions. From afar, the conflict in Spain appeared to support the assumptions of those, most especially in France and the Soviet Union, who believed that the next war would follow the general pattern of the 1914–1918 war—it would be a prolonged, positional war of attrition.

There were, of course, numerous changes in the nature of warfare at the tactical level, evident primarily in the use of armor and aircraft. Both sides used tanks in an infantry-support role, not an independent role, much as tanks had been used in 1917 and 1918. The Germans deployed their newest tanks to Spain, mostly Pz Kw Is and later a few Pz Kw IIs, as part of the Condor Legion's panzer battalion. Experience demonstrated that the Pz Kw Is were unsuited for modern combat, being too lightly armored and armed, especially compared to the Soviet T-26 tanks with their 47mm guns. The Italians learned the same lessons, as most of their armored-led attacks petered out with heavy losses before they had reached their objectives. The Germans frequently employed antiaircraft guns alongside comparatively weaker antitank guns, both to halt heavier Soviet-built tanks and to function as offensive weapons. As a result, some French and Russian observers concluded that the tank's contribution on the battlefield of the future would be limited.

The Germans, however, drew very different lessons. They concluded that the keys to the successful employment of tanks were employment in mass of heavier and better-armed models, neither of which was available in Spain. The Germans also learned valuable lessons about (though not the solutions to) the difficulties of ensuring effective air-ground cooperation.

It was in the air that the Germans, and the Soviets, probably learned the most valuable lessons. During the course of the Spanish Civil War, the fighter pilots of the Condor Legion, whose number included many of the early aces of the *Luftwaffe*, developed more modern multiplane tactics for air-to-air combat. The successes of the Germans bombers, however, led them to conclude that fast bombers could operate with little or no fighter escort, an assumption that would cost the *Luftwaffe* during the Battle of Britain. Moreover, German successes taught the Soviets that they needed more modern fighters. Another lesson learned by the Germans involved strategic bombing. Condor Legion bombers did attack several Spanish cities, most notably Guernica, during the course of the war. The *Luftwaffe* judged these raids mostly ineffective, if not counterproductive. The damage inflicted on Spanish industry was minimal, nor was there much evidence to suggest that the bombing had broken the will of the Republicans to resist. The experience of the Condor Legion thus served to reinforce the German presentiment against the concept of strategic bombing.

to develop a coherent combined-arms doctrine, chose instead to form separate tank brigades equipped with slower and heavier tanks dedicated to an infantry-support role.

In the British scheme, there were, thus, two different types of tanks carrying out two very different roles. The heavy "I" tanks operated in support of the infantry, but lacked the speed to exploit a breach made in an enemy line. The roles of exploitation and reconnaissance fell to the newly mechanized cavalry regiments and their "cruiser" tanks. As for British tanks themselves, they all seemed to possess at least one of several unfortunate attributes— they were slow, under-gunned, weakly armored, or mechanically unreliable. Infantry-support tanks generally carried only high-explosive ammunition and were nearly useless against opposing tanks, whereas the speedier "Cruisers" carried armored-piercing rounds, but no high explosives.

By 1938 the British had formed what could be described as two very different mechanized arms: mostly former cavalry regiments outfitted with light tanks and the smaller Royal Tank Regiment equipped with heavy tanks. In 1939, on the eve of war, Great Britain's sole mobile division was an extremely tank-heavy armored division consisting of mostly lighter tanks.

During the interwar period, the British failed to develop a comprehensive military doctrine that optimized the employment of armor. British experimentation with armored forces did, however, lead to recognition of the need for improved communications and the provision of motorized logistical support. These were major developments and ones not adopted by the French, who more narrowly viewed their use of tanks. Moreover, the failure to focus on armor ensured that the British infantry developed as a far tougher and mobile force, second only to the German infantry on the European battlefields of 1939 to 1941.

The French believed that they had mastered the lessons of the Great War. They, of course, had entered the Great War with one of the most offensive-minded doctrines of any of the combatants and had suffered crippling casualties. Well into 1917 the French army continued to embrace the offensive, but tempered its doctrine. Failures along the Chemin des Dames led to the virtual refusal of some units to adopt anything other than a defensive posture. In 1918, cautious infantry attacks supported by massed artillery and swarms of tanks secured victory. The French, having turned their collective backs on the offensive doctrine of 1914, easily made a transition to a defensive doctrine. As a result, defensive-mindedness shaped French planning, training, and acquisition during the interwar period.

After the Great War, there were occasional calls for the development of a broader mechanized force capable of independent, and possibly offensive, operations. In the mid-1930s, a French army officer, Charles de Gaulle, went so far as to propose the establishment of a small, mechanized, and professional army to supplement the mass army that France had relied on throughout the history of the Third Republic. De Gaulle's plan was a Gallic version of a somewhat similar proposal in Britain advanced by retired Captain Basil Henry Liddell Hart, who had suggested the conversion of the entire army into a professional mechanized force. While De Gaulle's call for the development of a professional mechanized army appears reasonable, it was politically unacceptable and demographically and fiscally unrealistic. France was already committed to the development of the Maginot Line (see "The Maginot Line"), and given the lean years—the demographic population hole caused by the casualties suffered during the Great War—there were not enough men to support both forces. As a result, resistance came not only from most of the army's senior commanders, but also from a broad spectrum of political leaders. Nor were the French people clamoring for such a development. De Gaulle's proposal, whatever its military virtues, was inconsistent with the concept of a nation in arms and lent itself to offensive operations.

The French army remained committed to the defensive and the 1918 formula—what became known as the "methodical battle." The high command envisioned tightly controlled engagements marked by heavy reliance on massed artillery and the commitment of infantry offensively, in short bounds, led by heavy support tanks, only when the prospects of victory were overwhelming and the likelihood of casualties much reduced. Given this doctrinal mindset, in combination with the popular revulsion to the horrors of the last war, it was easy for the French to adopt the defensive not solely as a doctrinal posture, but also as national policy.

It would also have been very difficult to alter that doctrine. First, under the French system during the 1920s and the early 1930s, draftees served for only a single year and then entered the reserves. Extensive reliance on the reserves during a general mobilization made it difficult, and disruptive, for the French to stage large-unit maneuvers to test new equipment and doctrine. Thus, the French rarely undertook divisional-level or higher training as often as did the Germans. Nor were the regulars in the army long enough to digest new ideas and concepts. Second, until the advent of Adolf Hitler's rise to power in 1933, subsequent German rearmament, and the formation of the first armored panzer divisions in 1935, the French army had no reason to suspect that its doctrine might be inadequate. While the Germans were able to quickly add an additional armored component to an already coherent military doctrine, the French faced the prospect of a veritable chaotic doctrinal and organizational revolution on the eve of crises that could easily lead to war.

Adherence to a predominantly defensive doctrine also had a deleterious impact on the development of French armored forces. For most of the interwar period, French tanks remained under the control of the infantry arm. Only slowly did the other arms participate in a broader mechanization. Nevertheless, by the mid-1930s, the French had developed a fair number of excellent armored fighting vehicles. In 1933, the French formed their first *division légère mécanique* (DLM), a converted cavalry division equipped with 240 armored cars, tanks, and other motorized vehicles, designed primarily to play a reconnaissance role. (The Germans had yet to form their first panzer, or armored, division.) As stocks permitted, additional cavalry divisions slowly made the conversion to the new mechanized form. When the French published a new doctrinal manual in 1936, the DLMs' mission expanded to include employment in the main battle itself. Nevertheless, the heavier French tanks remained committed to infantry support, and the DLMs lacked infantry, possessing only four battalions of motorized dragoons. As a result, when war began in 1939, the French had as many tanks as the Germans, but the tanks were not concentrated in powerful units capable of sustained combat. Not until 1940, after the fall of Poland, did the French hastily form their first *division cuirassée de réserve*, or armored division. By May 1940, when the Germans struck west, the French had formed three such divisions, with a fourth still forming. Unfortunately, at that time, the French had not yet fully developed a doctrine to employ their armored units.

Nor were many of the French tanks designed for mobile warfare. Most French models were well built and heavily armed and armored, especially compared to German tanks. In some technical respects—electric turret traverse and transmissions—French tanks were superior. But the heavier French models were designed primarily for infantry support during a slow-moving methodical battle. All but command tanks often lacked radios. In some models, tank commanders doubled as gunners. In fast-paced tank-versus-tank actions, French tank commanders quickly found themselves isolated and overwhelmed, unable to maintain a sense of what was happening while simultaneously attempting to sight their gun.

This doctrine also had a negative impact on the development of French infantry. The goal of the methodical battle was to limit friendly casualties through set-piece tactics that relied primarily on artillery and supporting tanks to suppress and destroy enemy positions. Infantry played a tertiary role in this formula. The basic French infantry platoon possessed fewer machine guns and generated far less firepower than its German counterpart. As a result, when the higher-than-expected tempo of operations of the spring of 1940 left French infantry without tank or artillery support, those units were at a severe disadvantage, not only unable to hold off German armor, but also unable to handle German infantry attacks.

Russian military thought was much better developed before and during the Great War than most in the West realized. It is true that the Russian army often did not perform well at the tactical level (and the same could later be said of the Soviet army). Nevertheless, Russian troops often fought stubbornly, and at the highest strategic levels, Russian commanders were conversant with the military thinking of the day. During the Great War, the Russians crushed the Austrians in Galicia in the fall of 1914. They fought the Germans to a standstill around Warsaw during the winter. In 1916, the innovative Brusilov offensive threatened to take the Austro-Hungarian Empire out of the war. In fact, the Russians held more German prisoners in 1917 than the French and British combined. While the Russians technically left the war in March 1918 following the treaty of Brest-Litovsk, their conflict had, in fact, continued in the guise of a civil war that lasted into the 1920s.

The Russian experience differed markedly from that of the western front. Warfare in the open eastern theater was more mobile. Even cavalry played an important role. The Russians achieved their greatest successes—Lvov in 1914, the Brusilov offensive in 1916, and several campaigns during the civil war—on the offensive, whereas they suffered their greatest defeats on the defensive. Offensive operations allowed the Bolsheviks to reestablish their control over most of the former tsarist empire. They lost control of Finland, Latvia, Estonia, Lithuania, parts of Poland, and the province of Bessarabia, but reconquered Byelorussia, the Ukraine, the Crimea, Georgia, and Kazakhstan.

After the civil war, the Bolsheviks ruled a state with virtually no natural borders that was surrounded by hostile neighbors. Their most likely enemy would be Poland, probably aided by France during the 1920s or by the Germans during the 1930s. Whatever the scenario, the best strategic course of action was to launch an offensive to knock Poland out before allies came to its aid. To implement that policy, the Soviets needed an army capable of offensive action.

Soviet military development during the interwar period took place within a larger internal political context. Revolutionary ideology motivated the Bolsheviks and spilled over into other areas, including the military. The concept of the relationship of war and diplomacy to the state differed within the Soviet context: since capitalism was the root cause of conflict, there could not be, and should not be, an end to warfare until capitalism could be destroyed. Wars, as the experience of Russia demonstrated quite well, could work to the advantage of socialism.

But how were these wars to be fought? Initially, most Bolsheviks expected to wage a revolutionary conflict with a people's militia as a prelude to a wider global revolution. But during the civil war, the Soviets relied heavily on "specialists"—that is, former officers and noncommissioned officers (NCOs) from the imperial army. Because these potentially reactionary elements could not be trusted, the Bolsheviks established the practice of dual control—namely, the appointment of political commissars as cocommanders at all but the lowest levels of the command hierarchy. (While this practice was unconventional, it was nothing more than an established western concept—civilian control of the military—carried to the extreme.) By the end of the civil war, many leading Bolsheviks, most notably Lev Trotsky, had become convinced that war required more of a scientific approach than a revolutionary one. Russia needed to reestablish an army organized along more traditional lines. Since the state did not have the means to develop a large professional army, a philosophical "center" developed, around Mikhail Tukhachevsky, that favored a compromise: the development of an elite professional cadre backed by a system of territorial-based militia units. M. V. Frunze, who replaced Trotsky as commissar for military and naval affairs in January 1925, pushed successfully for one-man command—that is, the end of the commissar system. Frunze subsequently underwent a forced operation for an ulcer and died under mysterious circumstances. His wife promptly committed suicide.

Josef Stalin then became the leading figure in the Soviet political hierarchy. He recognized the international reality: socialism existed, and was likely only to exist for some time, in one country—the Soviet Union. To defend the socialist motherland, Stalin increasingly relied on a professional army rather than a militia. Following the adoption of the first five-year plan in 1928, Stalin expanded industrial production to provide for a larger professional military cadre. In 1935, the Soviet Union formally adopted a professional army and the following year passed a law for obligatory military service throughout the Union of the Soviet Socialist Republics.

In the midst of these debates, Red Army commanders attempted to develop a coherent military doctrine. There is evidence of some foreign influence. As far back as the tsarist period, the Russian army had looked to the French for direction. After the Russo-German Treaty of Rapallo of 1922, which brought a formal and official end of differences dating back to 1918, German influences, along with German land and air units avoiding the strictures of Versailles, also found their way into Russia. Red Army leaders did review the work of foreign military writers. Nevertheless, Soviet military thought was far more original than derivative, and it reflected the Russian experience of open and mobile warfare.

That more fluid experience shaped the attempt to incorporate armor into the Soviet army. Some officers favored the defensive, a reflection of what could be termed the influence of the Russian "national school" dating back to the days of Mikhail Kutusov and the War of 1812. Tanks would be employed according to what could be considered the French method—armor supporting infantry, with tank battalions attached to individual infantry divisions. But Soviet success with cavalry during the civil war suggested the need for mobile, mechanized formations. In 1932, the Red Army began to form mechanized corps—mostly tank brigades, with an attached brigade of mechanized infantry—which were the largest units of their kind at that time. These were largely tank-heavy formations, organized somewhat along British lines.

Beginning in the late 1920s, the Soviet military began to focus on the problem of sustained operations. One of the lessons of the Great War and the civil war was that breakthrough forces rapidly lost their ability to sustain an offensive tempo. In 1928, Red Army commanders began considering what they termed "successive operations." The concept was simple: to defeat a defense in depth, an attacker had to attack in depth—attack with successive waves of assault elements maintaining pressure on the defenders to prevent their recovery. Mechanized forces were best suited to perform such a role.

Subsequent development led to the establishment of a comprehensive doctrine that included the orchestration of armor, mechanized and leg infantry, motorized and self-propelled artillery, and close air support. The Red Army also pioneered the development of airborne paratroopers, who would also participate in the planned offensives. The Soviet goal was not only to break through an enemy position, but also to defeat its second and reserve echelons and shatter the front as a prelude to decisive battles of encirclement. As was the case with most things Russian, these operations would take place on a tremendous scale.

By the mid-1930s, the Soviets had developed a comprehensive military doctrine that was one of, if not the, most advanced in the world. The outlines of many of the concepts that would figure prominently in Soviet military operations in the latter years of World War II, and subsequently in the Cold War period (including deep battle and operational maneuver groups), were evident in the 1930s.

However, not all Russian political and military leaders were in accord. Many believed that the next war would be an attenuated struggle of attrition in which population, productive capacity, and the ability of a state to mobilize the will of the people would be paramount. In such a struggle, defensive operations would be crucial. Armored forces should not be concentrated, but dispersed to support the infantry. Nevertheless, the reformers survived these initial attacks. The increased output that accompanied industrialization permitted the formation of large mechanized forces *and* independent tank formations committed to infantry support.

Unfortunately for the people of the Soviet Union, as the world moved toward war, the paranoid Stalin came to distrust the commanders of his army. In May 1937, Stalin reinstituted the practice of appointing political commissars at all levels of command. That same year, he extended the series of purges that had swept other elements of Soviet society to the military. Tukhachevsky and his followers disappeared in the abyss along with a quarter to a third of the officer corps. While the purge gutted the army, the surviving officers struggled to decipher the lessons of the Spanish Civil War. The length of that struggle and the lack of mobile operations appeared to support the views of those commanders who believed in more a defensive posture for the army. As a result, on the eve of war, Soviet military doctrine was in a state of flux. An army designed and trained for one type of war was not prepared for employment in a very different posture. The confusion for a relatively young force was a recipe for disaster.

Despite the doctrinal and organizational confusion, in 1939, the Soviets possessed superb tanks. While it was true that Soviet doctrine for the employment of armored forces, thanks to Stalin, was well behind that of the Germans, the same cannot be said of Soviet tanks. The Russians designed several models to support infantry and other models to participate in more mobile "deep" operations.

The Russian motor industry lagged behind that of the West. Not until 1924 did the Russians manufacture their own trucks. Factories turned out the first tanks, modeled on French Renault types, in the late 1920s. Soviet tankers considered the French models unsatisfactory for service in Russian conditions and turned to British and American manufacturers for alternatives. The first heavy Russian tanks were based on British models, but for medium tanks the Soviets chose the American Christie design and developed the various BT types. Still in use into 1942, the BT-7, armed with a 47-mm antitank weapon, outgunned most

continued on page 142

The Maginot Line

The history of France's Maginot Line is one of the most misunderstood chapters of the Second World War. Historians often portray reliance on this system of fixed fortifications as evidence of the inability of the French military to come to grips with the realities of modern war. In such accounts, the Maginot Line becomes the figurative sand into which the French buried their ostrichlike heads as the Germans prepared to strike.

Historically, it is true that reliance on fixed defensive works has rarely been successful. The Great Wall of China is perhaps the premier monument to the limitations of static defenses, no matter the scale on which they are constructed. Nevertheless, there is nothing inherently wrong with static defensive systems. The French were not alone in their reliance on such. In 1943 and 1944, the Germans, despite their blitzkrieg victory over the French in May–June 1940, continued work on the construction of their own fortification system along their western border—the Siegfried Line, also known as the Westwall. The Germans also poured resources into the construction of their Atlantic Wall along the Channel coast of France.

While static systems, no matter how elaborate, cannot ensure a successful defense, they do offer three advantages: they complicate the task of the attacker, they gain time for the defender, and they allow the latter to economize force—that is, to hold the fortified line more thinly while concentrating forces elsewhere. When the French decided to construct the Maginot Line, they sought not perfect security, but to benefit from these advantages. The line would shield France against a surprise strike, ensuring that the nation would have time to mobilize. The French, who expected to be outnumbered when war came, could practice economy of force—that is, they could secure their border with Germany with fewer troops, while the more mobile elements of the French army prepared for combat farther north to meet the expected German drive through Belgium and the Netherlands.

Between 1930 and 1940, the French worked to complete the line, named after the minister of defense in the former year, André Maginot. The defensive system was extensive and mostly subterranean. It included fifty-eight major works in the north, with another fifty along the Alpine front facing Fascist Italy. There were over four hundred infantry casemates, shelters for reserves, and observations posts. Artillery positions numbered over 1,600, including over 150 revolving turrets. Over a hundred kilometers of underground galleries linked various points. Barracks, dining facilities, hospitals, and entertainment facilities were all part of the system.

When war came, the Maginot Line performed as expected. It deterred a German thrust directly across the border. The Germans instead chose to outflank the fortress line by thrusting through Belgium and Holland. French failure to extend the line to the English Channel was not an oversight, but part of a coherent strategy. Both the Dutch and the Belgians had erected their own defensive systems along their borders with Germany. In the event of a German thrust in the north, the more mechanized elements of the French army, trusting the Maginot Line to provide security in the south, would rush forward to join the Dutch and Belgians.

The subsequent collapse of France was not the fault of the Maginot Line, but of other factors. The French retained too high a proportion of their army in and behind the Maginot Line. Some of these forces could more profitably have been employed elsewhere, especially along the weakly held front in the Ardennes. The Germans penetrated the Dutch and Belgian frontier defenses more quickly than anticipated and before the arrival of French and British troops. This breakthrough was partly the Dutch and Belgians' failure to appreciate the speed with which the Germans could move, but it was also the result of foolish diplomacy: the search for perfect neutrality doomed the Belgians and Dutch to defeat. The more sensible diplomatic course, especially for Belgium, which had been invaded by the Germans in 1914, would have been an alliance with France that would have permitted French troops to enter Belgium *before* the Germans invaded.

The Maginot Line's existence reinforced what subsequently became known as the Maginot mentality. Reliance on fixed fortifications reinforced French defensive-mindedness. But it is a mistake to blame the development of that mentality on the Maginot Line, for it was the mentality that led to the construction of the line.

Another aspect of the Maginot mentality concerns its impact on the conduct of French foreign policy. One facet of the doctrinal debate before both world wars involves the link between military doctrine and national policy. In 1914, given the alliance structure, all the major powers had to commit themselves to offensive military postures; to do otherwise would allow an opponent to seize the initiative and to concentrate its effort against one's ally. Had France, for example, adopted what might appear to be a more sensible defensive military stance in 1914, the Germans could have done the same on the western front and thrown the rest of their army against the Russians in the east. That is not to suggest that the embrace of the offensive by European militaries before 1914 was something forced upon them by their political leaders. But the realities of the alliance systems reinforced the need for offensive doctrine. The same forces were at play after 1918. Civilian antiwar sentiment and the French army's defensive-mindedness were mutually reinforcing, and that mutual reinforcement was epitomized by the construction of the Maginot Line. But reliance on these fortifications in the 1930s was a clear and unequivocal announcement that, in the event of war, the Germans would be free to concentrate their efforts in the east without fear of a major French offensive. Given France's Great War experience, a defensive military doctrine may appear sensible, but such a doctrine made it less likely that France would have an eastern ally if war came. As a result, France would face the Germans alone, except for the small British Expeditionary Force and Dutch and Belgian allies of dubious reliability.

Despite conventional wisdom, the defensive system that bore the name of André Maginot failed neither the French army nor the French people. It was France that failed the Maginot Line.

of the Germans tanks in use in 1941. Soviet tanks generally had wider tracks and more evenly distributed weight than comparable western tanks (ideal for the muddy conditions in the east), were more heavily protected with thicker and sloped armor, and were powered by reliable diesel engines. Nevertheless, Soviet tanks were not without shortcomings. They had cramped turrets, poor optics, and unreliable transmissions, and the poor machining of tracks caused breakdowns. Except for command vehicles, Soviet tanks also lacked radios.

Overall, a Soviet military gripped by doctrinal confusion was unprepared for war in 1941. Nevertheless, there remained a cadre of officers within the army familiar with the doctrine developed in the early and mid-1930s. The Soviets also had at their disposal a huge industrial base capable of producing enormous quantities of equipment, especially good tanks well suited not only to conditions in the east, but also to the deep operations that the Soviet army would eventually mount along the road to Berlin.

For the Germans, much like the Russians, the war did not end in 1918. Well into 1919, German soldiers were still fighting from the Baltic to the Black Sea. Organized in *Freikorps*, German soldiers struggled to contain Bolshevism and to secure the eastern border with the newly formed Polish state. When peace finally came, the Versailles treaty restricted the Weimar Republic, which had replaced the kaiser's Second Reich, to an army of 100,000 men, a force easily outnumbered by the Poles. Nor were the Germans permitted to have tanks, heavy artillery, or aircraft. They even had to dismantle their infamous general staff.

The Germans, a defeated nation defended by a small army and surrounded by potential enemies, had little choice but to focus on questions of national defense. At the level of national policy, there were two available options. The first was to rely on diplomacy and international agreements. The second was to adopt the more traditional approach of reliance on the military. Despite the fact that the German military could not possibly defend the country while remaining within the bounds of the Versailles treaty, the military insisted, and the Weimar Republic's political leaders chose, to pursue this second option.

But the question remained, how could the German military defend the German state? Here again there were two options. The first was the concept of *Volkskrieg*, or "people's war." Advocates of such proposals argued that modern war had so blurred the distinctions between the military and civilian sectors that a future war should be entrusted to the people. Only masses of armed citizens could hope to defend, primarily through defensive and guerrilla operations, the homeland. *Volkskrieg* concepts (there were many variations on the theme) had parallels in other European countries during the interwar period, most of which struggled with the question of whether they should rely on a smaller, more mechanized professional force or a larger, militia-type force. Americans had wrestled with that question as early as the 1790s. General Hans von Seeckt, acting chief of the German general staff in 1919 and subsequently the head of the *Truppenamt* (troops office, a disguised general staff) that replaced it, argued for a more traditional approach and reliance on a small, but professional and efficient *Reichswehr* (army). Ultimately, it was Seeckt's argument that prevailed.

Strategically, Seeckt could not conceive of a traditional approach that could hope to secure Germany's borders in the event of the most likely war scenarios. With 100,000 men, the Germans could not hold off the forces of France or even Poland, let alone a likely combination of the two. This reality had three consequences. First, the *Reichswehr* focused its attention on warfare at the operational and tactical levels. That is not to say that the Germans ignored the study of strategy during the interwar years, but only that its study was tertiary. Second, Seeckt and the Germans were inclined to seek ways to circumvent and ultimately eliminate the strictures of Versailles. Only such an outcome could ensure that the chosen national policy could, at some point in the future, make possible the defense of Germany's borders. Third, the Germans focused on offensive operations, even in the event that they were forced onto the strategic defensive. In the most likely scenario, a war against Poland, the Germans would have to strike quickly, either to knock the Poles out of the war before anyone could come to their assistance, or to disrupt a Polish offensive before it could reach Berlin.

The Germans were the first of the major powers to undertake a comprehensive effort to identify the lessons of the Great War. Seeckt directed a broad range of studies between 1919 and

1923. The Germans concluded that the *Stosstruppen* tactics that had worked well in 1917 and 1918 were fundamentally sound. German experience demonstrated that reliance on the offensive, maneuvering, concentration of effort, surprise, small tactical units possessing substantial firepower, combined arms, and the exercise of initiative at all levels of command were the key to success. The first *Reichswehr* tactical manual, published in two parts in 1921 and 1923, included discussions of the encirclement battles favored by Seeckt's predecessors, Moltke and Schlieffen, but also embraced breakthrough-penetration operations as a means to create flanking situations. Seeckt sought to enhance the effectiveness of such operations through the application of new technologies and the enhancement of existing ones.

Germany in the 1920s and 1930s was one of the world's leaders in the field of wireless radio. The incorporation of improved wireless technology by the German armed forces led to tactical improvements in the field forces. The Germans developed excellent lightweight shortwave radios that allowed units to remain in communication with higher headquarters in the event of a successful breakthrough. By the mid-1920s, even prototype tanks included provisions for radios.

The Germans made good use of trucks and tractors to motorize selected artillery and support elements, as well as a few infantry formations. Nevertheless, motorization remained one of the stumbling blocks along the road toward the full mechanization of the Germans armed forces.

Despite the treaty restrictions on the *Reichswehr*'s employment of heavy artillery, in the 1920s, the Germans designed and adopted prototypes of the guns that would enter production in the 1930s and serve throughout the Second World War. These guns included standard German 105mm and 150mm howitzers as well as the 75mm and 150mm field guns used by the German infantry.

In another related area of development, antiaircraft artillery, the Germans quickly established a significant lead. Denied their own air force, the Germans in the 1920s expected to operate without air cover. As a result, they developed a substantial and effective array of antiaircraft weapons and incorporated them into their overall doctrine in a manner unmatched by the militaries of the other major powers.

The essential building block of the *Reichswehr*'s strength remained, of course, the infantry. During the 1920s and 1930s, the Germans further enhanced the firepower and communications of their infantry formations. In 1939, the German infantry squad, armed with several light machine guns, possessed greater firepower than the squads of any other European state. Only the American infantry squads, armed with the semiautomatic M-1 carbine and the BAR, could approximate the firepower of the German squads.

Despite the strictures of the Versailles treaty, the Germans early on began to develop their own tanks and the doctrine to guide their employment. Initially, the Germans designed mostly light tanks for infantry support. But by late 1920s, they moved toward the adoption of heavier medium tanks as their standard and, much influenced by the British, considered the use of armor as an independent and decisive arm.

In general, historians have distorted the tale of interwar German armored development. In many accounts, Heinz Guderian, one of the leading proponents of armored forces in the German army, is seen to almost single-handedly move that service toward its embrace of the tank. Historians have also exaggerated the influence of British theorists, primarily Basil Henry Liddell Hart. Recent scholarship has demonstrated that while J. F. C. Fuller did influence the Germans to a degree, Hart's importance was primarily the creation of imaginative postwar German accounts, especially the English-language edition of Guderian's distorted and self-promoting memoirs. Guderian was only one of several German officers—including Ernest Volkheim, Oswald Lutz, Alfred von Vollard-Bockelberg, and many others—whose labors during the interwar period helped to develop German armored doctrine.

The high command of the *Reichswehr* did not fail to support these developments in the armored forces, although the developments did not progress at the speed that some armor advocates wished. Since the Germans had to train (in Germany, at least) with dummy tanks throughout the 1920s, this slow advancement ought not to be a surprise. As technology improved and the motorization of the other arms advanced, the Germans steadily refined and expanded their doctrine for armored warfare. Cooperative Swedish and secretive German manufacturers, and the ability of the *Reichswehr* to operate an armored training establishment between 1927 and 1933 in Kazan in the Soviet Union, aided developments.

Another extremely important contribution of the *Reichswehr* in preparing the German armed forces for war was reliance on large-scale maneuvers for training and as a means to work out doctrinal questions. Starting in the 1920s, the *Reichswehr* conducted regular field exercises, including large multidivisional affairs. No other European power attempted comparable undertakings on anything approaching a regular basis. The continuation of this practice during the 1930s ensured that German officers had far more practical experience than their Allied counterparts.

Despite these developments, German doctrine of the 1920s was not armored focused. Tanks and aircraft remained infantry-support forces. The central tactical goal remained the combination of existing arms on the battlefield. By the mid-1920s, however, the Germans had developed a coherent military doctrine into which armored forces could very easily be inserted in a fashion that would allow them to play a more substantive, and eventually leading, role.

When the Nazis came to power in 1933, German rearmament accelerated and became more public. In the field of armored development, the Germans were in many ways behind. The British had already begun forming tank brigades, and the French the DLMs. But the performance of German mechanized units in the 1935 field exercises led to the formation later that year of the first three panzer divisions. Subsequent exercises allowed the Germans to test, adjust, and refine their armored doctrine. When maneuvers demonstrated that the armored force was too tank heavy, the number of tank battalions in each panzer division declined, and the number of infantry battalions increased. While the strength of panzer divisions varied, the ideal initial paper ratio of sixteen tank companies to nine infantry companies shifted to a balance of twelve each. Despite the Germans' late start, by 1939, they had formed six panzer divisions.

Doctrinal development proceeded apace. The doctrine that guided the employment of the panzer divisions combined two roles that were considered distinct by most other major armies, requiring separate types of tanks and tank formations for each purpose. The British, French, and Russians, for example, fielded heavy-tank units to support infantry breakthroughs. Subsequent exploitation of tanks was the responsibility of cavalry-like mechanized forces designed for mobile operations. In contrast, the German panzer division was designed to perform both roles, breakthrough and exploitation. German armored theory developed as a subset of an existing comprehensive combined-arms doctrine that ensured that the panzer division was seen as a more mobile force of all arms, rather than a mere collection of tanks.

The actual tanks available to the Germans in September 1939 were developed during the years following Hitler's ascension to power in 1933. Most German tanks were lightly armored and often lightly gunned. The heaviest tank-mounted antitank gun was the 37mm, a weapon lighter than the heaviest weapon employed by most other armies. The early models of the German *Panzerkampfwagen* ("armored fighting vehicle," or *Pz Kw*) IV mounted a 75mm gun, but this was a short-barrel, low-muzzle-velocity weapon meant to fire high-explosive, not armor-piercing, rounds.

Nevertheless, German armor proved superior during the initial stage of the Second World War. The Germans employed their armored forces in mass. German mechanized forces were better trained, were guided in their operations by superior doctrine, and were led by officers accustomed to demonstrating initiative and seizing opportunities as they developed.

But there were grave weaknesses in the German military. Strategic thinking was not as well developed as the operational and tactical. German tanks were, in some ways, inferior. Motorization was uneven. In fact, one could argue that two German armies took the field in September 1939: the first was a modern motorized force, while the other remained a nineteenth-century army bound to the horse. If the war that began in the fall of 1939 could be kept short, the impact of these weaknesses would be limited. But if the war dragged on, these shortcomings could become fatal.

The most significant military developments during the interwar years came in the changing nature not of ground warfare, but of air warfare. The capability of aircraft to wreak havoc, on both other aircraft and on targets on the ground, increased tremendously. Air power went from being a support element of marginal utility to a near-decisive weapon.

During the Great War, air power had evolved along two lines. First, aircraft had functioned in a support role for the ground war either indirectly, by observing enemy forces or spotting for artillery batteries, or directly, by bombing or strafing troops or other targets. Of these functions, the last-named was the least important, although the effectiveness of direct ground attack improved markedly during the final year of the war. Second, aircraft (both planes and zeppelins) had conducted strategic bombing raids against enemy cities and industries. Technological limitations ensured that such raids had limited effectiveness, and their effects more psychological than physical. Cutting across both forms of air warfare was the role of the fighter, employed against bombing and observation aircraft and against other fighters.

The challenges militaries faced during the interwar years were twofold. First, the air services had to explore the impact of technological development on air warfare. Second, national leaders had to decide how to apportion limited available resources to either line or to both lines of development. The fact that air power evolved in different forms is attributable to a variety of political, military, and economic factors.

In 1919, the Germans, as they had with ground warfare, undertook a systematic study of their Great War experience in the air. These *Luftsreitkräfte* ("air service") reviews all but ignored strategic questions and focused on the tactical—namely, support of ground operations. The reasons were simple: first, strategic bombing had been ineffective during the war; second, strategic air warfare only made sense for a nation planning a protracted war, the type of conflict German national policy sought to avoid.

The Germans concluded that they had performed well in the air. They had downed more aircraft than they had lost, despite being outnumbered. In the latter stages of the war, specially designed and organized attack aircraft had provided ground forces with effective assistance. But the reviews were not uncritical: they concluded that the Germans' defensive doctrine—the decision to fight along or behind their own lines—had reduced losses, but had nonetheless been a mistake, yielding the initiative to the Allies.

Analysis led to several recommendations. First, at some point in the future, Germany should establish an independent air force. Second, that force should be guided by offensive doctrine. The objective of air warfare was to engage and to destroy the enemy air force in the air and, preferably, on the ground. Third, after the air force achieved this primary goal, it could then conduct operations in support of ground or naval forces.

To build the foundation for a future air force, German military aviation leaders, working within the *Truppenamt*, adopted several policies. First, the would-be air staff did its best to stay abreast of developments abroad. Second, the military relied on German civil aviation firms to cooperate, secretly, with the military to design and adopt aircraft that could be converted to martial use. Erhard Milch, head of Lufthansa and a future *Luftwaffe* general, epitomized this type of cooperation. Third, the Germans established a research and evaluation center in Russia, at Lipetsk. Fourth, the Germans tested their air theories and refined their doctrine during maneuvers and exercises.

By 1926, the Germans had developed a doctrine for air warfare. The primary task of the air force was to gain air superiority and then to support the army. That support would fall into one of two categories: direct tactical support on the battlefield and operational support—that is, attacks against headquarters, artillery positions, depots, reserves, road junctions, bridges, and other bottlenecks behind the front lines.

Despite a tactical and operational focus, the Germans did not ignore strategic air warfare. They were well aware of developments by foreign air forces, but were not prepared to commit major resources of their own to develop such an arm. Moreover, the Germans rightly considered the strategic capabilities of contemporary European air forces grossly exaggerated.

In 1933, with Hitler and the Nazis coming to power in Germany, the strategic picture changed dramatically. In 1934, Hitler established the new and independent *Luftwaffe*. Former *Reichswehr* officers and industry leaders, such as Milch, joined the new service. Rearmament meant that a successful defense of Germany against likely enemies was rapidly becoming a possibility.

Not surprisingly, the *Luftwaffe* began to give more serious consideration to strategic bombing. In 1935, a new doctrinal manual expanded the discussion of strategic efforts, although it also diluted the term to include attacks on any target that lay beyond the front lines. Destruction of the enemy armed forces, and especially its air force, remained the primary objective of the *Luftwaffe*. This dilution of doctrinal focus, the poor performance of the first German four-engine bombers, and the death of Major General Walther Wever (the *Luftwaffe's* chief and primary advocate of strategic bombing) ensured that the strong suite of the German air force remained in support of the army.

Even under Wever, the *Luftwaffe's* primary doctrinal goal had remained the development of effective close air support. Improved radio communications and the assignment of air force forward observers (FLIVOS—*Fliegerverbindungsoffiziere*) to frontline units ensured that the *Luftwaffe* possessed an effective doctrine.

continued on page 156

Naval Developments During the Interwar Period

The paucity of major naval battles, not only during the First World War, but also since Trafalgar in 1805, ensured that the lessons of the 1914–1918 conflict remained subject to debate and reinterpretation during the 1920s and 1930s. The Great War had offered a glimpse of changes to come. By 1918, naval warfare had become three dimensional, as aircraft operated above and submersibles operated below the ocean's surface. Advocates for aviation and submarines appeared in all of the world's militaries, but these men were often as premature in their expectations as their opponents were assured of the centrality of the battleship.

Post–World War I navies also wrestled with the political realities of arms control, which focused on the limitation of navies because of their expense and the widely held belief that the Anglo-German naval race had helped to precipitate the Great War. While capital ships—dreadnoughts—had caused few casualties, they became the principle focus of naval arms control and reduction. Submarines, which had wreaked havoc, escaped limitation, save for the restrictions of the Versailles treaty applied to Germany.

During 1921 and 1922, the major naval powers met in Washington, D.C., to discuss naval arms limitations and assorted Asian security matters. Britain, France, Italy, Japan, and the United States reached an agreement in the Washington Naval Limitation Treaty. The signatories agreed to a ten-year moratorium on capital-ship construction, limitations on some other ship types and armaments, and a halt to the fortification of installations in the Pacific. The agreed tonnage ratio was 5:5:3, respectively, for Britain, the United States, and Japan. France and Italy accepted ratios of 1.75. The Japanese, who had sought a ratio of 10:10:7, left Washington less than fully satisfied.

In 1930, the London Naval Treaty continued the ratio system from the Washington treaty, extended it to cruisers, extended the moratorium on capital-ship construction for another five years, limited the number and displacement (tonnage) of aircraft carriers, and placed limits on the gun size and displacement of submarines, which were henceforth bound by international law to the limits imposed on surface raiders when attacking merchant vessels. In other words, the treaty banned unrestricted submarine warfare. The Japanese, Italians, and French left London dissatisfied. Shortly thereafter, the assassination of the prime minister brought on a governmental crisis in Japan. In 1931, leaders of Japan's Manchurian army staged an incident and seized Manchuria, now reestablished as a puppet named Manchuko.

In late 1934, Japan announced that it would not renew the naval limitations in force since 1922 when they came up for renewal in 1935. A new naval race ensued among the great powers. In 1937, the Japanese began construction of the world's largest battleship, the 72,000-ton Yamato, armed with nine 18.1-inch guns.

In Europe, the British feared an all-out naval race and chose to contain through diplomatic action a possible German naval threat that might toss aside the existing treaty structure. In 1935, the British agreed to the Anglo-German Naval Agreement, which allowed Germany to construct a navy with a tonnage equal to 35 percent of the Royal Navy, and to construct a submarine force to parity. By 1936, the Germans had begun construction on a 50,000-plus-ton dreadnought—the *Bismarck*.

While these treaties constrained naval construction, they did not do the same to doctrinal development and experimentation. In fact, the limitations on battleships helped to push navies, especially those of Japan and the United States, toward the development of carrier aviation.

A central doctrinal issue involved command and control. The course of the Great War demonstrated that the fruits of the Industrial Revolution had finally begun to reshape what could be termed the technology of command and control at sea. Wireless telegraphy played a major role in shaping naval strategy, operations, and at times even tactics during the Great War. But could these technological advances hope to offset the impact of concurrent technological advances in myriad naval platforms, which were placing additional strains on commanders-in-chief? At Jutland, both Jellicoe and Scheer discovered that the challenges of command at sea exceeded those of the age of sail. Navies moved more quickly, covered more ocean, included a far more complex mix of forces, and could strike at distances unimaginable a century earlier. While the technology of command had advanced with the telegraph and wireless, had that progress been more than offset by the narrowing of a commander's decision-making window?

For the Americans, the U.S. Navy's 1924 war instructions reflected what could be termed "David Beatty's lessons learned from the battle of Jutland." The Americans were committed to a "vigorous offensive" to destroy the enemy fleet. The aggressive and post-Jutland character of the instructions is evident in the paragraph on the "torpedo menace": in the event of an enemy attack, American ships were to turn toward and not away from the threat, as had Jellicoe, in conformity with his own prebattle doctrine, at Jutland.

The Americans, and the British, also learned an important lesson from their wartime experience. British success in breaking the German naval codes caused the British and Americans to reduce radio communication to the minimum possible. To compensate, the Americans rethought their formations and deployed the battle fleet in a series of concentric rings to permit visual communications throughout the formation.

The lessons of the Great War did not, however, change the fixation of most senior leaders on the dreadnought. Advocates of the big-gun battleship dominated all the major navies and were reluctant to recognize new directions apparent in naval warfare. Recalcitrance impeded the development of new weapons platforms along with appropriate tactics and doctrine. Nevertheless, many proponents of new weapons systems, such as the airplane and the submarine, offered exaggerated and premature claims. Despite the protestations and showmanship of the American air-power advocate Brigadier General William "Billy" Mitchell, in 1921, land-based aircraft did not yet pose a dire threat to warships.

The history of interwar submarine development provides an example of the overestimation of the capabilities of a new technology. Had, for example, Adolf Hitler embarked in the mid-1930s on a massive submarine building program, the course of the battle of the Atlantic during the early years of World War II might have taken a different course. It is easy to look back at the course of the war and consider Hitler's failure to support a massive submarine building program as idiotic. But Hitler's decision was part of a larger national policy for his Third Reich. He planned to fight a blitzkrieg war, waged and won on the continent. Within the context of such a strategy, why would Hitler expend scarce resources on the construction of U-boats that would only be useful in a long war of attrition? The same was true of the Japanese. The U.S. Navy was also unhurried in its development of a submarine arm, but that policy was perfectly consistent with the realities of American national policy, which considered the use of submersibles as commerce raiders a violation of international law.

The same lack of development was less true of the aircraft carrier. The Royal Navy pioneered the carrier during the Great War, but failed to capitalize on its lead after 1918. Nevertheless, British experience during the Second World War demonstrated that they actually had a limited need for big carriers in the European theater. Moreover, the limitations of the aircraft carrier were marked. The ineffectiveness of carrier-based aircraft, relative to their land-based counterparts, ensured that the carrier emerged as a fully developed weapons system only on the eve of the Second World War. Neither the Japanese nor the American navies deployed powerful, well-armed, capable, modern, monoplane carrier-based fighters until 1940—the Mitsubishi A6M2 Zeke (the infamous Zero) and the Grumman F4F-3 Wildcat, respectively. The same was true of the British, Italians, and Germans.

Nevertheless, the world's navies, however slow they might have been to embrace the submarine and the aircraft carrier, were well aware of the evolution and steadily growing importance of these platforms. During the interwar years, navies struggled to find ways to incorporate these novel weapons systems into a comprehensive scheme of doctrine and tactics. As had been the case during the nineteenth century, rapid technological change during peacetime made such doctrinal and tactical developments a guessing game.

The Germans also benefited from experiences gained during the Spanish Civil War. At its peak, the *Luftwaffe* maintained a force of about a hundred aircraft and five thousand personnel in Spain. Perhaps the most important innovation came in air-to-air fighter tactics. The *Luftwaffe* jettisoned the "V," or "Vic," formation, built on groups of three planes, and adopted tactics based on pairs of two-aircraft elements. This seemingly minor doctrinal change vastly improved (by 50 percent) the offensive power of German squadrons. A group of twelve aircraft now included six shooters with six wingmen providing cover. A comparable twelve-plane squadron from other air forces included only four shooters with eight wingmen providing cover. The Germans also learned the effectiveness of mass—that is, the concentration of effort along one part of the front—and interdiction. Direct ground support, despite its centrality in German doctrine, proved far more difficult in practice than it did during exercises. Nevertheless, the Germans refused to give up and continued to work on the problem.

On the eve of war, the *Luftwaffe* had the most comprehensive doctrine and was the best-trained air arm in the world. The German air force was well suited to the immediate task at hand: participation in the blitzkrieg campaigns upon which the Germans were about to embark. Ironically, the *Luftwaffe* was also the only air force in the world capable of conducting strategic air warfare. The Germans possessed substantial numbers of good medium bombers, albeit with limited range and payload, as well as the blind bombing techniques and radio-beam navigation capabilities to guide the bombers to large targets at night. As inadequate as the strategic capabilities of the *Luftwaffe* were, those of its enemies were even less adequate, despite two decades of focus on air doctrine development.

The concept of strategic bombing had enamored British and American airmen since the Great War. In 1916, the British were the first to initiate what could be termed "strategic" attacks when they bombed industrial sites in the Saar. The following year, the Germans struck with their zeppelins against London. The German attacks helped lead to Great Britain's establishment of its Air Ministry in 1917, and eventually to the conversion of the Royal Flying Corps (RFC) into a third service—the Royal Air Force (RAF)—intended, in part, to strike at German industry. By 1918, the British were raiding Germany at night with heavy Handley Page bombers. In June 1918, these squadrons of night raiders formed the core of the Independent Force, the forerunner of Bomber Command. In August 1918, the Allies formed the Inter-Allied Bombing Force, a combined British, French, and American command that planned a more extensive and methodical bombing campaign against German targets. The war ended before the Allied plan could be put into effect with heavier four-engine bombers with the range to reach Berlin.

The post-1918 public reaction against war had the least impact on the air arms of the various major powers. Fascination with flight, still a novel activity in 1919, proved stronger than the revulsion often felt toward the military. While the public perceived the war in the trenches as a struggle without glory, fought amidst muck and horror, many viewed the air war as a boundless arena in which gallant knights of the sky dueled in a mechanized form of chivalric, if deadly, aerial jousting.

Novel theories of air warfare developed within a perceptual context that offered strategic alternatives in which the plane provided the means of avoiding a repetition of the Great War. Aircraft could soar over the trenches and reach deep into the heart of an enemy state. A modern industrial nation, some of the new advocates of air power argued, could be destroyed from the air, easily, quickly, and cheaply.

The foremost proponent of the new air power theory was an Italian army officer, Giulio Douhet. During the war, Douhet was an advocate for Italy's fledgling air arm and an outspoken critic of the Italian high command. The army court-martialed Douhet, but despite a prison sentence, he returned to service early in 1918 as head of the Central Aeronautical Bureau. In 1921, Douhet, now a general, began publishing his ideas about the future of air power with the first of two editions of *Il Dominio dell' Aria* (*The Command of the Air*; second edition, 1927) and continued to write until his death in 1933. Only posthumously were Douhet's works published in translation, although the substance of his concepts spread among the air advocates of the major air forces a decade earlier.

Douhet's theory rested on several assumptions. The Great War had destroyed, in his mind, the distinctions between soldier and civilian. Armies and navies were no longer capable of producing decision in other than long and costly wars of attrition. He believed that in the near future air power would become far more formidable than it had been in 1918 and that there would be little defense against large-scale air attacks. Civilian morale would be unable to withstand such aerial bombardments. Thus, the key to future victory would be the possession of a large bombing force able to strike enemy industrial and population centers at the beginning of the conflict.

Douhet's theories were not without problems. He underestimated the ability of land and naval forces to embrace new military technologies, including air power, and to regain their ability to produce decision. He overestimated the amount of damage and terror that bombers could inflict, although Douhet had assumed that air attackers would employ poison gas as well as incendiaries and high explosives. Who can say what impact chemical bombs would have had on civilian morale had such weapons been employed during World War II? Douhet also believed that his "battle plane," a heavily armed bomber, would be virtually unstoppable. Writing in the 1920s, he could not have foreseen the advent of radar or the development of high-speed, heavily gunned, monoplane interceptors capable of overtaking and destroying bombers. Nor had Douhet, the theoretician, foreseen the technical problems and costs of building the requisite numbers of heavy bombers.

While Douhet had many things wrong, his predictions became more prescient with the passage of the decades. Multipurpose fighter-bombers have become ubiquitous among the major air forces. Precision-guided munitions have made attacks more accurate. The marriage of the airplane and nuclear power in 1945 could be viewed as the fulfillment of Douhet's concepts.

But in the 1920s, limited budgets and technological realities remained the determining factors in aviation development. Italy, despite Douhet's influence, lacked the necessary resources. German airmen focused mostly on supporting the army and navy. The Soviets did likewise, and not surprisingly, since they were too distant to contemplate strikes against the industrial infrastructure of any of the major powers. Thus, it was left to the British and the Americans to pursue the concept of strategic bombing.

That Douhet-like concepts found their fullest expression in Britain and the United States should not come as a surprise. Both were insular sea powers that intuitively understood the fundamental ideas that underlay strategic air warfare. Until the advent of nuclear power, naval warfare was a form of conflict for the patient. Navies routinely employed strategic warfare in the form of the economic blockade.

But even in Britain and the United States reality checked development. For the RAF, the 1920s was a decade of tight budgets and few threats. The service's primary struggle was to survive as an independent entity. Despite vicious interservice wrangling, the RAF did remain a separate service, primarily because of the strong leadership from men such as Air Marshal Sir Hugh "Boom" Trenchard, and the marketing of a not-so-effective, but relatively inexpensive concept of imperial policing from the air, employed in the Middle East.

Amidst this turmoil, the RAF maintained a handful of bomber squadrons. Crews practiced night flying and bombing, with poor results. Target recognition remained the primary unsolved problem.

When rearmament began after 1932, the British poured resources into the RAF. Fighter Command became an effective force, relying on an advanced radar net, a coordinated system of command and control, and modern eight-gun fighters, such as the Hawker Hurricane and the Supermarine Spitfire. As the capabilities of bombers improved, the RAF argued for more aircraft to strike Germany, many of the main industrial centers of which were conveniently placed along its western border. The bomber option was politically attractive. It allowed politicians to contemplate offensive action without committing themselves to send the BEF to the Continent. Unfortunately for the British, the bombers available in the late 1930s were inadequate. At night, they could not find the target, hit it if they found it, or inflict much damage with their light bomb loads. Daytime raids were impossible since there were no long-range escort fighters. Fighter Command had proposed the development of an escort arm, but Bomber Command had shown no interest. As a result, in 1939, Bomber Command was an ineffective military force. However committed some British airmen were to the concept of strategic bombing, they did not possess the tools, training, or doctrine to put their theories into practice.

Many American airmen in France during the Great War had become converts to British bombing concepts. Nevertheless, the American political environment was initially less conducive to the development of strategic bombing. Americans could reasonably ask, who is it that we need to, or could possibly, bomb? In 1918, the American air arm's primary mission remained to support ground forces, although had the war continued, plans existed to employ strategically a force of over a thousand bombers. The end of the war wrecked such grandiose plans and replaced them with abysmally low peacetime budgets.

Since American air doctrine had never fully developed during the war, the early postwar experience ensured continued doctrinal disarray. Analysis of aerial warfare, conducted by the U.S. Army's general staff, concluded that strategic bombing had been ineffective. Doctrinal focus, such as it existed, remained fixed on support of the ground forces.

The Air Service, however, was otherwise inclined. In 1921, the chief of the Air Service published a report, parts of which were probably lifted directly from Douhet's writings, at that point not yet translated into English. But the Air Service was caught in a doctrine-procurement cyclical trap. The focus on support of ground operations during the Great War drove procurement decisions—that is, judgments about the types of aircraft needed. Postwar analysis demonstrated that close support worked, whereas bombing, an effort conducted by an improperly equipped force, had failed. As a result, the postwar army bought more observation aircraft and fewer bombers.

But there were individuals determined to break this cycle. One of the most prominent was William "Billy" Mitchell, an army officer who had transferred to the air arm in 1916. By the end of the war, Mitchell commanded the largest operational force of American aircraft in France. Mitchell was an air advocate well before the end of the Great War. While Douhet's theories probably influenced those of the American during the postwar decade, Mitchell was no Douhet clone. The American airman, who had practical experience commanding large air units in battle, focused less on the purely strategic, but also went further than Douhet in other areas. Mitchell viewed aerial warriors as a "special class" of "armored knights." He argued that an air force could destroy not only the enemy's economy, but also its army and navy. Unlike Douhet, Mitchell believed that an air force would need fighters and not just bombing "battle planes." He foresaw the need to secure "air superiority" in the initial stage of an air campaign. He supported concepts of aerial defense, an un-Douhet-like posture, but one with some appeal to Americans. After all, some argued, how else could an enemy get at the United States if not by air? Mitchell acknowledged the problems of distance facing the United States, but argued for very long-range bombers, advocated for the development of island bases in the Pacific, and suggested the viability of polar routes over the Arctic, three decades before they became reality.

If Douhet was the theoretician of air warfare, Mitchell was the popularizer. But like Douhet, Mitchell also ran afoul of his high command. His aggressive arguments and public political drive for the creation of an independent Air Service angered superiors and even many in the Air Service who disagreed with his tactics. Perhaps Mitchell's biggest errors were his exaggerated claims that air power would soon make armies and navies virtually useless. It was one thing to build up one's own service; it was another to threaten the existence of others. The army court-martialed Mitchell in 1925, and he resigned his commission the following year.

Mitchell's professional demise did not, however, signify the defeat of the Air Service's vision of its future. In 1926, the army formed an air corps and established the Air Corps Tactical School (ACTS) to study air-warfare concepts. Strategic bombing quickly became the major focus; the objective was not the destruction of the enemy's armed forces, but the morale of the enemy population. By 1932, air corps doctrine had identified a set of priorities: the destruction of the enemy's air force, strategic bombing of enemy industry, the coastal defense of the United States (historically the responsibility of the army and navy), and, lastly, air support of ground and naval forces. By 1933, students at the school were reading Douhet in translation. By 1935, studies concluded that an air campaign could secure victory unaided.

By the mid-1930s, the army's air corps had identified precision daylight bombing as the path to victory. Daylight attacks solved the problems the British faced with finding and hitting targets. ACTS studies also focused on economics and business organization in an effort to identify bottlenecks in an enemy economy.

Commitment to precision attacks had two political advantages. First, it allowed the air corps to avoid the public-opinion pitfalls of what would otherwise have appeared to be unrestricted attacks against a civilian population. Second, precision allowed the air corps to argue before Congress that it could achieve its goals with a fleet of bombers that the politicians were more likely to fund.

During the mid- and late 1930s, uneven technological advances weakened the air corps' commitment to the concepts of air defense and the achievement of air superiority as a preliminary stage. Fighter development lagged in the United States. Poorly armed biplanes with low service ceilings remained in use well into the late 1930s. The new bombers, such as the four-engine Boeing B-17 armed with the remarkably accurate Norden Mark XV bombsight, could fly higher and faster than contemporary fighters. As a result, American airmen concluded that bombers could operate unescorted and, once over enemy territory, could inflict significant damage in precision strikes. Doctrinally, both the concept of air defense and the effort to achieve air superiority appeared to be unnecessary.

As a result, on the eve of war, American air doctrine was well developed, but flawed, though not fatally. The Americans overestimated both the defensive and offensive capabilities of their bombers. The belief that an enemy state could be defeated without engaging and destroying its armed forces (or at least the air element) was not only a repudiation of Clausewitz, but also of Mitchell. The Americans, however, had many things right. They had also, unlike the British, developed a cadre force and a doctrinal framework that, with a few substantive alterations, could be made to work.

The price of the Anglo-American focus on strategic bombing was the failure to develop an effective doctrine for close air support. Both air forces struggled throughout the war to find effective ways to support their ground and naval forces.

The RFC and RAF had performed fairly well in support of the British army during World War I. Postwar analysis, however, indicated that losses to ground fire had been high, and the impact of such attacks on enemy ground forces was impossible to measure. Moreover, RAF leaders viewed continued attention to ground support as a recipe for a return to army control. As a result, the RAF paid virtually no attention to close air support during the interwar years. Fighter doctrine envisioned the possibility of sporadic ground attacks. But no doctrine for the coordination of such efforts by the two services existed. Nor did the RAF train its pilots in ground support.

The American Air Service had likewise worked diligently to support the army during the Great War. But the postwar focus on securing service independence (or at least autonomy), planning for strategic bombing, and ensuring that Congress funded large numbers of expensive bombers allowed the close air support function to atrophy. Air Corps doctrine in the mid-1930s envisioned light bombers striking not enemy troops, but airfields in support of the air campaign. Doctrine limited ground support to interdiction strikes against targets behind the front lines, such as road junctions, rail yards, supply depots, and headquarters. Between the wars, the Air Corps, like the RAF, failed to develop a doctrine to support engaged friendly ground forces.

Any attempt to determine the preparedness level of the European military forces on the eve of war in 1939 must first consider the unprecedented scope and scale of World War II. Despite expectations that the conflict would be quick and decisive, the Second World War was neither. It was a titanic global struggle that lasted longer and was more costly in both human and materiel terms than the Great War.

There can be no doubt that the Germans (and the Japanese in the Pacific theater) were the best prepared for the war in its opening stages. The Germans were well trained and employed superior doctrine, both on the ground and in the air. But another element in the equation was the simple fact that Germany had begun its preparations earlier than Great Britain, France, and the United States. Political purges had gutted the Soviet army and thrown its doctrine and organization into confusion. The Allies could, and would, gradually and at great cost, make up that lost time.

There also remains another consideration: there is a difference between being prepared for war and being prepared for the war that actually began in 1939. The ultimate failure of the Germans and their allies to win the war quickly left them engaged in a prolonged struggle for which they were *not* prepared, and for which, in many ways, they were actually less prepared than the Allied powers, especially the Soviet Union and the United States.

Despite the Germans' tactical and operational superiority early in the war, strategic failures ensured that there would be no quick end to the conflict. The Germans began the struggle in 1939 lacking the strategic vision and "reach" necessary to ensure victory. The Germans had spent the 1920s thinking about how they could defend their country against France and, primarily, Poland. After Hitler came to power in 1933, existing defensive concepts were easily translated into offensive schemes ideal for use against Germany's neighbors. In 1939, the Germans crushed Poland; in 1940, they overran France and the Low Countries. But the Germans could not leap the English Channel to complete their victory by defeating insular Britain. The following year, logistic and mobility limitations prevented the Germans from defeating both Stalin's army and the vastness of the Soviet Union in a single "blitz" campaign. When the United States joined the Allies in December 1941, the Germans lacked the military power to strike across the Atlantic with anything more than a handful of submarines.

While in purely operational and tactical terms Germany's enemies may not have been well equipped for war in 1939, they were, in fact, better prepared in other areas, most notably the strategic (both air and naval) and the organizational (primarily logistical and industrial). As the war lengthened, the importance of these Allied advantages became more marked and ultimately helped to pave the road to victory.

CHAPTER V

World War II, 1937–1945

HISTORIANS CONTINUE TO DEBATE THE EXTENT to which the Treaty of Versailles set the stage for the Second World War. Some argue that it was too harsh, others that it was not harsh enough. Nevertheless, Europe a decade after Versailles was in the midst of economic, social, and political recovery. Many Europeans and Americans believed that they had witnessed the last world war. Virtually all the major states were signatories to the 1928 Pact of Paris, best known as the Kellogg-Briand Pact, which renounced the use of aggressive warfare as a means of national policy.

But a variety of forces too numerous to discuss initiated a drift toward more belligerent policies. In 1929, an economic depression of broad and deep severity struck the world. Two years later, Japan occupied Manchuria. In 1933, Hitler and his National Socialist (Nazi) party came to power in Germany. The Nazis repudiated the Versailles treaty and began open rearmament. In 1935, the Anglo-German Naval Agreement marked Great Britain's de facto acceptance of the Germans' decision to expand their navy beyond the limits of Versailles. That same year, Italy invaded and conquered Ethiopia.

Economic sanctions failed to help the Ethiopians, but made Italo-German cooperation more likely. In 1936, the Germans reoccupied the Rhineland, an area demilitarized under the terms of Versailles. France failed to act. Civil war erupted in Spain. Germany and Italy sent considerable aid to Franco's Nationalists, while Soviet Russia aided the Republicans. By 1939, the Nationalists had triumphed, in part thanks to the military aid they received, but primarily because of the political infighting within the Republican camp. As the Spanish Civil War raged, the Germans occupied Austria in what they termed the *Anschluss*—connection or annexation. Italy, the only European state able to help the Austrians, stood aside.

German territory now surrounded Czechoslovakia, a hybrid, multinational state that included ethnic Germans. In 1938, Hitler made a series of demands on Czechoslovakia, among them a call for the German annexation of the Sudetenland—the mountainous border region in which Germans predominated—where the Czechs had constructed most of their defenses. Turning over the Sudetenland would render Czechoslovakia defenseless. War appeared imminent, but British and French leaders balked. In late September, Hitler and Benito Mussolini met in Munich with British prime minister Neville Chamberlain and French premier Édouard Daladier. The resultant accord called for the Czechs to yield the areas in question by mid-October, and Britain and France guaranteed the rump of what remained. The Czechs, totally isolated, yielded, thus temporarily avoiding a European war.

Despite hopes of peace, the old world was well along the road to war. In March 1939, the Germans occupied the rest of Czechoslovakia as Britain and France stood by, despite their promises and guarantees. Great Britain and France, expecting Hitler to move against Poland, pledged their support to the Poles. In April, the Italians overran Albania. In May, Italy and Germany signed a military pact, forming the Rome-Berlin "axis." Over the summer, the Germans began a war of nerves against Poland, demanding the return of the "free" city of Danzig and areas of western Poland that formed that state's corridor to the sea.

Hitler worked to isolate Poland diplomatically, much as he had isolated Austria and Czechoslovakia. On 23 August 1939, Germany and the Soviet Union signed a nonaggression pact that ensured Russian neutrality (in return for the eastern third of Poland). There was little that Britain or France could do to save the Poles. Nevertheless, it was politically impossible for British and French leaders to back down as they had at and after Munich. Despite the fact that few people wanted war, the French and British announced their decision to stand by the Poles. Hitler, confident that the *Wehrmacht* (the German armed forces) could destroy Poland quickly, made the decision to invade.

Thus began the second European war. The Poles were heavily outnumbered on the ground and in the air. Germany deployed 1.25 million men and nearly three thousand tanks against the 800,000 men of the still mobilizing Polish army, which numbered its tanks in the hundreds. The *Luftwaffe* had over 1,500 modern aircraft in the east, the Poles had between 400 and 500 obsolescent models. The *Wehrmacht* was better trained and employed superior doctrine.

Geographically, the Poles were isolated and surrounded, their industrial vitals exposed in salients they felt compelled to defend. Poland's eastern neighbor, the Soviet Union, was prepared to intervene, but on Hitler's side. Even the weather favored the Germans: September 1939 was unseasonably dry, offering good flying weather for the *Luftwaffe* and hard ground for the panzers.

Nevertheless, the Germans needed to win quickly before the French fully mobilized. Operationally, the Germans intended to hold in the center and to break through the Polish defenses on the right and left flanks with offensives led by mechanized formations. These advancing prongs would meet near Warsaw, the capital, destroying the bulk of the Polish army west of the Vistula. The Germans would then occupy the remainder of the country as they shifted forces westward.

Tactically, the Germans employed the doctrine derived from the *Stosstruppen* of the Great War, refined under Seeckt's leadership during the 1920s, and enhanced by mechanization during the 1930s.

To defeat the Poles, the Germans relied on surprise, speed, use of combined arms at all levels, decentralized command and control, mission-type orders (*auftragtaktik*), and reliance on the initiative of subordinate commanders to make the most of opportunities as they presented themselves.

On the whole, the campaign went according to plan. The new German tactics, now termed *blitzkrieg*, proved decisive. The Poles lost almost a million men, including 700,000 who became prisoners of war, in the short campaign. German casualties were much lower, about 43,000. German mechanized units, often organized in panzer corps, broke through Polish defenses and drove deep into the rear. On the first and second days of the campaign, the *Luftwaffe* struck the Polish airfields and air force and quickly gained air superiority. On the third day of the campaign, the *Luftwaffe* turned its attention to interdiction and close support of the army's advance. In the air, the German JU-87B "Stuka" dive-bombers, with their gull wings and eerie sirens, epitomized the fury and terror of the new German tactics. On the ground, the dark gray German panzers crushed the poorly equipped Poles and drove through their lines. The speed and ferocity of the German attack disrupted Polish plans, communications, defenses, and mobilization. The *Wehrmacht* crushed the bulk of the Polish army in a fortnight. On 17 September, Hitler began shifting forces to the west. Three days later, the Soviets occupied eastern Poland. On 27 September, Warsaw, besieged for nearly two weeks, surrendered. While some Polish units fought on into early October, and guerilla operations continued throughout the war, Poland had been defeated in less than a month.

But all had not gone as planned, either diplomatically or militarily. On 3 September, Great Britain and France declared war. The localized conflict Hitler sought became a European war. Despite successes, the *Luftwaffe* had yet to master close air support and in a short campaign had exhausted half its stock of bombs. And while the *Luftwaffe* had quickly gained air superiority, it had done so more by default and because of its overwhelming superiority than it had by its attacks against Polish airfields. Many of the more recently mobilized German army units were inadequately trained. The four light divisions proved to be too light for sustained combat and were subsequently converted into panzer divisions. German armored units lost almost a quarter of their strength to mechanical problems, and the panzer divisions lost over two hundred tanks to Polish 37mm antitank guns and to infantry armed with antiquated antitank rifles. The dichotomy within the German army—the existence of fast, mechanized, panzer units alongside more traditionally equipped infantry divisions still overwhelmingly reliant on draft horses—also caused problems. Infantry divisions fought extremely well, but strained to keep pace with the motorized formations. Unfortunately, the slow infantry columns filled up the few Polish roads and blocked the path of the motorized supply units trying to reach the armored formations. Only the unseasonably good weather, the limited geographic scope of operations, and the brevity of the campaign saved the Germans from a logistical nightmare. The campaign also demonstrated that German infantry needed their own tracked armored weapons to assault entrenched or fortified positions. The Germans began the development of assault guns and what they termed *jagdpanzers*—respectively, direct-fire artillery and antitank guns mounted on the chassis of obsolete tanks.

After a brief diplomatic interval that failed to end the conflict, Hitler decided to launch an assault in the west, but poor weather, the need to rearm, and the reluctance of the German generals forced a delay until the spring. In the interim, the armies in the west—German, French, and the British Expeditionary Force (BEF)—idly faced each other in what became known as the Phoney War or the *Sitzkrieg*. The Allies were such reluctant belligerents that they preferred to drop leaflets on the Germans in lieu of bombs. The Germans were similarly restrained, happy to be left free to prepare their forces for a spring offensive.

Fighting, to the surprise of many, next erupted in the east. Stalin, after invading eastern Poland, set his sights on Finnish territory that lay close to the Baltic city of St. Petersburg, renamed Leningrad by the Bolsheviks. The Soviets struck on 30 November when the Finns refused to yield. By February, despite a few isolated successes, the main Russian drive against the Finnish defenses northwest of Leningrad—the Mannerheim Line—stalled. The Finns, fighting in near-Arctic conditions, slaughtered tens of thousands of Soviets while thousands more froze to death.

Ultimately, the Soviets learned hard lessons and massed an overwhelming force along the border. In February, they launched a set-piece attack that ground down the outnumbered Finns, who yielded in March. Finland suffered 25,000 killed or missing and another 43,000 wounded. Russian casualties can only be estimated, but are believed to have included at least 200,000 dead.

The results of the Winter War were many. The Soviets began restructuring their army, a process that would accelerate after the fall of France in June 1940 and would be incomplete in June 1941 when Hitler struck, with his Finnish allies at his side. The poor Soviet performance in the campaign also reinforced German assumptions about the inferiority of Stalin's military. Stalin's attack on Finland also led France and Britain to view the Soviet Union as Hitler's de facto ally. In fact, had the Winter War lasted, the Allies were planning to send a relief force to the Finns through neutral Norway and to bomb Soviet oilfields in the Caucasus from Middle Eastern air bases.

The focus on Scandinavia hastened a German invasion of Denmark and Norway. The latter was important to Hitler for two reasons. Swedish iron ore from northern mines made its way overland to the Norwegian port of Narvik and thence by ship along the coast to Germany. If the British moved into northern Norway, this route would be cut. German naval strategists also considered Norway pivotal. During the Great War, the Germans had been trapped in the North Sea. Interwar studies suggested the occupation of Norway as a means of outflanking the British blockade.

In February, a small staff at the headquarters of the *Oberkommando des Wehrmacht* (OKW)—the German multiservice high command—began planning Operation Weser, one of the more difficult undertakings the Germans conducted during the war. *Weser* required interservice—army, navy, and air force—cooperation to a degree unparalleled in German military history. The plan involved *Kriegsmarine* (German navy) and *Luftwaffe* support for amphibious and airborne operations conducted at great distance in the face of the superior Royal Navy.

Weser, launched on 7 April 1940, was a stunning, though near-run, success. Denmark fell in hours and Norway in six weeks. But on several occasions the operation came close to failure. The German navy suffered heavy losses. Allied expeditionary forces sent to aid the Norwegians initially gained ground and in the north retook Narvik. At one point, Hitler nearly ordered the withdrawal of the German mountain units from Narvik. But the perseverance of those troops and the crisis that developed in France in May eventually led to a complete Allied withdrawal and German victory.

As the Scandinavian campaign ebbed, the Germans completed their final preparations for their offensive to the west: Operation *Gelb* ("Yellow"). The original proposal was an updated version of the Schlieffen plan of 1914—a right hook through Belgium and Holland. The Allies expected such a move and planned to rush their own left wing into the Low Countries to meet the Germans as far forward as possible.

For a variety of reasons, the Germans changed their plan and, at Hitler's prompting, adopted a more daring strategy. They would advance instead with their center, driving a panzer group, containing most of the panzer divisions, through the Ardennes—a wooded region that spanned Luxembourg, Belgium, and France. This armored juggernaut would break through Allied defenses, cross the Meuse, race east to the Somme, and follow its valley to the Channel, trapping the bulk of the French and British armies against the sea.

The offensive began on the morning of 10 May 1940. The opposing forces were evenly matched in terms of men and materiel. The Allies actually possessed more and heavier tanks, but the Germans employed theirs with superior organization and doctrine. Everywhere the Germans were successful. In the north, they overran Holland. A specially trained glider detachment seized the fort of Eben Emael, opening the Belgian plain to the German flood. Near Hannut on 13 May, elements of two German panzer divisions clashed with two French DLMs. The French tankers fought hard, but could not match German combined arms and tactical proficiency.

With Allied attentions focused up north, the Germans moved *Generaloberst* Ewald von Kleist's panzer group through the Ardennes. Many prewar analysts considered the Ardennes impassable by a modern army. The region, heavily wooded with few north-south roads, was not ideal tank country, as events would demonstrate in December 1944. But in May 1940, the Ardennes front was barely defended, allowing the Germans to motor virtually unopposed through the area along good east-west roads. Three panzer corps, commanded by generals Hermann Hoth, Georg-Hans Reinhardt, and Heinz Guderian, met little substantive resistance until they reached the Meuse River, by which time they had left the Ardennes behind. On 13 May, the motorized German infantry attached to the panzer divisions seized several bridgeheads across the Meuse, most notably at Sedan where *Luftwaffe* Stukas delivered the most impressive display of air-ground support witnessed to that point in the war. Engineers quickly built bridges and ferried tanks across the river.

By 16 May, the Germans had driven a bulge into the middle of the French line. Allied reserves were mostly committed elsewhere. Communications broke down. Panic seized the French high command, neither doctrinally nor mentally prepared for the fast tempo of operations. The French abandoned their methodical battle and became belated converts to defense in depth. But the situation was beyond redemption, despite the often hard fighting of French soldiers. By 21 May, the German advance had reached the Channel, fending off a handful of poorly executed Allied counterstrokes along the way.

Over the course of the next five weeks, the Germans completed their victory. As the French collapse became complete, Mussolini, on 21 June, joined the fray. Even a section of the Maginot Line fell. The following day, the Germans granted a French request for an armistice. Fighting continued for a few more days, but the campaign had effectively ended.

The "temporary" armistice gave the Germans control over two-thirds of France, including Paris and the Channel and Atlantic coasts. A rump state, with its capital in Vichy, ruled over southeastern France, including the Mediterranean coast, the navy, and the colonies.

In six weeks, the *Wehrmacht* had achieved what the kaiser's army had failed to accomplish in four years. Germans were elated. Much of the rest of the world stood in shock. Stalin, who had expected a long war of attrition between the fascists and capitalists, was stunned, although he made the best of the situation by grabbing the Baltic states—Estonia, Latvia, and Lithuania—and Bessarabia from Romania.

But the German triumph, despite appearances, was incomplete. Between 26 May and 4 June, the Royal Navy had evacuated 340,000 Allied troops, including 215,000 men of the BEF, from Dunkirk along the French Channel coast under the cover of the RAF. The British left all their equipment and vehicles behind, but saved the cadre of their army. The *Luftwaffe* was unable to prevent the escape. The vulnerability of the lightly armored German tanks remained a problem, as did their inadequate armament. On several occasions, the heavier French and British tanks forced the Germans to tackle the behemoths with 88mm antiaircraft guns. Problems caused by uneven mechanization and logistic shortcomings, evident in Poland, remained. Gaps frequently developed between the rapidly advancing panzer corps and the slower-moving infantry. Fortunately for the Germans, the Allies were unable to take advantage of these situations. Nevertheless, Hitler, who had refrained from interfering with the conduct of operations during the Polish campaign, did intervene during the drive toward the Channel, halting the panzers more than once and setting a bad precedent for future operations. Nor had the victory been cheap: German casualties totaled over

continued on page 179

The Battle of Kursk

The true turning point of the war in the east was not Stalingrad, but the epic battle of Kursk—the largest tank engagement of the Second World War. Axis defeat at Kursk marked the end of Hitler's dreams of victory over the Soviet Union.

When Manstein's February–March 1943 counterstroke in the Ukraine stalled in the spring mud, a large Soviet salient jutted westward into the Axis front near the city of Kursk. This salient became an obvious target for a renewed German offensive, and planning began in April for such an eventuality. The Russians, too, saw the likelihood of such an attack, a surmise confirmed by intelligence sources. As a result, throughout the spring and into the early summer, both sides prepared for the third German summer offensive around Kursk.

Several aspects of German planning attest to the Germans' declining fortunes. In 1941, the Germans had struck on 22 June along the entire front from the Baltic to the Black Sea. In 1942, the Germans struck on 28 June, a week later, and limited their offensive to the southern sector of the front. In 1943, the Germans did not attack until 5 July and then only along a limited portion of the front around Kursk.

Nor were the Germans of one mind as they planned their offensive. There was a consensus that Kursk was the best place to strike. To pinch off the salient would shorten the German line and produce a haul of prisoners. But there were divisions between those generals who wished to strike as soon as possible and others, with Hitler's support, who wished to delay the offensive until more units could be outfitted with new heavy and medium armored vehicles, most notably the Panther tanks. As delays mounted, some generals became more and more pessimistic about the prospects of success. Nevertheless, recent scholarship in Soviet archives suggests that the debate was moot. The strength of the Soviet forces in the rear of the exposed salient in May and June 1943 was far greater than the Germans knew.

The Axis plan was simple: to strike at the haunches of the salient from both the north and the south. The Ninth Army would strike from the north, from its positions south of Orel. Army Group South's Fourth Panzer Army would strike from the area near Belgorod along a northern axis. Originally scheduled for 4 May, the offensive was repeatedly postponed because of rains, a desire to wait for more tanks, and the need to send reinforcements to Italy after the Axis collapse in Tunisia.

Soviet plans for Kursk were innovative. Even Stalin had learned the lessons of 1942 and accepted the fact that it was best to allow the Germans to strike first rather than to preempt them before their forces had been weakened. In that sense, the buildup around Kursk suited Soviet strategy. Having resolved to accept a defensive posture, they developed a defense in depth to meet the German attack and planned an ambitious series of follow-on offensives meant to crush the German front in the center and the north.

Tactically and operationally, the Soviet army of 1943 was vastly superior to the forces that took the field in 1941 and 1942. Moreover, the Soviets achieved their successes in 1943 and 1944 when they no longer possessed the technological superiority they had held in 1941 and 1942, when their T-34 tank was the best armored fighting vehicle on the eastern front. By 1943, the T-34 was in many ways inferior to the newer German medium tanks—the up-gunned medium Pz Kw IVs, Panthers, and heavy Tigers—and would remain so for the rest of the war. But the Soviets had developed superior tactical proficiency and ability to employ combined-arms tactics on the battlefield.

Soviet preparations to meet the expected German blitzkrieg were well thought out. The Russians arrayed their defense in layers to a depth of forty miles. They dug in troops, tanks, guns, and communication lines. Antitank guns and minefields dominated likely approaches. The Soviet high command positioned mechanized reserves to respond to crises that might develop along any axis. Even the Soviet air force prepared to challenge the Germans for local air superiority from the first day of the operation. Moreover, as the battle developed, the Soviet plan envisioned the use of reserves offensively to disrupt the Axis offensive. Gradually, these local counterattacks would expand until they became a counteroffensive that would wrest the initiative from the Germans.

In execution, the battle of Kursk followed Russian and not German expectations. In the north, the German Ninth Army made disappointing progress, suffered heavy casualties, and within four days had ground to a virtual halt. Two days later, the Soviets began assaulting the left flank of the offensive, forcing Army Group Center to shift its reserves and ending all hopes of a continued drive by the Ninth Army. The Germans made better progress in the south. Despite hard going, the Germans nearly drove through the defensive belts. But if Manstein's troops broke in, they could not break out. In their weakened state, they had to contend with the fresh Soviet mechanized reserves. Moreover, as the mobile battle began, Allied troops landed in Sicily. Hitler now had to contend with a threat to Italy, and the necessary reserves could only come from the eastern front.

The climatic fighting centered on the town of Prokhorovka. For several July days, the SS Panzer Corps and the Soviet Fifth Tank Army traded blows in a bloody battle of attrition. But attrition was Stalin's game. On 13 July, Hitler decided to end the offensive and shift troops to Italy. Manstein wished to keep attacking, not in the expectation of a victory, but as a means to exhaust Soviet tank reserves. Hitler agreed to allow limited offensive action for this purpose, but basically *Zitadelle* had ended, and the Germans had lost.

For decades after the war, many historians argued that Hitler lost a great opportunity by prematurely closing down his Kursk offensive. More recent studies using available Soviet documents suggest that Hitler was wise to bring the operation to an end. Manstein was not exhausting Soviet reserves; he was exhausting his own, just as the Soviets hoped that he would before they unleashed their own offensives. On 17 July, when the Russians went over to the offensive on Manstein's right flank, it became apparent that there was no point in continuing the German effort.

If the Germans did make a mistake, it was to attack at all, or to attack into an area where they knew the Russians had prepared defenses. But Hitler and his generals shared the same misplaced confidence in the operational and tactical superiority of their forces. Few Germans seem to have considered it possible that the Russians could stop a German summer blitzkrieg dead in its tracks.

The ability of Stalin's army to do just that was more than a defeat: it marked the eclipse of a tactical doctrine the Germans had thus far applied with success. The Russians had not only turned the tide of the war in the east, but they had also demonstrated that a well-prepared blitzkrieg could be defeated. As the follow-on Soviet offensives opened, the Soviets also confirmed that they had developed improved offensive tactics of their own. Soviet infantry and artillery led the assault, and only then did tank and mechanized formations exploit the holes. By mid-1943, not only the strategic, but also the operational and tactical assumptions upon which the Germans had gone to war in 1939 were no longer viable.

150,000. This was a rate of loss much lower than that suffered during the Great War, but the casualties were concentrated in the divisions that bore the bulk of the combat. Officers, who led from the front, made up about 5 percent of the total.

Nevertheless, Adolf Hitler stood at the apogee of his power. The self-styled artist and architect visited Paris as a tourist, gawked at the Eiffel Tower, and stood silently before the tomb of Napoleon I. But the conqueror of Poland and France had exhausted the strategic inheritance of the *Reichswehr*. Hitler was virtually clueless about what to do next. The obvious option was to cross the English Channel as soon as possible, but few of Hitler's senior commanders—air, land, or naval—seemed enthusiastic about an invasion of England. Nor could the führer be certain of the assurances offered by the *Luftwaffe*'s pompous and vainglorious commander, *Reichsmarshal* Herman Göring, who had assured Hitler that the British would never escape from Dunkirk. Admiral Erich Räder favored a *guerre de course* and the extension of the war to the Mediterranean, but the commander-in-chief of the *Kriegsmarine* spoke a language all but foreign to the continental-minded former army corporal, and the prospects of a prolonged war did not hold much appeal for Hitler. Alternatively, he could fall back on the vapid, pseudogeo-political rantings he had published in his own *Mein Kampf* and strike east against the Soviet Union to crush Bolshevism and gain the *Lebensraum*—"living space"—that the German people neither needed nor wanted.

Hitler initially directed the *Wehrmacht* to prepare for a cross-Channel invasion, given the unwillingness of Great Britain, led by Winston Churchill since 10 May, to make peace. But the führer also toyed with the idea of shifting operations to the Mediterranean or to the east. In July, planners began sketching out a preliminary scheme for an invasion of the Soviet Union. In the midst of this strategic debate, the Germans began demobilizing their army, and the armaments industry remained uncertain about its priorities. Should industry be producing ships and aircraft for a war with England, or tanks and guns for a ground war in the east?

Hitler's three strategic options were all viable. It is impossible to say which he ought to have chosen. What can be said with certainty is that the decision should have been made *before* the French campaign, and the fact that it was not demonstrates a failure of strategic foresight. The German navy had begun preliminary planning for an invasion of Britain in November, but the army, air force, and the armed forces high command had remained focused on tactical and operational issues. The Germans had failed to ask the obvious question: if we win in France, what then? After the French armistice, Hitler only gradually moved toward a final decision, at times drifting in all three strategic directions at once.

In mid-July, the OKW directed the armed services to prepare for an invasion of Great Britain, codenamed Operation *See Löwe* ("Sea Lion"). While German preparations were real, the historical record remains less than clear about Hitler's commitment to launch the invasion. If he was sincere, he was also extremely reticent and eager to grasp any excuse to cancel the planned invasion.

What became known as the Battle of Britain began in July when the *Luftwaffe* undertook preliminary operations against British shipping and ports, meant also to test the response of the RAF's Fighter Command. The main operation would begin on *Adler Tag* ("Eagle Day"), initially scheduled for 9 August 1940. The Germans expected to destroy British fighter defenses in the south in four days and shift their effort north as British defenses crumbled. Once they gained air superiority, a task estimated to take four weeks, the invasion would begin, as the *Luftwaffe* prevented interference by the Royal Navy.

The British air-defense system was formidable. A state-of-the-art radar net warned of approaching German aircraft. A superb command and control system, linked to those the radar sites, ground spotters, airfields, and squadrons, allowed the selective and advantageous response to incoming raids. As a result, the British did not need to keep planes on patrol and RAF fighters were hard to catch on the ground. Fighter Command also possessed nearly 600 modern fighters—Hawker Hurricanes and Supermarine Spitfires, armed with eight .303 Browning machine guns.

German planning for the campaign was flawed, strategically, operationally, and tactically. The Germans were using the *Luftwaffe*, however superb, for a mission for which it was not designed. The problem was not that the German air force was incapable of strategic warfare, but that operationally the *Luftwaffe* was woefully unprepared for the campaign. The Germans lacked accurate intelligence. They could count aircraft well enough, locate most of the British airfields, and mark the sites of the British radar stations on a map. But the *Luftwaffe's* senior leadership had little appreciation of how the British defensive system worked. And they were not aware that British factories were already producing more fighters than German industry. Tactically, the Germans' greatest weakness was their lack of escorts for the bombers. The Messerschmitt Bf-109E was an excellent fighter, superior to the Hurricane and on par with the Spitfire. But the Bf-109 had limited range and could just reach London. The German twin-engine destroyer, the Bf-110C, possessed the necessary endurance, but could not compete with the more nimble British fighters.

Bad weather delayed *Alder Tag* until the afternoon of 13 August. The Germans struck with two air fleets based along the Channel coast and another, smaller air fleet in Norway. The *Luftwaffe* had nearly 2,800 aircraft at its disposal, including 1,300 bombers, 280 Stuka dive bombers, and 250 twin-engine and 760 single-engine fighters.

The initial operations did not proceed as planned. The Germans hit British airfields in the southeast, but dirt airfields were easy to repair, and the British had backup facilities prepared. The Stukas, which for the first time met serious opposition in the air, proved to be so antiquated and vulnerable that they had to be withdrawn from the campaign. The armament of the German medium bombers was inadequate, leaving them vulnerable to British fighters. The presence of Spitfires or Hurricanes often forced German Bf-110 long-range escorts to form defensive circles to save themselves. The Bf-109s performed well, but usually at a disadvantage, operating at the limits of their endurance and tethered to the bombers they escorted. British losses were heavy, but German losses were even heavier. Nor did Fighter Command appear to be on the verge of collapse.

On 2 September, the *Luftwaffe* switched its operational focus and began the day and night bombing of cities, especially London. The new goal was to terrorize Britain into surrender. But this effort failed as well. *Luftwaffe* medium bombers could not deliver the heavy payloads necessary for such tactics. Fighter Command, now spared attacks against its infrastructure, recovered and soon made the German daylight attacks too expensive to continue. On 17 September, Hitler postponed *See Löwe*. By October, the Germans had given up their daylight raids, but the Blitz, as the night bombing became known, continued until May 1941.

In late September, Hitler turned his attention to the Mediterranean. He planned a diplomatic offensive to bring Spain and Vichy France into a collaborative front in the Mediterranean.

The momentum the Germans had possessed in the summer had aleady dissipated. On 4 October, Hitler met Mussolini at the Brenner Pass and discussed the details of the new strategy. The führer met next with Franco on 23 October, but the *caudillo* set an extremely high price for Spain's entry into the war—one Hitler chose not to pay. The next day, Hitler met with Marshal Henri Phillippe Pétain, the Vichy leader and hero of Verdun. Pétain offered verbal support, but was likewise reluctant to pursue active operations. Shortly after the meeting, Hitler learned that the Italians were poised to attack Greece, an action that would upset the führer's plans. He met with Mussolini in Florence on 28 October, but that morning the Italian army invaded Greece.

Mussolini blundered, simultaneously launching two offensives: the first from Libya into Egypt in September, and now the second from Albania into Greece. The Italians lacked the resources to ensure victory on either front and risked defeat on both. The attack in the Balkans, launched on the eve of winter, was likely to provoke the dispatch of British ground and air forces to Greece, providing the RAF with bases from which it could bomb the Romanian oil fields, Germany's primary source of petroleum.

Mussolini's actions might have drawn Hitler into an expanded war in the Mediterranean basin. But the failure of the Italian offensive against Greece, reports from a German military mission in Libya of Italian incapacity in North Africa, and Hitler's disgust with Mussolini's actions led to a decision against direct support for the Italians. Hitler did, however, set in motion a military buildup in Bulgaria, from which he could attack Greece.

Hitler was already beginning to lean toward his eastern option when on 12–13 November he met with Vyacheslav Molotov, the Soviet foreign minister, in Berlin. Hitler's goal was to convince the Russians to push south in order to threaten the British imperial positions in the Near East and South Asia. But in meetings punctuated by British air raids, the acerbic Soviet foreign minister remained unconvinced of ultimate German victory. While the Soviets had expansion in mind, they were focused on Finland and the Baltic, Turkey and the Dardanelles, and Romania and Bulgaria. The talks failed to produce agreement, and thereafter Hitler leaned inexorably toward the east. On 18 December 1940, he signed Directive Number 21—Operation Barbarossa—committing the Third Reich to an invasion of the Soviet Union.

Hitler's fatal decision was not made as part of any comprehensive analysis of available options. The failure to identify a strategic course in July, or preferably earlier, allowed German policy to drift for six crucial months. Hitler ultimately adopted an eastern strategy by default, as his other options seemed to evaporate. But he never pursued either of his strategic alternatives—an invasion of Britain or a shift of operations to the Mediterranean—with the relentless focus so evident in his earlier policies toward Austria, Czechoslovakia, Poland, and France.

Having made his decision, Hitler now rushed to prepare for what he knew would be a life-and-death struggle. The OKW concentrated German forces in the east, while Hitler lined up his allies—Italy, Finland, Hungary, Romania, Bulgaria, and Yugoslavia—for a spring offensive in the Balkans against Greece and the summer offensive against Russia. But in December, in

Egypt the British drove Mussolini's army back west toward Tripoli. The Greeks drove the Italians back into Albania. In February, Hitler ordered the dispatch of a force of two panzer divisions, under the command of Erwin Rommel, to Libya. Thus was born the famed *Afrika Korps*. But the British had already halted their offensive and in early March began sending troops to Greece. Then, on 27 March, a British-sponsored coup in Yugoslavia, which had just joined the Axis, further complicated the Balkan situation.

German operational and tactical excellence allowed Hitler to master a deteriorating situation. In April, Rommel drove the British to the Egyptian border, besieging, but failing to take, Tobruk. In the Balkans, the Germans struck on 6 April and in eleven days crushed Yugoslavia. By 30 April, Greece had been overrun and the British forced to evacuate. The Germans followed their victory with a costly, but successful, airborne invasion of Crete (from 20 to 30 May).

While operations in the Balkans and Libya once again demonstrated the capabilities of Hitler's ground and air forces, limitations remained. Logistic constraints brought Rommel's offensive to a halt in the desert. Hitler was unable to concentrate his army for the coming decisive blow as he had a year earlier. In May 1940, Hitler had concentrated 136 (87 percent) of his 157 divisions—all ten panzer divisions, 2,400 tanks, and 3,600 aircraft—against France and the Low Countries. Of the remaining 21 divisions, most were fighting British and French troops in Norway. By late June 1941, the German army had expanded to 205 divisions, but 38 divisions were garrisoned in France, 13 in Scandinavia, and 7 in the Balkans. Two of Hitler's panzer divisions were with Rommel in Libya. Hitler deployed 145 divisions (70 percent) against the Soviet Union and only 2,770 aircraft. The Germans had more than doubled the number of panzer divisions from 10 to 21, but the 19 panzer divisions earmarked for Russia possessed only 3,200 tanks—only a third more than had invaded France the year before.

Nor was the German plan for Operation Barbarossa, despite its grandiose title, as well developed as Operation *Gelb*. Planning for Barbarossa revealed the *Wehrmacht*'s strengths (operational and tactical expertise) and weaknesses (strategy, logistics, and intelligence). The Germans knew little about the Soviet Union; maps were poor, and the output of Soviet factories was a matter of guesswork. The Germans estimated that the bulk of Soviet industry lay in the south, and that if those areas were overrun, Stalin would be unable to wage a protracted war. The Soviet army was known to be large, about 150 to 160 divisions, but it was also believed to be ineffective. The qualitative estimate was close to the mark, although the quantitative was off by more than 200 percent.

Within this context, German planners began their work. They quickly identified the peculiar logistical problems they faced. The Soviet Union was enormous, and the area to be occupied was huge. Hitler planned to advance to a line that ran from Archangel in the far north to Astrakhan on the Caspian Sea. The terrain in the south favored armored operations, but most of the roads and railroads were in the north. Most of the economic objectives also lay in the south, but the political objectives—Leningrad and Moscow—were in the north. As the Germans advanced, they would face two other problems: the limitations of motorization already evident in the Polish and French campaigns, and the fact that Soviet railroads were not that well developed and were built to a different gauge than the German railroads. This track would have to be relaid. Given these logistic constraints, the Germans could expect to drive about 300 miles before their offensive ground to a halt.

Since the Germans believed that the bulk of the Soviet army was concentrated near the border, an offensive along the entire front would lead to the encirclement and destruction of the enemy before it could withdraw into the interior. The Germans concluded that, despite logistical handicaps, they could defeat the Soviet Union in a single campaign. The Bolshevik regime would collapse, and a reduced force of sixty to eighty divisions would mop up and push east to the Archangel-Astrakhan line.

But the Germans failed to consider several possibilities. What if Stalin's army avoided destruction? What if Stalin's reserves were more numerous than expected? What if the Soviet government did not collapse? If subsequent operations were necessary, what objectives would guide the advance? The German armed forces were totally unprepared for any of these contingencies. Armaments production remained far below capacity. Preparations for winter were limited, given the estimate that less than half the troops would remain in the east. If further operations became necessary, Hitler favored an advance in the south to seize the Soviet economic region. The army high command—*Oberkommando des Heeres* (OKH)—favored a drive on Moscow, the Soviet Union's political-military center of gravity and the state's primary rail hub. The Germans deferred a final decision. Not only Hitler, but also his generals, were awestruck by their own successes.

Barbarossa began on 22 June 1941. From the Baltic to the Black Sea, the Germans and their Finnish, Hungarian, Romanian, Italian, and Slovak allies drove relentlessly east. Within three weeks, German troops reached the approaches to Narva, Smolensk, and Kiev. The Axis destroyed or captured thousands of guns and planes, tens of thousands of tanks, and hundreds of thousands of prisoners. On 3 July, the chief of the general staff, Franz Halder, wrote in his diary that the campaign had already been won. The OKH held in Germany replacements earmarked for the Russian front.

But Halder's optimism was misplaced. By mid-July, the Germans had identified over three hundred Soviet divisions, twice the expected number. The Germans, at the end of their supply tether, fended off constant Soviet counterattacks and in the center were unable to advance. Soviet tanks—such as the heavy KV models and the medium T-34, with its thick, sloped armor and 76mm gun-caused German tankers problems. Casualties kept mounting. In both July and August 1941, the heyday of blitzkrieg in Russia, the Germans lost over 50,000 men killed—the total number the United States would lose in three years in Korea (1950 to 1953) and eleven years in Vietnam (1964 to 1975).

Since neither Hitler nor his generals would accept the failure of their plan and instead hunker down for the winter, they had to decide in which direction to continue their advance. The OKH argued for a thrust for Moscow; Halder and his generals argued that the Soviets would concentrate their forces before the capital, where they could be engaged and destroyed. But Hitler preferred to drive on the flanks: to isolate Leningrad, to link up with the Finns, and to seize the Ukraine and overrun the Soviet's industrial region in the south.

Historians will long debate whether Hitler's plan or his generals' was better. Perhaps the proper course would have been to delay any advance and prepare for winter. But an argument can be made that the decision actually reached was the worst one possible: a compromise that had the Germans first striking on the Baltic and Ukraine flanks, and then reconcentrating their forces in the center and beginning a belated drive on Moscow. Following this course, the Germans failed to achieve any of their objectives. In the north, they isolated, but could not take, Leningrad. In the south, Kiev fell, and two German panzer groups captured over 660,000 prisoners. But before these victories could be fully exploited, the OKH recalled the panzers to the center for the drive on Moscow.

On 30 September, the Germans began their offensive, codenamed *Taifun* ("Typhoon"). Three armies and three panzer groups (soon to be redesignated panzer armies) drove toward the Soviet capital. The Russian defenses collapsed, and the Germans collected another 658,000 prisoners. But the autumn rains began on 7 October. The advancing formations slogged forward through the mud. When the rains stopped and the ground froze in early November, the panzers regained their mobility, but only briefly. Temperatures continued to drop and by the end of the month were reaching lows of minus 40°F. Snow replaced rain.

The Germans had not designed their equipment, or their lubricants, to operate in such extremes. Since September, overworked and overstretched *Wehrmacht* transport units had given priority to ammunition and fuel. Now, as the Russian winter hit full force, the trucks were unable to move from the rear to the front the winter clothing the soldiers needed. Frostbite incapacitated more Germans than the Russians. From the Baltic to the Sea of Azov, the Axis advance ground to a halt. Barbarossa had failed.

As the Germans reached the end of their strength, the Soviets went over to the offensive. Despite the loss of nearly 5 million men, including 3.9 million prisoners of war, Stalin still had reserves at his disposal. The Russians struck in the south in mid-November, retaking Rostov on 28 November. By 6 December, the Russians had seized the initiative in the north and center. For three months, Stalin kept up the pressure, trying to break the Germans along the entire front.

Amidst the disaster, recriminations flew amongst the Germans. Senior commanders resigned, were forced to resign, or were fired. The generals wished to retreat and to regroup. But Hitler, who himself replaced Field Marshal Walther von Brauchitsch as commander-in-chief of the army, ordered his troops to hold their ground at all costs. By extraordinary efforts, the Germans held on until the spring thaw and avoided complete collapse. But the costs had been high, and the German army would never fully recover its striking power.

By January 1942, the European war that Hitler had begun in September 1939 had become the world war he had hoped to avoid. On 7–8 December 1941, the Japanese struck British, Dutch, and American possessions in the Pacific. Hitler, although he was not compelled to do so, declared war on the United States on 11 December. The Germans correctly calculated that it would be some time before the Americans could make their weight felt in the European theater, although Hitler grossly miscalculated the capacity of the American armaments industry and the impact its effort would have on the ultimate course of the war.

Whatever the capabilities of the Americans, Hitler faced the same problem he had confronted in July 1940: how to bring the war to a successful conclusion. In both Russia and North Africa, the Allies were on the offensive. In November 1941, the British had launched a counteroffensive—Operation Crusader—and broken Rommel's siege of Tobruk, driving the *Afrika Korps* into Tripolitania. Hitler believed that his armies would weather the immediate crisis and regain the initiative. But to what end?

Hitler, having committed himself to an eastern strategy, saw no alternative to the destruction of Soviet Russia. The failure of the German offensive against Moscow strengthened his belief that the Achilles heel of the Soviet Union was its economic heartland in the south. Moreover, given the reality of a protracted and global war (a victory in Russia in 1942 would not force an end to the conflict since Britain had a new ally in the United States), the Germans needed to seize the resources of the Donets River basin and the oil fields in the Caucasus. In April 1942, Hitler directed that as soon as the ground hardened, the Germans would begin a series of offensive operations to secure the Crimean peninsula, to eliminate a salient near Kharkov, and then to mount a two-pronged drive toward Stalingrad on the Volga River and the oilfields in the Caucasus. The Germans, as they had the previous year, expected to break through the Soviet defenses, destroy the opposing Russian armies, and then exploit eastwards. But, as had been true the previous year, the Germans underestimated Soviet reserves and productive capacity. Hitler and his generals also underrated the growing capabilities of the Soviet army.

Despite the huge losses suffered during the 1941 campaign, by the spring of 1942, the Soviet army was better equipped, better organized, and better led. In 1941, Stalin had ordered the dismantling of Soviet industry in areas threatened by the German advance. By the summer, these industrial assets, now shifted to Siberia, were beginning to produce tanks, artillery, and aircraft at rates beyond current German levels of production. The Soviet army had also learned many lessons from its early defeats. The Russians formed new tank and mechanized corps, and they revised the Soviet army's doctrine to incorporate both lessons learned *and* many of the old operational concepts from the mid-1930s, such as successive attacks. As early as the winter of 1941–1942, when the weather negated German tactical superiority, the Soviets had performed well operationally and strategically.

Stalin intended to seize the initiative as soon as the ground hardened—a move that at the minimum would disrupt the Germans' plans for their own offensive. But the Germans struck first, on 8 May, although only in the Crimea, where they began an operation that concluded on 2 July when they captured the fortress of Sevastopol. Four days later, the Soviets attacked further north, driving from a salient near Izyum toward Kharkov. The Germans, who had planned to eliminate the salient, counterattacked on 17 May and took nearly quarter of a million Soviet prisoners.

On 28 June, the Germans launched their main offensive, codenamed *Blau* ("Blue"). The Germans met stiff resistance on their extreme left flank near Voronezh, but along the rest of the line the Soviets pulled back, avoiding encirclement. They recognized that they could not hold their ground in the open against fresh, up-to-strength German divisions. Stalin and his generals adopted a traditional Russian strategy: make good use of available space, retreat, and turn to fight only after the Germans had exhausted themselves or when they could be engaged in terrain—urban or mountain—in which their tactical superiority would be reduced.

In the summer campaign of 1942, superior Soviet strategy negated German operational and tactical advantages. The Germans drove east, but took few prisoners. As the Germans turned south into the Caucasus, their line lengthened. Contingents from Germany's allies—Romanians, Hungarians, and Italians—filled the gaps between Hitler's armies. In late August, the Soviet defense stiffened, and the Germans suddenly found it hard going in the Caucasus. Fighting intensified in Stalingrad—an urban environment in which superior German mobility meant little. By the fall, the German offensive had lost its momentum. Casualties grew. Both sides kept feeding troops into Stalingrad, by now reduced to rubble. Then came the autumn rains and mud and, after that, another Russian winter. By November, the German offensive had failed. Again, recriminations began. Hitler fired Halder and took personal command of the troops in the Caucasus.

In North Africa, the Germans regained the initiative earlier than they did in Russia. In February, Rommel's *Afrika Korps* counterattacked and reached the Gazala–Bir Hacheim line west of Tobruk, along which the two armies built up for the next round of fighting. On 26 May 1942, Rommel struck. The course of the battle ebbed and flowed for a fortnight, after which the British position collapsed, and the Germans seized Tobruk in a coup de main. Rommel chose to exploit his victory and struck eastward toward the Suez Canal. His decision led to the cancellation of Operation Hercules—a planned airborne and naval assault against Malta, a British controlled air and naval base located south of Sicily and directly athwart Axis supply lines.

Strategically, there was little to be gained by a continuation of the offensive. Rommel's primary mission was to prop up Mussolini's tottering African empire until the Germans achieved victory in Russia. If the *Afrika Korps* could reach the Suez Canal, Britain's position in the Middle East would be weakened, but such a defeat would hardly have been decisive. An advance to the oilfields of the Persian Gulf was a virtual logistic impossibility, and even if by some miracle Rommel reached the gulf, there were no means available to ship the petroleum back to Europe. Nor were the oilfields of the region vital to the Allied war effort. During World War II, oil production in the Persian Gulf actually declined as the Allies, short of tankers, capped wells. The vast majority of the petroleum products consumed by the Allies came from the Western Hemisphere, especially the United States. But Rommel, promoted to field marshal for his conquest of Tobruk, refused to accept the limited role accorded his German-Italian panzer army.

By late July, the advance had exhausted itself. Commonwealth troops of the Eighth Army dug in along the Al Alamein line—a narrow, forty-mile-long front from the Mediterranean coast to the impassable Qattara Depression in the south. There were no flanks to turn, and Rommel's army, starved of supplies at the end of an extremely long logistical tether (in part because of a resurgent Malta), lacked the strength to penetrate the enemy front. Rommel

continued on page 197

Strategic Bombing

In the spring of 1941, as the bulk of the German air force shifted to the east in preparation for Operation Barbarossa, only a handful of German fighter *Geschwader* (wings) remained in France to face Britain's Fighter and Bomber Commands. The Germans found themselves on the defensive in the air in the west well before they had actually lost the initiative in the war. During the interwar era, the Germans had considered the possibility of air defense, and they had developed powerful antiaircraft forces designed to cooperate with the army. But despite these strengths, strategic air defense, especially against night bombing, was an area of air combat for which the Germans had not fully developed a comprehensive set of doctrine.

The British had recognized early in the war that it was not practical to launch daylight bombing operations. Daylight operations—termed circuses, rodeos, and rhubarbs—were attempts by Fighter Command to draw the outnumbered Germans into combat. In general, the Germans ignored these operations and preserved their strength, which by that time included the new FW-190A Focke-Wulf radial-engine fighter armed with cannon. Bomber Command struck at night, but although the raids were an embarrassment to the *Luftwaffe*, they were not very successful. In the summer of 1940, the Germans began forming a night-fighter force, relying on modified Bf-110s and, in the fall, a ground-based radar warning system, later known as the Kammhuber Line.

Several problems handicapped Bomber Command's early efforts. The British lacked an effective means to locate targets in the dark. The RAF did not yet possess a good heavy bomber. Bomber Command crews were poorly trained, and both personnel and aircraft were drawn off and sent to Coastal Command to hunt U-boats. As a result, the British night-bombing campaign remained ineffective and failed to prompt a serious reexamination of German air strategy.

The British effort underwent a major transformation in early February 1942 when Arthur "Bomber" Harris took over Bomber Command. Harris was single-minded in his determination to build up a force capable of winning the war in

Douhet fashion: independently by destroying the German industrial infrastructure, including the German civilian workforce, through area bombing. Historians continue to debate the efficacy, and morality, of Harris' strategy.

In the spring of 1942, Harris launched several major strikes, including the first thousand-bomber raid against Cologne on 30 May 1942. Bomber Command now employed a radio-beam device—Gee—that helped direct the bomber stream to the target. But the Germans reacted effectively to these raids and inflicted heavy losses on the raiders.

In May 1942, the American Eighth Air Force began deploying to Great Britain with its four-engine heavy bombers—Boeing B-17F Flying Fortresses and Consolidated B-24D Liberators, both equipped with the Norden bombsight. Early precision attacks were successful, but German fighter opposition suggested a need for escorts. When the Eighth Air Force's bombers ventured into Germany without escort, they suffered heavy losses. The Eighth Air Force conducted most of its raids against targets within the limited range of the P-47 Thunderbolt, the principal American fighter. Most of these early targets were in France.

During this critical 1941–1942 transition stage of the air war in the west, the Germans met the Allied challenge with minimal alterations of existing practices. Air operations in Russia and the Mediterranean caused the *Luftwaffe* its heaviest losses. As a result, as the Anglo-American air forces began to deploy the first of the thousands of aircraft being produced by Allied aircraft assembly plants, the overconfident Germans failed to scale up their own aircraft production and pilot-training efforts. As a result, when the British and American air attacks increased in ferocity in late 1943 and early 1944, the *Luftwaffe* was unable to survive what became a war of attrition. By the time the Germans reacted and increased fighter production in mid- to late 1944, they had lost air superiority, not only at the front, but also over the Reich.

There was nothing inevitable about this outcome. The Germans lost the air war because of myriad poor decisions, the results of gross managerial incompetence and political infighting amongst the responsible ministries. As the Germans demonstrated in late 1944, they could have produced over a thousand fighters each month, as well as more advanced types, such as the ME-262 jet fighter. Instead, once the Allied air offensive began in the second half of 1943, German losses mounted, and although aircraft production grew, transportation dislocation, fuel shortages, and reliance on hastily trained aircrews led to a steady diminution of *Luftwaffe* fighting power.

In January 1943, at the Casablanca Conference, the Anglo-American high command ordered their air forces to undertake a sustained offensive against the German industrial base. For the first half of the year, both the British and Americans struggled to destroy the Reich's industry, but with little success. In June 1943, the high command, concerned by these failures and the concurrent buildup of the German day and night fighter forces, issued a new directive: Operation Pointblank made the *Luftwaffe* and its supporting industrial infrastructure the focus of the air campaign.

The strategic air war began in earnest in August 1943. The Americans now deployed heavy bomber groups in both Britain and the Mediterranean. When the American bombers ventured beyond the range of their escorts, as they did in August raids against Schweinfurt and Regensburg, they suffered unsustainable losses. But they increasingly relied on fighter escorts—a combination of long-range P-38 Lightnings and P-47s Thunderbolts, now equipped with drop tanks—to strike more deeply against German targets. Simultaneously, the British night-bombing offensive gained momentum. The British began to employ their new four-engine Lancaster bombers, improved radio (Oboe) and radar (H2S) navigation devices to guide the raid to the target, and used pathfinding squadrons to mark the target and its approach with incendiaries, and "Window"—foil strips that blinded the German radar net. Bomber Command launched a massive firebomb raid against Hamburg on 24 July 1943.

Nevertheless, by the fall the Allied air offensives had failed to overwhelm the German defense. The British suffered heavy losses in their night raids, and the Americans did the same whenever they strayed beyond escort range. The Allies had two major problems. First, they needed a good long-range escort fighter. Second, the Americans were still employing an inappropriate strategy, attempting to defeat German industry and not the *Luftwaffe*.

To the Anglo-American high command, not only had the strategic bombing campaign itself failed, but also, and more importantly, that failure placed the cross-channel invasion at Normandy at risk. If the German fighter force continued to expand, the Allies might not possess the prerequisite for invasion—air superiority.

Once again the Allies altered their approach. Late in 1943, the Americans began deploying a nimble long-range escort fighter—the P-51 Mustang. Simultaneously, the Americans changed the organization and leadership of their strategic air forces. They formed the new Fifteenth Air Force in the Mediterranean and named James Doolittle, the hero of the March 1942 Tokyo raid, as commander of the Eighth Air Force in Britain.

Doolittle brought a new conception to the strategic air war. Using his new long-range escorts, he planned to launch a series of sustained attacks on the German aircraft industry as soon as the weather permitted. Doolittle sought to draw the *Luftwaffe* into battle in an effort to destroy its fighter arm. To further this aim, Doolittle also allowed his escorts to seek targets of opportunity on their return flights, crediting pilots with "kills" for aircraft destroyed on the ground.

In late February 1944, the Eighth and Fifteenth Air Forces launched a sustained air offensive known as Big Week. Historians continue to debate the impact of these attacks on the German aircraft industry, but there can be no doubt that the sustained nature of the offensive, by day and by night, quickly ground down the *Luftwaffe*. Despite rising production, losses outpaced deliveries, and the replacement pilots could not match the skills of the *Luftwaffe*'s rapidly diminishing pool of *Experten*, or aces. By May 1944, the Allies had secured total air supremacy in the west. On 6 June, there were few German fighters in France. Even though the Allies diverted their heavy bombers for months to support the Normandy invasion, the Germans never recovered. In the summer of 1944, the Allies resumed their air offensive and systematically destroyed the German oil industry and transportation network, and finally set out to level the Third Reich.

Historians continue to debate the significance of the overall strategic air campaign. But some things can be said with certainty: The air war devastated German industry and reduced production by as much as 40 percent. The supplies that were produced were difficult to move to the front because of attacks against the oil industry and the transportation network. The air campaign forced the *Luftwaffe* to concentrate on the production of fighters, to the near exclusion of bombers, robbing the German army of an important doctrinal support component. The Germans deployed thousands of heavy antiaircraft guns and hundreds of thousands of men for home defense, instead of moving them to the front, where they could have been employed against Allied tanks. The strategic air campaign also secured for the Allies air superiority on all fronts.

Nevertheless, the strategic air war was costly, both in economic and human terms. A third of all American battle deaths were airmen. More Eighth Air Force personnel were killed in action than were Marines killed in the Pacific theater.

And there were moral questions. The Americans began the war with the intention of hitting precision targets, but the British lacked the necessary technology and resorted to less discriminate area bombing. Bomber Harris talked frankly about "dehousing" German civilians. Without a doubt, the Allies *did* target civilians. But, of course, the descent along that path had begun earlier with the less-than-discriminate German terror attacks against Warsaw, Rotterdam, Belgrade, London, and Coventry. Even the Americans participated in area attacks on Dresden at the end of the war. The Allied bombing campaign killed an estimated 500,000 German civilians. This was less than the number starved to death by the British blockade of Germany during the Great War (an estimated 800,000). And the bombing figure, of course, pales in comparison to the number of civilian deaths caused by German actions, most notably the extermination of nearly six million Jews and seven million Soviet civilians.

Nevertheless, there can be little doubt that the strategic bombing campaign in Europe, in concert with Germans actions, lowered the wall that existed between the military and civilian sectors during wartime. By 1945, when the Americans faced key decisions about the course of their air campaign in the Pacific, that wall was extremely low and porous. When several factors worked against the employment of a "precision" strategic bombing strategy in the Pacific, the Americans resorted to night area bombing with incendiaries. In the late summer of 1945, when the Americans possessed the world's first atomic weapon, there would be few constraints on its use.

received some reinforcements, but the British received more. The Eighth Army, under General Claude Auchinleck, launched a series of limited counterattacks. The effort failed to destroy the Axis army, although the offensive did prevent Rommel from mounting an assault of his own. There followed a lull in the fighting as the two armies prepared for the next round. Churchill flew to the Middle East and appointed Sir Harold Alexander as the new command-in-chief, Middle East, and Bernard Law Montgomery ("Monty") as the new commander of Eighth Army.

On 31 August, Rommel attacked in the south, hoping to roll up the British left flank. But Montgomery was fully prepared, thanks in part to preparations begun by Auchinleck. The battle raged for a week around and south of Alam Halfa Ridge, but at no time were the British in danger.

By the summer of 1942, the Allies were beginning to profit from an incredible intelligence asset—Ultra. Before the war, the Poles had managed to acquire a German Enigma coding machine, which they later turned over to the British. Possession of this machine, along with early electronic computing devices, allowed the Allies to decipher high-level German message traffic. As the war progressed, the volume and regularity of Allied code breaking improved. But intelligence, no matter its quality, was no guarantor of victory. Even when the British knew what Rommel intended, they often lacked the means to do anything about it. But in the late summer of 1942, Ultra provided excellent information to Montgomery, a general who, unlike other Allied commanders, possessed the ability and willingness to make the best use of that intelligence and also the means to counter Rommel.

Montgomery prepared his own offensive—a set-piece battle code-named Operation Supercharge. Montgomery intended to avoid the fluid mobile engagement at which the Germans excelled and which had so often embarrassed the British.

On the night of 23 October, Monty struck, not in the south, as was usually the case in the desert war, but in the north. The battle did not go as planned, but it did remain a set-piece affair and a battle of attrition that the outnumbered Rommel could not win. On 2 November, Rommel decided to withdraw. He ordered a retreat and wired Hitler for permission. Orders came back from the führer's headquarters: stand fast! Rommel halted the retreat, but then realized it was too late. On 5 November, the retreat, this time approved by Hitler, began again. Only the motorized units now stood a chance to escape. Most of the Italian infantry units surrendered. On 8 November, Rommel learned that American and British forces had landed in the Vichy-controlled North African territories of Morocco and Algeria, in an operation codenamed Torch. Rommel now knew that he had to continue his withdrawal until he reached Tunisia, where the Germans were deploying new forces to block the Allied advance from Algeria.

Operation Torch had several objectives: to trap Rommel, to secure the whole North Africa coast, and, perhaps, to bring the Vichy French into the war on the Allied side. The operation was the result of a strategic compromise. The Americans favored a cross-channel invasion of France—the "second front" promised to the Soviets. But the British, who would supply most of the assets in 1942, balked for good reason. The Western Allies were simply not ready to undertake a cross-channel invasion. Torch allowed the Americans to fight the Germans on the ground before the end of the year, a self-imposed goal of the American president, Franklin D. Roosevelt, and to support their British ally in North Africa. The British agreed to allow an American, General Dwight D. Eisenhower, to command the Torch forces—the British First Army and the American II Corps.

The actual Allied invasion went well, but the Germans responded more quickly and forcefully than expected. Hitler ordered the immediate occupation of Vichy France and rushed troops into Tunisia. As a result, Allied exploitation faltered. Eisenhower's lead elements came within thirty miles of Tunis, but German counterattacks checked the advance and threw the British and Americans back. Both the Axis and Allies rushed reinforcements into Tunisia, but neither side could make more than minor gains with the arrival of muddy winter weather.

As the Allies and Axis sparred in Tunisia, Rommel continued his retreat, one of the longest in the annals of military history—a distance equivalent to that from Moscow to Paris. In February, he reached Tunisia. He left part of his force in the Mareth Line along the Tunisian-Libyan border, and with the rest, he advanced north, joined Axis troops already in Tunisia, and launched a counterattack against the Americans near Kasserine Pass. The Germans drove the Americans from the pass, but the setback was temporary and more of an embarrassment than a major defeat. Eisenhower replaced the commander of the II Corps with Lieutenant General George S. Patton.

Kasserine Pass was Rommel's last noteworthy success. In late February, Montgomery breached the Mareth Line, and the Allied ring closed around the Axis forces in Tunisia. The fighting in March was difficult, but in April and May, concerted attacks broke the Axis line. The final surrender came on 13 May. The Allies captured 275,000 Germans and Italians.

As the Axis position in North Africa collapsed, so, too, did the German front in Russia. In late September and early October, as the Germans spent themselves at Stalingrad and in the Caucasus, the Soviets prepared to launch major offensives intended to collapse the Axis front from Rzhev, on the upper Volga, to the Black Sea. The Soviets based their plan on the concept of successive operations. Operations Mars and Jupiter would tear a succession of holes in the front of the German central group of armies; Operations Uranus and Saturn would do the same to the German southern group along the Don River.

Uranus opened first, under the direction of Colonel General Aleksandr M. Vasilevsky. On 19 November, the Soviets struck Romanian formations both north and south of Stalingrad. The front disintegrated, and the Russians encircled the German Sixth Army at Stalingrad, threatening the entire Axis front north of the Caucasus.

Hitler placed Field Marshal Erich von Manstein in command of the newly formed Army Group Don. It was Manstein who had devised the German plan to defeat France in 1940 and who in the summer of 1942 had captured the Soviet Black Sea fortress of Sevastopol. Manstein's tasks were two: stabilize the front in the south and relieve the German Sixth Army, which had been ordered by Hitler to stand fast in Stalingrad. But throughout November and December, the Soviets kept feeding fresh reserves into the offensive and expanding its front, especially to the north. In late December, the Germans broke off their relief drive toward the Sixth Army and retreated toward the Donets River in an effort to hold Rostov, which would allow the German armies to withdraw from the Caucasus.

Farther north, the Soviet attack against Army Group Center, under Marshal Georgi K. Zhukov, failed. Operation Mars opened on 25 November, but the planned breakthroughs became break-ins in the face of concerted counterattacks. The determined Zhukov, who had directed unsuccessful offensives in the same area in July and August 1942, drove his forces relentlessly until late December, when Stalin ordered the end to the abortive offensive.

Stalin shifted the reserves intended to support Mars and Jupiter in the south to instead reinforce Vasilevsky's success. The revised Soviet plan now envisioned the destruction of the entire Axis southern front east of the Dnepr River by means of vast encirclement operations. In early February 1943, as the approximately 190,000 men who formed the remnants of the German Sixth Army surrendered in Stalingrad, the Soviet offensive spread across the southern front from Voronezh to the Black Sea.

In Moscow, success seemed assured. Stalin, at Zhukov's prompting, directed the movement of newly available reserves to the center with the intention of renewing the drive there and collapsing the entire German front. But this new scheme was as overambitious as it was daring. Along the central front, the Germans conducted a successful controlled withdrawal to shorten their lines and gain reserves. In the south, Manstein, reinforced with several fresh mechanized divisions, conducted a masterful counteroffensive against the overextended Soviets. The Germans retook Kharkov and regained most of the Donets line, except for a large salient around Kursk, before the spring thaw brought operations to a close.

Despite Manstein's notable successes in February and March 1943, the second German campaign in Russia had ended in failure. Hitler had neither knocked the Russians out of the war nor secured the economic objectives he had set for the campaign. Between March and July 1943, both sides worked feverishly to prepare for the renewal of operations in the summer, but the prospects of a decisive Axis campaign in the east in the summer of 1943 were nil.

For the Soviet Union, despite the setbacks west of Moscow and the failure to gain a complete victory in the south, the campaign of 1942–1943 had been a major strategic success. Tactically, the Soviet army could not yet manage the Germans on even terms. But the Russians demonstrated marked improvements in the conduct of their operations, perhaps most apparent in the failure of the Germans to capture huge hauls of prisoners. At the strategic level, the analysis and planning evident in the preparation of Mars-Jupiter and Uranus-Saturn were far superior to German planning for *Blau* or Barbarossa. The Soviets did outnumber the Germans—that is, they possessed what they termed a favorable correlation of forces. But in 1941, numerical superiority had gained the Russians nothing except the loss of millions of lives. By 1943, the Russians had learned how to offset the Germans' tactical advantages not only through superior numbers, but also through the development and execution of well-thought-out operational and strategic plans.

In early July 1943, the Germans launched their summer offensive at Kursk (see "The Battle of Kursk") codenamed *Zitadelle* ("Citadel"). The Soviets repulsed the attacks against the haunches of the salient and launched a series of counteroffensives. When *Zitadelle* failed to produce the expected results, Hitler broke off the attack on 13 July so that the remaining reserves could be employed to meet the ever-expanding Soviet counteroffensives. For the first time since the start of the war in 1939, the Germans were on the defensive in the summer.

The excuse for Hitler's cancellation of *Zitadelle* was the Anglo-American landing in Sicily. The Allies expected Husky, as the operation was codenamed, to keep the pressure on the Germans the Mediterranean theater, to secure maritime transportation routes in the Middle Sea, to strike another blow against Mussolini's regime on its home soil, and to secure a base for further operations against Italy proper.

Husky began on 10 July. The Italian defenders showed little fight, although the German units near the landing beaches counterattacked, unsuccessfully. By 17 August, the U.S. Seventh Army, commanded by Patton, and the Commonwealth Eighth Army, commanded by Montgomery, had cleared the island of its defenders.

On 3 September, the Italians signed a secret armistice, and that same day, elements of Montgomery's army crossed the Strait of Messina and landed in Italy. Operation Avalanche had begun. Six days later, the Allies' main force landed at Salerno, south of Naples. The Germans rushed troops to occupy northern and central Italy, while farther south spirited counterattacks threatened the Allies' landing in its initial stage, although the Allies held on and the Germans retreated. Fortunately for the Axis, the weather and the rugged Italian terrain negated Allied advantages of mobility and air power. The Anglo-American offensive ground to a halt along the lines of the Garigliano and Sangro rivers.

The Allies continued to slog their way north during the fall and winter, in fighting that had more in common with the trench warfare of the Great War than with blitzkrieg. In January, the British and Americans launched an amphibious assault at Anzio, south of Rome and well behind the German front, in an effort to break the stalemate. But the Allies failed to exploit their element of surprise, and the Germans sealed off the beachhead. Farther south, the Allied offensive stalled along the Volturno River line, the key position of which was a mountain peak near Cassino that was crowned by a Bendictine monastery. By March, the British and Americans had given up on their efforts to break out and began to prepare for new offensives in the spring and summer.

The Soviet summer offensives likewise ran out of steam when the autumn rains came to the Ukraine. But the Russians made substantive progress nonetheless. After the failure of the German offensive at Kursk, the Soviets expanded their offensive operations along the entire line in the south and then into the central sector of the eastern front. The largest gains came in the Ukraine, where the Soviets reached the Dnepr River and seized several important bridgeheads. While the Soviets failed to destroy the Axis armies east of the Dnepr, they did trap the German Seventeenth Army in the Crimea.

When winter froze the ground, the Russian advance resumed along the entire front. In the north, the Soviets relieved Leningrad after an epic thousand-day siege. Assaults against the German Army Group Center gained little ground, but in the south, the Russians shattered the German lines, temporarily encircled an entire panzer army, and drove toward the Carpathians, threatening to split the Axis front. But Manstein, and the spring thaw, stabilized the front, though not before the Russians had destroyed the German Seventeenth Army.

In the spring of 1944, the Germans stood on the defensive everywhere. In Russia, Italy, and Great Britain, Allied forces prepared for their offensives. Anglo-American strategic air forces assaulted the Reich in a coordinated, round-the-clock bombing campaign (see "Strategic Bombing"). In the Atlantic, the *U-Waffe* (submarine force) no longer posed a threat to the Allied shipping.

The Germans' options were few. They stood no chance to regain the initiative in the east. Italian terrain, while conducive to defensive operations, offered little prospect for an offensive. The Germans had only a single hope—one chance that might allow them to negotiate something less than the unconditional surrender the Allies had demanded at the January 1943 Casablanca Conference. Hitler expected the Allies to launch their long-awaited cross-channel invasion of France in the spring. If the Germans could destroy the landing, that victory might force the

continued on page 208

The Role of Sea Power in the World Wars

Historians debate the contributions of sea power to Allied victories in the world wars. There are almost as many views on this subject as there are historians. As noted in "The War at Sea" in Chapter III, sea power played an important role during the Great War, but it was hardly a decisive factor. Although the Allied blockade of Germany was effective, only a few extreme sea-power advocates have claimed decisiveness for it. The German submarine campaign of 1917–1918 clearly failed and did so after prompting American intervention. Some studies have raised serious doubts about the efficacy of the U-boat offensive, even if it had begun earlier and had greater resources.

During the Second World War, sea power played a far more important role in the overall Allied victory, especially in the Pacific theater, where the primacy of sea power was obvious. Nevertheless, Japan did not surrender, despite the near total elimination of its navy, until it faced the threat of invasion and two of its cities were reduced to rubble by atomic attack from the air, leading some historians to conclude that sea power was not, ultimately, decisive in the Pacific. Such arguments will continue to provide historians, and their readers, with unending debate.

Historians are more circumspect when discussing the role of sea power in the European theater during the Second World War. There sea power, while important, played a lesser role. In the Baltic and Black seas, German and Soviet naval power had little influence on the course of the campaigns in Poland, the Balkans, or Russia. Armies, primarily, and air power fought and won the war in the east. In western Europe, maritime forces were more important. Navies played a pivotal role in securing the sea lines of communications across the Atlantic and the Mediterranean. After securing these routes, Allied navies moved land forces, via amphibious operations, to the German occupied coasts of North Africa and western Europe. The naval mission could be described as enabling, in that it allowed the Allies to supply the Soviets and to build up the air and land forces needed to win the war in the west.

The crucial maritime campaign in the European theater during the Second World War was the Battle of the Atlantic, which pitted German U-boats against the surface and air forces of the Allies. Had the western powers lost control of the Atlantic to the Germans, the Allies' defeat probably would have been decisive. The same was not necessarily true for Allied victory. The war ultimately had to be won by the Allies on the ground and in the air.

The German concept of submarine operations that so alarmed the British and Americans was the brainchild of Karl Dönitz, a World War I U-boat veteran who commanded the German submarine force—the *U-Waffe*—in the years before the Second World War. Dönitz's experience convinced him that submarines facing escorted convoys were at a disadvantage. Subsequent interwar developments in detection technology—sonar, which the British called ASDIC—worsened the odds against the U-boat. The counter to the escorted convoy was the mass night surface attack, a concept termed *Rudeltaktik*—pack tactics, popularly known as the Wolfpack. Dönitz planned to deploy his U-boats in a scouting line across the approaches to Great Britain. When a U-boat located a convoy, it would radio the relevant information—size, strength of escort, course, and speed—to the controlling headquarters, *Befehlshaber der U-boote*, or BdU. BdU would vector—that is, direct—other boats in the scouting line and additional boats within range to intercept. The Wolfpack would concentrate and attack the convoy at night on the surface from all points of the compass. The escorts would be confused and overwhelmed; the gray wolves would massacre their prey.

Unfortunately for Dönitz, the *Rudeltaktik* concept had an Achilles heel: it relied on wireless telegraphy, or radio, which allowed the U-boats to transmit information to BdU, and Dönitz to concentrate his submarines in a pack. Dönitz understood that such reliance was dangerous; transmissions were subject to traffic analysis, direction finding (DF), and interception and decoding. Nevertheless, he remained convinced that a few shortwave signals condensed into a shorthand would yield transmissions abbreviated enough to prevent British direction finding or effective traffic analysis. Dönitz also trusted Enigma—a German machine that did not just encode, but also encrypted, wireless transmissions. It is clear that Dönitz's assumptions about the security of his radio communications were misplaced. Wireless transmissions from the boats were heavier than expected. The Allies developed advanced direction-finding gear, including sets small enough to be employed on escort ships. And, of course, the British managed to break and to read the German messages flowing from the Enigma machines.

Dönitz's concept for the submarine campaign in the Atlantic was also flawed in other ways. His tonnage-based strategy—*Tonnageschlact*—meant that the U-boats would have to sink Allied merchant ships faster than new ships were built. To Dönitz, it made no difference what, if any, cargoes the ships carried or where they were headed. Tonnage was tonnage. But that conception made sense only within the context of a protracted war of attrition—the conflict that Hitler was determined to avoid. Dönitz's too-oft-accepted claim that he could have defeated Britain had Germany begun the war with a force of three hundred oceangoing boats ignored several factors. Why would Hitler expend resources in pursuit of a strategy that would weakened the German army and air force, ensure British hostility, and result in a prolonged war? And how likely was it that the British would ignore such an ambitious German submarine-building program and fail to adjust their own resource allocations and defense polices?

The strategy also faced practical problems unforeseen by Dönitz. Locating Allied convoys in the North Atlantic was far more difficult than anticipated. Dönitz's prewar assessments had not fully appreciated the dangers posed by Allied antisubmarine aircraft patrols, nor the corresponding virtues of using German land-based aircraft to search for convoys. Long-range patrol aircraft, armed with depth bombs and, by midwar, outfitted with radar and search lights, posed a grave danger to German U-boats transiting on the surface in day or night and forced Dönitz to deploy his patrol lines ever farther from the approaches to British ports. As Dönitz deployed his boats farther and farther west, the arcs to be searched for convoys became longer, the number of U-boats needed to patrol a given line increased, and the task of assembling a pack in time for attack became more difficult. The constant need to reposition U-boats along these arcs provided the British with a constant flow of Dönitz's abbreviated, but also standardized and thereby predictable, radio traffic, which delighted Allied code breakers.

While a series of technological advances, including HF/DF (high frequency/direction finding) ashore and on ship, were responsible for turning the tactical tide in the Battle of the Atlantic, Allied code breaking played an important strategic and operational role in assuring Allied victory at sea. Allied efforts to break the German codes during the Second World War—"the Ultra secret"—have been well known since 1975. Code breaking allowed the Allies to reroute shipping; reinforce threatened convoys; disrupt U-boat patrols; sink critically important assets, such as the U-tankers needed to refuel and replenish the supplies of the U-boats at sea; and gain a remarkable insight into the workings of the German U-boat command structure.

At the tactical, operational, and strategic levels of warfare, reliance on radio proved the Germans' undoing in the Battle of the Atlantic. A highly centralized command structure failed because the enemy electronically penetrated the network of communications, thanks to insecure codes.

Not everyone within the *Kriegsmarine* high command, or even the *U-Waffe*, supported Dönitz's plans. A prewar naval-staff study argued that the necessary wireless traffic would prevent surprise and lead to the detection of the attacking U-boats. Eve-of-war maneuvers in the Atlantic exposed shortcomings of Dönitz's concept of operations. Post-war analysis indicates that the German U-boats achieved their greatest successes early in the war, at a time when their naval codes were not yet compromised and before they had begun operating in Wolfpacks. Until late 1941, most U-boats hunted alone, as they had in the Great War and as American submarines did in the Pacific. Not until the first quarter of 1943 were the majority of the Allied ships sunk by U-boats sailing in convoy. In the first twenty-eight months of war, nine hundred Allied convoys crossed the Atlantic, but Dönitz's U-boats achieved major victories—that is, sinking six or more confirmed ships—on only nineteen occasions. According to Clay Blair, who wrote a two-volume study of the German U-boat campaign in World War II, "Although occasionally successful, group or 'wolf pack' tactics were on the whole a failure. . . ." Blair's detailed study of the U-boat war revealed that the Germans, despite their many successes, actually sank less than 2 percent of Allied merchant shipping, while losing over 75 percent of their U-boats and crews. Such figures do not suggest that the Allied victory in the Battle of the Atlantic was as near-run a thing as it is often portrayed.

Allies to reconsider their policy, or at the minimum, delay full-scale ground operations in the west and allow Hitler to concentrate his forces against the Russians in the east.

While the point of decision for 1944 clearly lay in the west, the German high command was not of one mind about how to defeat an Allied invasion. The Germans rushed to complete their Atlantic Wall, but they could not fortify the entire coast. The key to the defeat of the invasion lay with the Germans' mobile, hard-striking panzer divisions, the scheme for the employment of which remained a subject of debate. Rommel, whose Army Group B controlled the coastal sector, drew on his experience fighting the British and Americans in North Africa. He was convinced that Allied air power would prevent the timely movement of an armored reserve to the coast. Rommel wanted the armored divisions deployed immediately behind likely landing sites. But there was an obvious problem: since the Germans were unsure where the Allies intended to land, the armored divisions would have to be dispersed, rather than concentrated. Generals with experience on the eastern front wished to keep their mobile reserves concentrated in a central location, from which they could be dispatched to meet the landing. As was often the case with the Germans' strategy, they adopted a compromise: Rommel controlled a few divisions deployed near the coast, but the rest were held in the OKW reserve and could be released only on Hitler's authority.

Thanks to Ultra, the Allies were aware of German uncertainty about the likely landing area. The British and Americans spent two years developing a detailed and comprehensive cover and deception plan—Fortitude South—designed to convince the Germans that the invasion was coming in the Pas de Calais region. The Allies even deployed an entire sham army group—the First U.S. Army Group, or FUSAG—commanded by the ostentatious George S. Patton, who was temporarily out of work after he slapped a shell-shocked soldier in Sicily. The Allies' reinforced their deception efforts by feeding inaccurate information to the Germans through double agents. Ultra allowed the Allies to monitor the effectiveness of their work. Fortitude South worked so well that even after the Allied landing in Normandy, weeks passed before the Germans realized that they were facing the primary invasion force, not a feint, there.

Throughout the spring of 1944, the Allied air forces helped prepare for the campaign by isolating the invasion beaches. Strikes against rail yards, rolling stock, and bridges would hinder the movement of German reserves and supplies to the beaches once the invasion began.

By the spring of 1944, the military buildup in the British Isles to support the invasion had been underway for almost two years, under the codename Bolero. The actual plan for the operation—codenamed Overlord—called for the landing of five infantry and three airborne divisions on the Normandy coast near the base of the Cotentin peninsula. Montgomery would command the Commonwealth forces on the left; Omar Bradley the American forces on the right. Eisenhower was overall commander. Once ashore, the Allies would secure a lodgment and seize the port of Cherbourg. Allied air power would assist the landing and, aided by the French resistance, interdict German movement toward the beachhead. The buildup would continue until the Allies were ready to drive to the Seine River, an objective to be reached by the ninetieth day after the landing. In mid-August, a second landing operation—Anvil-Dragoon—would take place in the south of France. These two advances would link up in central France and push together toward the Rhine.

The Anglo-American spring offensive opened on 11 May 1944 under an umbrella of total Allied air superiority. Within a week, the Allied offensive broke the German front in Italy. Polish troops finally gained the Cassino position on 17–18 May, while Anglo-American forces broke out of the Anzio beachhead and advanced along the western coast of Italy. American troops entered Rome on 4 June—a major victory soon overshadowed by the Normandy landing.

At that point, the Allied high command decided not to exploit the victory, but to redirect, as planned, assets from the Mediterranean toward the main drive in France. Forces from the Italian front were withdrawn to refit in preparation for Anvil-Dragoon. As a result, the Allied advance in Italy bogged down again north of Rome against the Germans' Gothic Line. The Allies would not break this line until April 1945.

The Allies launched Overlord on the night of 5–6 June, after a twenty-four-hour postponement caused by bad weather. Going ahead on the sixth was risky, since conditions were still less than ideal, but Eisenhower's decision paid off, since the Germans believed the weather to be too poor for an invasion. Rommel was home celebrating his wife's birthday when the landings began.

Overlord was a complete surprise—and a success. The Allies met stiff resistance at only one of the five invasion beaches—Omaha, in the American sector. The battle was nonetheless chaotic, and the Allies did not reach all their objectives. The inevitable German counterattacks came soon enough to contain the invaders, but, as Rommel had feared, too late to destroy the Allied beachhead.

From mid-June until mid-July, both sides fed reserves into a static attritional meat grinder. Normandy may have been an excellent choice for landing beaches, but once ashore, the Allies discovered that the terrain, marked by the thick and tall hedgerows that divided the fields of the Norman farmers, was perfectly suited to defensive operations. Cherbourg fell on 27 June. British forces did not take Caen, expected to fall on D-Day, until 19 July.

But while the Germans halted the more immediate threat posed by Montgomery's advance on the Allied left, the Americans on the right were on the verge of a breakout. Bradley's U.S. First Army launched Operation Cobra near St. Lô on 5 July. Within a week, the Americans had shattered the German front and reached Avranches, the key road junction leading westward into the Brittany peninsula. At this point, the Americans activated the U.S. Third Army, under Patton, for a planned drive into the Brittany peninsula to secure the major French Atlantic ports. But the collapse of the German front presented Eisenhower with an opportunity to destroy the German field armies deployed against him. Ultra indicated that the Germans, rather than retreating, were preparing a counter-stroke to close the Avranches gap. Eisenhower decided to send Patton east, rather than west, in a movement designed to annihilate the Germans. Unfortunately, the Allies failed to spring their trap. Many Germans escaped, although without their heavy equipment. The Allies had destroyed German striking power west of the Seine and now began a rapid drive across France. French troops entered Paris on 19 August.

The Allies had more than made up the time lost slugging it out in Normandy and were well ahead of schedule. Unfortunately, their rapid advance also placed them ahead of the supply buildup planned to support a drive to the German border. As a result, the Allies conducted their operations in France and the Low Countries during the late summer and fall of 1944 on a logistical shoestring.

Supply limitations shaped the strategic debate about the course of future operations—a debate perhaps more important for its political ramifications than its strategic merits. Montgomery believed that the supply shortages dictated the need for a more focused advance. He suggested that Eisenhower halt the American advance and funnel available supplies to the British and Canadian forces on the Allied left, where the terrain was more suited to mobile operations. For obvious reasons, such a proposal held few attractions for the Americans, who argued for a continued advance on a broad front.

There were advantages and disadvantages to both strategies, and it is impossible to say with certainty which was better from a purely military point of view. But Eisenhower recognized that Montgomery's strategy was politically dangerous. Such a decision would infuriate the American public, place a huge burden on the British-Canadian forces that would henceforth bear the brunt of the casualties, and risk a weakening of the heretofore solid Anglo-American alliance. By now, the Allied invasion in southern France had begun (5 August), and by the end of the month, advance elements had reached Grenoble. Eisenhower hoped that this second supply corridor would help alleviate the logistical crisis before the Germans recovered.

Unfortunately, the Allied broad advance slowed and then stalled. In September, Eisenhower agreed to allow Montgomery to try to break the Rhine River line in the Netherlands by using three Allied airborne divisions to seize a series of bridges leading to the main crossing at Arnhem. But the daring operation failed, principally because the Germans had already recovered their equilibrium. The Allied advance continued along the front from the Channel to the Swiss border, but the fighting was more attritional than mobile. Allied hopes that the war might end before Christmas were dashed.

As the western Allies struggled to break out in Normandy, the Soviets opened their summer 1944 offensive. On 23 June, the Russians launched Bagration, an operation designed to destroy the German Army Group Center. In six weeks, a series of successive and deep attacks encircled and destroyed the bulk of an entire German army group. By 1 August, the Soviets were on the outskirts of Warsaw. Much of German Army Group North was trapped in Estonia and Latvia. In August, the Soviets struck farther south and broke the German lines, overran most of Romania, and drove into Bulgaria and, later, Yugoslavia and Hungary. In the fall, the Russians closed up on the East Prussian border in the north, but remained idle in the center while the Germans destroyed the Polish resistance in Warsaw.

Hitler, facing disaster on all fronts, decided to gamble. During the fall, the Germans had built up a sizable reserve of panzer divisions. He knew that these divisions would be quickly consumed in the east, but their impact in the west would be substantial. He planned to strike through the Ardennes, split the Anglo-American front, and recapture the main Allied supply port of Antwerp.

The Germans struck on 16 December along the American front in the Ardennes, achieving near-complete surprise. Bradley's troops were caught off balance and with few reserves. The situation was an embarrassment for the American high command, and Montgomery did little to spare their feelings.

But despite initial success, the operation was a forlorn hope. The Germans had thrust through the Ardennes in May 1940, but at that time had motored unopposed through a virtually undefended region. The Americans defended their positions in the Ardennes, and whatever the faults of their high command, the troops were dogged in their determination. German panzer leaders quickly discovered that the Ardennes was not, in fact, prime tank country. They were tactically road-bound and unable to move quickly. The advance fell behind schedule, and fuel supplies ran short. Initially, poor weather kept the jammed roads safe from Allied air attacks, but when the skies cleared on the 23 December, the dreaded Allied fighter-bombers appeared. On the northern flank of the Bulge, as it became known, the Americans, backstopped by the British, held firm. In the south, Patton masterfully redirected his Third Army from an easterly to a northerly orientation and drove into the German flank. On 26 December, Patton relieved the Americans at Bastogne, a major road junction that had held out in the German rear. The Allies spent the rest of December and January eliminating the Bulge and, with it, Hitler's final hope for something other than complete and utter defeat.

The Soviets, to help take the pressure off the Americans in the Ardennes, stepped up the timetable for their own offensive. Along the front from Hungary to the Baltic, Soviet advances shattered the German line. By mid-February, the Russians had reached the Elbe, less than fifty miles from Berlin. Hitler shifted his reserves from the west to the east, counterattacking in Hungary. But gains were few, and the German counterattacks were quickly over-whelmed by broader and heavier Soviet offensives. Vienna fell on 13 April. Stalin's armies were poised for their final offensive toward the Nazi capital.

In the west, the Allies unleashed a series of offensives designed to bring their armies into position along the entire length of the Rhine. By early March, they had succeeded, taking ever-larger formations of Germans prisoner. By late March, the Allies were across the Rhine in the British sector in the north and in the sectors of the First and Third American Armies. Within a week, the Americans encircled the Ruhr and, with it, an entire German army group. In late March and early April, Allied forces began a race across Germany. Eisenhower, for sound political and military reasons, decided not to drive toward Berlin.

On 16 April, the Soviets began their final offensive, comprising two fronts driving for Hitler's capital. By 25 April, the Russians had surrounded Berlin. Hitler committed suicide on 30 April, and by 2 May, the Russians had extinguished resistance in the city. On 7 May, Admiral Karl Dönitz, Hitler's successor, surrendered. The Second World War had come to an end in the European theater.

The western democracies had triumphed, but only through their alliance with Stalin's Soviet Russia—a regime no better, and arguably worse, than Hitler's Germany. The fate of Poland symbolized that pact with a devil: Poland was not liberated, but exchanged the domination of Germany for that of the Soviet Union. Stalin retained his ill-gotten gains in eastern Poland, and the Allies compensated the Poles with new territories in the west. These territories were cleared of their German inhabitants in a regimen of ethnic cleansing that put millions of Germans on the roads of Eastern Europe, and approximately two million of these refugees perished. The alliance was such a marriage of convenience that even before Hitler had spared the world his further presence, the British and Americans were already quarrelling with the Russians. By the spring of 1946, contentiousness had taken on crisis proportions, and the Cold War had begun. For the next half century the former Allies confronted each other along the Iron Curtain, which stretched from Stettin on the Baltic to Trieste on the Adriatic.

But the very fact that a cold war followed the "hot" war of 1939–1945 reveals the most important element that lay behind Allied victory. Great Britain, the United States, and the Soviet Union, despite very real differences, had forged an effective military alliance. Such coalitions are rare in the annals of history. And there can be little doubt that in the absence of such an alignment the outcome of the war could have been disastrous.

Nevertheless, Allied victory did not come cheaply. The Second World War was the most destructive conflict in the history of humankind. Deaths, military and civilian, totaled in the tens of millions. Scores of cities lay in ruins. As Allied armies marched into central Europe, they discovered unbelievable horrors. Over eleven million European civilians died in German death factories, nearly six million of them Jews swept up from the corners of the new German empire in a genocidal effort to achieve a "final solution" to the "Jewish question" that guided Nazi policy. If Verdun symbolized the tragedy of the First World War, Auschwitz epitomized the tragedy of the second.

In retrospect, it is tempting to conclude that the effective Allied coalition was itself sufficient to secure success. Combined, Russia, the United States, and Great Britain outproduced Germany in every military category. But quantity, while important, was itself no guarantor of victory. Excepting the Polish campaign, early on the Germans were usually outnumbered and won nonetheless. Ultimately, all the production in the world could not have defeated the *Wehrmacht* unless that output had been applied judiciously and effectively.

At the level of grand strategy, the Allies demonstrated clear superiority. Whatever their early mistakes, they planned for the long war they fought. The United States, despite the post–Pearl Harbor debacle and public desire to refocus the American war effort in the Pacific, stuck to its prewar Europe-first strategy, rooted in the correct assumption that Nazi Germany posed the far more serious threat than Japan. That the Allies enjoyed a production advantage in the final stages of the war was no accident: it was a planned outcome. Few leaders in Moscow, London, or Washington held illusions about the costs or the length of the war.

In the strategic realm, there can be little doubt that the Allies were much wiser than their Axis counterparts. Generals such as Eisenhower may never have commanded a unit in battle, but they possessed the diplomatic and management skills to wage coalition warfare effectively on an oceanic and continental scale.

A general with Eisenhower's background would never have risen to such a position of prominence in the German army, but then Eisenhower would never have waited until the campaign in Tunisia was concluded before considering his next move to Sicily, in the fashion that the German generals in the spring of 1940 thought no further than the immediate defeat of France. Even Soviet strategic military planning after 1942 was more thoughtful and analytical than that of the Germans.

At the operational level, the Germans excelled, but their advantage eroded gradually and was often undermined by poor strategy. By midwar, the Allies often displayed operational excellence. Russian operations during 1943 and 1944 demonstrated an evolving level of skill and appreciation of the realities of war, including the tactical limitations of the Soviet army. The Russians made the most of their numerical superiority, but numbers had not guaranteed victory in 1941 or 1942. They did so between 1943 and 1945 because of an improved level of operational effectiveness.

Tactically, the Germans retained their superiority until the end of the war. But here, too, the German advantage declined as the war progressed, and Allied tactics improved as their armies learned from experience much of what the Germans had learned from study during the 1920s.

In the air, the Germans lost the initiative earlier than they did on the ground. During the Battle of Britain, the *Luftwaffe* and the industrial base upon which it was built displayed their limitations. This failure was central to the Axis defeat. German combined-arms doctrine envisioned close cooperation between ground and air elements. When the Germans lost the initiative in the air, in 1942 in the west and 1943 in the east, they lost a fundamental component of their military machine. While Allied doctrine for close air support never became as effective as that of the Germans, the Anglo-American air forces excelled in interdiction and the isolation of the battlefield.

In the realm of strategic air warfare, the Germans were at a disadvantage. By 1942, faced with a protracted struggle, the

Luftwaffe lacked the capability to retaliate. Geography was a major factor: even possession of a bomber comparable to the B-17 would not have allowed the Germans to strike distant American factories. But the Germans possessed the means to develop a fighter force capable of defending the Reich. The Battle of Britain had demonstrated that successful air defense was possible. But lack of strategic direction, and technical and administrative incompetence and mismanagement, assured German defeat in the air.

Nazi Germany lost the war because it failed to continue the pace of innovation so evident in the 1920s. The Nazis, during their twelve years in power, were unable to build on the strategic, operational, and tactical inheritance of the *Reichswehr*. In April 1945, they were still relying on Enigma coding machines that the Allies had learned to read six years earlier. Blitzkrieg was in many ways nothing more than the addition of steel tanks to an existing combined-arms doctrine that had employed cardboard substitutes. The Germans developed their air doctrine primarily before the advent of Hitler. In the strategic realm, Hitler and his generals failed to look beyond the defeat of Poland and France, as envisioned almost two decades earlier by Seeckt, until it was too late. In 1944 and 1945, operationally and tactically on the ground, in the air, and at sea, the Germans were often doing things the same way that they had done them in 1939 and 1940. The same could not be said of the Allies.

Conclusions

During the second half of the nineteenth century, as the full impact of the Industrial Revolution impacted warfare, the widely held conceptualization was that conflicts were becoming less likely and that those that did break out would be short, decisive, and, for those reasons, less costly than previous conflicts. European wars waged between 1859 and 1913 did little to undermine such assumptions. As a result, when a general European conflict began in August 1914, the Europeans marched off to a struggle they expected to end in short order. The kaiser assured German troops about to entrain for the front, "You will be home before the leaves have fallen from the trees."

Clearly, the kaiser's and other Europeans' expectations for a quick war were misguided. No single climatic battlefield engagement secured victory in the Great War, which became a gigantic struggle of attrition that lasted over four years and caused the deaths of the over sixteen million soldiers, who succumbed to wounds and disease.

Why? The reason is simple enough: many of the leading military minds of Europe believed that they had found in their experiences and in their studies of history a formula for quick and decisive victory. Historian Russell F. Weigley, in his work

The Age of Battles, termed that quest "elusive"; I think it could be more properly termed "chimerical." It is perhaps best epitomized by Schlieffen's fascination with Hannibal's 216 BCE triumph at Cannae—a victory so "decisive" that the Second Punic War continued for another fifteen years and ended with Hannibal's defeat!

It was to the great misfortune of the Europeans that the mid-century short wars of Italian and German unification overshadowed the experiences of the prolonged American Civil War and held out the prospect of apparent battlefield decisiveness. It was likewise a grave misfortune that the Germans and their general staff believed they had discovered within warfare's nature and the advent of industrialization some magical formula that would ensure quick decision.

There were many reasons why the mid-century European wars were decisive, quick, relatively cheap, and exceptional. The Austrian Empire was in decline, and its leaders were reluctant to risk much on the battlefield. They were unwilling to contest both French military power and local nationalism in Italy, or employ more than an army or risk more than a single major engagement to challenge Prussia in Germany. In 1870, the crushing defeat of Napoleon III's army ended his fragile dynasty, although it did not bring about an immediate defeat of France. The siege of Paris continued into early 1871, lasting longer than the seven-week-long mobile and decisive phase of the conflict. Moreover, Bismarck's adroit diplomacy kept both Austria and France isolated. Russia and Britain had been allies of Prussia and enemies of France since the late eighteenth century. All that would change with the Prussian military triumphs and the Second Reich's assumption of a new status in Europe. But it was only in retrospect that Europe's leaders and, later, historians saw clearly the dangers in the ascent of Prussia vis-à-vis France. When the shift in the balance of power became apparent with the formation of the Second Reich in 1871, Europe slowly began to realign itself. France would not be isolated again.

Prussia's quick and decisive military victories became the model for the European powers. The conflicts fought after 1871 in the Balkans, South Africa, and the Far East were bloody slaughters that for the most part lasted longer than the Austro- and Franco-Prussian Wars. But this fact could be, and was, explained away because the combatants had taken months to mobilize and bring their forces to bear in distant theaters—the Far East or South Africa—or in the Balkans, where communications remained primitive. A war in the heart of Europe would be fought by armies that would be fully mobilized along their respective frontiers and in direct proximity of the enemy in a matter of days. Moreover, these "other wars" had nevertheless been short, lasting a year or months; they had not dragged on for twenty, ten, or even four years.

The history of all the European wars fought between 1859 and 1913 did demonstrate the importance of seizing the initiative and taking the offensive. The various Balkan wars had nearly driven the once mighty Ottoman Empire from Europe and secured the independence of numerous Balkan peoples. Japanese casualties in their Manchurian campaign against the Russians had been heavy, but Japan had won battle after battle and secured its objectives.

The fact remains that the pre-1914 expectation that the wars waged by modern industrial states would be shorter *was* accurate. While the First World War lasted longer than expected, it was, nevertheless, more abbreviated than the general European wars of the eighteenth century. The French Revolution and subsequent Napoleonic Wars lasted over twenty years (from 1793 to 1814/1815), Great Britain's global struggle for America eight (from 1775 to 1783), the Seven Years' War seven (from 1756 to 1763), the War of Austrian Succession over eight (from 1740 to 1748), the Great Northern War twenty-one (from 1700 to 1721), the War of Spanish Succession almost fourteen (from 1701 to 1714), and the War of the League of Augsburg just short of a decade (from 1688 to 1697). The fuller industrialization of

European conflict between 1914 and 1945—the period historian Martin Van Creveld termed, in his *The Transformation of War*, the second Thirty Years' War—failed to produce cost-effective results, but nevertheless hastened the process of attrition that more quickly brought one side or the other to the negotiating table or to the brink of collapse. Military thinkers of the late nineteenth century were correct: modern warfare did yield results more quickly. Unfortunately, the actual process remained attritional, and the full mobilization of state and society yielded even longer casualty lists and far higher civilian death tolls than the pre-industrial wars. For example, during the two decades of the French Revolution and subsequent Napoleonic Wars, a European population of about 150 million people suffered the deaths of between 3.5 and 6.5 million soldiers from combat or disease. It took over twenty years to kill off combatants numbering about 3.5 percent of the population. During the Great War, thanks to greater industrialization, it took only four years to slaughter combatants representing about 5 percent of the population.

Millis wrote in *Arms and Men* that by the campaign of Waterloo conflict war had begun "to lose its one virtue—its power of decision." In fact, during the seventeenth and eighteen centuries, warfare had rarely yielded quick, decisive victories. An examination of history through the ages reveals that decisive battles—of the type that yielded results in a single afternoon—were the exception rather than the rule. While several of Napoleon I's campaigns ended with a battlefield triumph—Austerlitz in 1805, Jena-Auerstadt in 1806, and Wagram in 1809—looked at as a whole, the wars of Napoleon ended in a decade-long attritional defeat for the Empire of France. The campaign that began with the June 1812 invasion of Russia continued until March 1814 and Bonaparte's first abdication, and it forms a prolonged and extended whole that swept from Poland, to Moscow, and back across central Europe to Paris. The impact of the fuller industrialization of warfare was to concentrate and accelerate the speed with which societies could destroy each other, resulting in shorter, but still attritional, wars marked by higher casualties rates and rising levels of physical destruction.

The expectation that wars could be decided quickly and cheaply was a fantasy, and no European state spent more time and effort in pursuit of that fantasy than Germany. Historians have long noted the traditional German desire to avoid long and costly wars—a desire rooted in their vulnerable geographic position in central Europe and the weaknesses of the Brandenburg-Prussian state as it emerged. But historians generally fail to inquire whether after 1871 a unified, industrialized Germany was as vulnerable as the Prussian state of the seventeenth and eighteenth centuries. Why did the Germans' strategic horizons fail to expand along with German power? Germany acquired colonies and built a large and powerful navy—traditionally a long-war asset—but remained wedded to its quest for short wars.

Consider, by comparison, American history. The fledgling United States began life as a weak confederation strung along the Atlantic coast of North America. By the 1820s, American diplomats were expressing concern that led to the Monroe Doctrine. By the 1840s, the Americans had expanded across the continent to the Pacific and had occupied Mexico City. Roughly a century after achieving independence, the United States, by then the strongest industrial power on the globe, was involved in the Caribbean and the Philippines. Not long afterward Americans were at the Rhine. As American power grew, strategic horizons expanded, and national strategy transformed along with it. In little more than a century, Americans adjusted their strategic horizon from the Atlantic coast to the Elbe River.

While German national horizons grew along with its industrial might—evidenced by the pursuit of colonies in Africa and Asia and the transition from a coastal defense to a blue-water navy—military strategy remained primarily, if not purely, continental. No matter how much larger and powerful the Germans became during the wars they waged successfully during the seventeenth, eighteenth, and nineteenth centuries, they continued to envision themselves as the inhabitants of some poor, weak state surrounded by enemies. Their inability to recognize fully their changed status after 1871—that they had become, in fact, Europe's most powerful nation—prevented them from understanding the ever-increasing insecurity of their own neighbors and hamstrung the development of a national military strategy capable of taking fuller advantage of German industrial and military might.

As a result, the Germans committed two fundamental and interrelated errors. First, from 1890 to 1945, they believed that their armed forces had attained a level of relative excellence that would quickly secure decisive battlefield victories; so armed, they pursued unswervingly short-war strategies. Second, they assumed that they lacked the wherewithal to wage a protracted war and failed—or refused—to plan for one. Actually, the Germans had it backward. The decisive victories they sought proved to be elusive, and the history of the two world wars suggests that Germany did possess the capability to fight a prolonged war.

Despite the fact that Germany was home to Clausewitz and innumerable other notable military thinkers, and despite the fact that the Germans demonstrated consistently remarkable dexterity at the operational and tactical levels of warfare, their grand strategy remained vestigial. When the offensive of the summer of 1914 failed in Belgium and France, the German general staff had no fall-back plan for an extended war. Likewise, the German navy had no plans for a conflict that *did not* begin with a rash and what would probably have been a suicidal assault by Britain's Royal Navy on the German fleet in its bases. Here was how German strategic thinking and the expectation that a war would be, and had to be, quick had polluted its naval strategy. Navies rarely win wars in weeks! When in 1918, Crown

Prince Rupprecht of Bavaria asked Ludendorff about the operational goal of his forthcoming spring offensives, Ludendorff replied, "We make a hole and the rest will take care of itself." That strategy had worked in the east against the Russians who were on the brink of collapse, but it led to disaster on the western front and ensured Germany's defeat in the Great War.

How might the Great War have progressed if Germany had embraced the prospects of a protracted multifront war and followed the more cautious and initially defensive strategy adopted by the elder Moltke in the 1870s and 1880s? The Germans could certainly have contained a French offensive confined to the relatively short and well-fortified Franco-German border. If the Germans had refrained from marching through Belgium, would Britain have intervened? In the absence of British intervention, or "the rape of Belgium," what would the Americans have done? How much earlier than March 1917 might Russia have collapsed if the Germans had adopted a defensive posture in the west in 1914 and launched with consistency a series of offensives along the eastern front? Can there be any doubt that if the Germans had adopted a long-war, eastern-front-focused strategy, they would have fared better than they did in the Great War as fought? In 1914, the Germans threw away a realistic chance for victory in a longer conflict in exchange for a high-risk gamble, both in military and diplomatic terms, that they could knock France out of the war in six weeks. In early 1917, they made the same mistake again, unleashing their U-boats in an unrestricted campaign that they knew would lead to American intervention in the expectation that they could bring Great Britain to its knees in six months.

Nor did the Germans learn from their mistakes. When a new European war began on 1 September 1939, they again displayed their tactical and operational brilliance and demonstrated that modern warfare could be quick, decisive, and, compared to the Great War, inexpensive. In quick succession, the Germans overran Poland, Denmark, Norway, Holland,

Belgium, Luxembourg, and most of France. They suffered about 45,000 casualties during the Polish campaign, 6,000 during the Scandinavian campaign, and another 160,000 during the campaign in France and the Low Countries—a total of about 211,000 casualties to overrun much of central and western Europe. By comparison, in 1916, the Germans suffered over 330,000 casualties at Verdun and another 600,000 along the Somme—just short of one million—and achieved nothing.

Despite their successes, or perhaps because of them, the Germans repeated their strategic and conceptual errors. In 1933, Hitler inherited the *Reichswehr*'s defensively oriented strategic concept developed during the 1920s when Germany was confined by the military restrictions of the Versailles treaty. The strategy was basic: the army would knock out the Poles and turn on France and hope for the best, while the navy secured Norway to outflank another British naval blockade in the North Sea. Neither Hitler nor the reborn German general staff, despite the repudiation by Germany of the Versailles treaty and the subsequent massive expansion of the military establishment after 1933, built on or beyond the *Reichswehr*'s strategic concept. As a result, by late June 1940, a primarily defensive strategic concept, given an offensive edge by German military expansion, had yielded a series of decisive victories. Unfortunately for the Germans, they had exhausted the *Reichswehr*'s strategic inheritance and had no plans for what to do next. *In 1914, the German general staff had no plan for defeat; in 1940, it had no plan for victory.*

Hitler wasted months before he reached a strategic decision. After a half-hearted attempt to invade Britain and an uninspiring diplomatic effort to take full advantage of Britain's weakness in the Mediterranean, Hitler chose to turn east and to attack the Soviet Union. Moving east was the direction Hitler had always wanted to go, but *Mein Kampf* was hardly a substitute for a clearly thought out national military strategy. Once again the Germans convinced themselves that their campaign, if it were to be successful, had to be, and could be, concluded in a single season—the summer of 1941. No doubt German success in France suggested that the *Wehrmacht* could annihilate the Russians armies deployed along the frontier. But the distances in Russia were so great, the lack of internal communications so marked, the weather so perilous, and the state of intelligence on the Soviet armed forces so primitive, that the Germans, in a commanding position within Europe, were committing themselves to another high-stakes gamble. In retrospect, the Germans would have done better had they tried to make their way to Leningrad and Moscow in two campaigns.

And what of the adoption of a long-war strategy in the summer of 1940? Was Nazi Germany, given its control of Europe from the Atlantic to the Niemen, and from Norway to the North African coast, actually too weak to risk a prolonged war with Great Britain? Even if one assumes Soviet intervention at some point, could the Germans conceivably have fared worse than they did in the war as actually fought between 1941 and 1945?

As if the costs and the destruction—human, physical, financial, political, and social— associated with this second Thirty Years' War were insufficient to question the utility of conflict, the advent of atomic weapons, meant to be employed against Germany, but first used by the United States against the Japanese empire in August 1945, convinced Europeans of the futility of war as a means to resolve great-power disputes. A thermonuclear conflict might well be quick, but the costs are likely to be prohibitive—akin to two people armed with grenades locked in a closet. As Van Creveld noted, if *the* Thirty Years' War (from 1618 to 1648) demonstrated the inability of the Europeans to resolve religious differences through military conflict, the second Thirty Years' War (from 1914 to 1945) did the same for political disputes.

The collective European experiences of the German wars, combined with the atomic revolution, brought to an end and exposed the realities and limitations of the classical era of Western warfare. What looked good on the pages of a book rarely worked out as promised on the battlefield. The British and Americans learned that Giulio Douhet's concept—that air power could secure victory while avoiding the horrors of the trenches—proved far more difficult to employ in practice than in theory. Only the addition of atomic weapons to aerial arsenals suggested the likelihood of quick conflicts, but at almost unthinkable costs.

But before readers applaud the end of an era marked by such brutal conflicts, they need to recognize that the technology of warfare—the military application of the fruits of scientific industrialization, epitomized by atomic weapons—remains and continues to advance. And the fact that European—now broadened to Western/modern—states no longer believe in the possibilities of short, quick, decisive wars, does not imply an end to human conflict. The second Thirty Years' War demonstrated not only the recognition of the chimerical nature of Western military thought between 1859 and 1945, but also the collapse of the constraints Europeans had attempted to place on warfare between 1648 and 1945. How else can you explain the butchery and death of millions of civilians on the Russian front or the Holocaust and the industrialization of genocide? We have mistakenly considered Western warfare as a total, and everything else as a lesser and limited, form of conflict, to the extent that many people refuse to consider the West's struggle with global jihadists to be war and prefer to view it as a criminal enterprise . The reality is that modern Western warfare is limited, and the "lesser" forms are total. As Lawrence H. Keeley wrote in *War Before Civilization*, primitive warfare as practiced since prehistory is the more total form of conflict. Primitive war—known in the modern era as guerrilla, low-intensity-conflict, asynchronous warfare or, in its modern Islamic form, jihadism—is, in fact, total war. It draws few, if any distinctions between soldiers and civilians; it aims to totally destroy its enemy, be it a limited goal such as French colonial rule in Indochina or the broader objective of crushing all non-Islamic societies as a prelude to the establishment of a global caliphate. As Keeley argues, Westerners wage limited war with unlimited means, while others wage unlimited war with limited means.

The reality of Western warfare is not only that it has lost its ability to produce decisions at an acceptable cost as a means to resolve inter-Western disputes, but also that non-Western states cannot compete on the battlefield in western-style warfare. In effect, since 1945, while Europe has not seen a major war, conflict has been pushed into the recesses of the non-Western world. Since local peoples cannot compete successfully with Western military power on a traditional battlefield, they have wisely resorted to the lesser forms of warfare, occasionally with success. Compare, for example, the failures of Saddam Hussein's vaunted Iraqi army in 1991 and 2003 with the successes of the ongoing insurgencies in Iraq or Afghanistan.

We witness daily the new reality. Westerners, armed to the teeth, but with their own history fresh in their minds, remain reluctant to resort to force, whereas assorted non-Western groups eagerly embrace their weapons and unabashedly revel in their willingness to butcher without distinguishing between military and nonmilitary targets. The West, with all its power, remains wedded to its self-imposed strictures governing warfare as if it were refighting the Franco-Prussian War. Whereas assorted non-Westerners, having rejected Western ideals and political and cultural assumptions, follow their own rules and are branded as terrorists.

What will happen if, or more probably when, the "terrorists" get their hands on a weapon of mass destruction and gain the ability to wage their form of total war with, for example, nuclear weapons? How long will the self-imposed restraints hold (international law is an almost wholly Western invention) when a major American or European city suffers an attack that kills hundreds of thousands of its citizens?

The German wars brought to an end and revealed the short-comings of the classical era of modern Western military thought. But the regressive slide toward premodern and primitive warfare, in combination with the fruits of the industrial and scientific revolutions, places the world on the edge of an abyss.

Acknowledgments

CONCEPTUALLY *THE GERMAN WARS* WAS BORN during the 1980s when I worked as a historian for the U.S. Navy in Washington, DC. I was somewhat taken aback by the near worship of things German by myriad personnel in the U.S. military. I understood that the Germans epitomized tactical and operational excellence on the battlefield, but I nevertheless found it odd that people so often overlooked the fact that the Germans had managed *to lose two world wars*, whereas the Americans had actually been on the winning side of both. In response, I wrote a short satirical piece published in 1989 in *Military Review.**

I thought at the time that someday I would write something larger that would examine how it was that the Germans, despite their oft-proclaimed "genius for war," choked in the big games. Over the next twenty years, as I read more, wrote more, and taught about warfare, I gradually began to shape a two-part thesis. First, the Germans, unlike the Americans, failed to mature strategically as their nation grew and became more powerful. Second, the Germans, along with virtually everyone else, misinterpreted the lessons of their own successes against Denmark (1864), Austria

*"If Nelson Spoke German?" Military Review 69 (January 1989): 98-99.

(1866), and France (1870) and concluded that they had to and could successfully wage short, decisive wars in the age of industrial warfare. Reality caught up with them during the years of 1914 to 1918 and 1939 to 1945, and the world, the Germans included, paid a horribly steep price for that mistake.

I wish to thank several individuals for their help and support with this project. First, my friend of two decades and literary agent Fritz Heinzen once again helped me find the appropriate publisher. I enjoy working with Fritz because our historical interests coincide, a fact that makes him an excellent sounding board for ideas. I wish to thank Richard Kane, editorial director at Zenith Press, whom I knew from his days at Presidio. Steve Gansen, my editor at Zenith, was helpful, supportive, and did an excellent job cleaning up the manuscript. I have been blessed over the years with good editors.

I would also like to thank my friend and former East Carolina colleague Ylce Irizarry. She helped keep me focused when my concentration wavered; I thrive on her constant encouragement.

Otto Eduard Leopold von Bismarck (1815–1898). This portrait of Bismarck
shows him as a man in his prime during the 1860s, when as Ministerpräsident
he guided Prussia through its unification struggle and toward the establishment
of the Second Reich in 1871. Bismarck then became chancellor. He was a master
of political manipulation, with regard both to internal Prussian/German politics
and international relations. He and Helmuth von Moltke formed quite a team but,
unlike the next generation of German politicians, tempered their aggressiveness with
a sense of caution born of experience in a Germany that was not Europe's greatest
economic and military power. *Library of Congress*

Alfred von Schlieffen (1833–1913).
Schlieffen served as chief of the
general staff from 1891 to 1906.
During his tenure, German plans
shifted from an initially defensive-
focused effort on both fronts toward
a strategy aimed at defeating France
in a quick campaign before turning
on the Russians. This shift in strategy
ensured that any conflict that began
in the east (the most likely scenario)
would become a European war. The
concept was high risk and based on
myriad assumptions, many of which
were unfounded. Schlieffen is also
famous for his interest on Hannibal's
classic double-envelopment at
Cannae in 216 BCE. Schlieffen and
other Cannae enthusiasts failed
to note that the Second Punic

War continued for another fifteen years and ended in Carthaginian defeat, despite
Hannibal's "decisive" victory. *Hulton Archive/Getty Images*

**Erich von Falkenhayn
(1861–1922).** Falkenhayn
succeeded Helmuth Ludwig
von Moltke (the Younger)
as chief of the general staff
following the German defeat
at the Battle of the Marne in
September 1914. Falkenhayn's
strategic focus remained locked
on the western front, despite
the Austro-German successes
gained against Russia in 1915.
In February 1916, Falkenhayn
launched his offensive at
Verdun. The offensive, which
lasted from February through
December 1916, failed to take
the town and bled both armies.
French casualties totaled about
371,000; German about 331,000.
The failure of the campaign,
combined with complaints by
other German commanders,
most notably Hindenburg and

Ludendorff, about lost opportunities in the east, led to Falkenhayn's dismissal in
August 1916. *Library of Congress*

Hans von Seeckt (1866–1936). Seeckt was a career officer and World War I veteran who became one of the central figures of the German army between the world wars. From 1920 to 1926 Seeckt served as Chef der Heeresleitung of the Reichswehr, virtually army commander-in-chief. Under Seeckt's guidance the Germans gathered and digested the lessons of the First World War on the ground and in the air. The Reichswehr became a small force of long-serving, well-trained professionals. When Hitler came to power in 1933, the Reichswehr served as the cadre for the expanded Wehrmacht. Hitler also inherited the strategic concepts worked out by German interwar strategists, for example knocking out Poland quickly and then turning on France, and the idea of capturing Norway to prevent the Allies from bottling up the German navy in the North Sea. By June 1940 these concepts had proven their worth, but neither Hitler nor his generals and admirals had any plans for how to exploit the victories gained. *Library of Congress*

Paul Ludwig Hans Anton von Beneckendorff und von Hindenburg (1847–1934), Friedrich Wilhelm Victor Albert, Kaiser Wilhelm II (*1859–1941*), and Erich Friedrich Wilhelm Ludendorff (1865–1937). The German brain trust of the Great War pose in January 1917 before a table spread with maps, the Kaiser's withered left arm hidden behind his back. By the end of the war, Hindenburg and Ludendorff were virtually running Germany, although Hindenburg was primarily the front man. Luderndorff was largely responsible for Germany's defeat. He supported the early 1917 decision to launch the unrestricted submarine-warfare campaign that brought the United States into the war. He threw away the German advantages gained through the defeat of Russia in the east. The series of offensives launched in the west in the spring of 1918, while tactical successes, served no larger operational or strategic purpose. Ludendorff infamously remarked to his subordinates that he would make a hole and the rest would follow. They made the holes, but what followed was German defeat. *National Archives*

Alfred von Tirpitz (1849–1930). Tirpitz was the chief figure in the development of the pre–World War I German navy. He oversaw its transition from a small force focused on coastal defense to a major navy embracing the blue-water doctrines of Alfred Thayer Mahan. While Tirpitz, with the Kaiser's support, gained great political success in Germany, his theories and expectations regarding what Imperial Germany could accomplish with the world's second most powerful navy were wide of the mark. The buildup of the German fleet led to the Anglo-German naval race and made war with Britain more, not less, likely. Nor did the powerful navy-in-being prevent the British from blockading Germany after 1914. Tirpitz's mighty navy proved to be an enormous waste of resources. *Library of Congress*

Adolf Hitler (1889–1945). Hitler delivers a rambling speech to the Reichstag on 11 December 1941, hours after Germany declared war against the United States. As usual, Hitler railed against Roosevelt, Churchill, "plutocrats," Communists, and Jews. His decision to enter the war alongside Imperial Japan, which was not mandated by the Tripartite Pact of 1940, made it easier for Roosevelt to keep the American war effort focused on "Europe First" after the debacle at Pearl Harbor on 7 December. Hitler's decision was one of the worst of the many German blunders of the war. *National Archives*

Franz Ritter von Halder (1884–1971).
At the start of the Second World War, Halder was the chief of the German general staff and Walther von Brauchitsch was commander-in-chief of the army. From 1939 to 1941, as the war went well, Hitler, Halder, and Brauchitsch muddled along. But in the mid-summer of 1941 when the debates began within the German army about the prosecution of the Russian campaign, Halder and Brauchitsch differed with the Führer but lacked the ability to consistently stand up to him.

Brauchitsch suffered a heart attack in December 1941 and was promptly relieved of his command. Halder lasted into the summer of 1942 and was replaced in September as the German campaign in the south of Russia stalled. *Hulton Archive/Getty Images*

Erich von Manstein (1887–1973). Manstein may have had the best operational mind in the German army during the Second World War. He conceptualized the thrust through the Ardennes in May 1940; he commanded a Panzer corps during the drive on Leningrad; his Eleventh Army captured Sevastopol in July 1942; he rescued the collapsing German southern flank in his famed riposte of February-March 1943; and he commanded the southern wing in the Kursk offensive of July 1943. Hitler relieved Manstein of command in March 1944. *Interfoto/Alamy*

Bernard Law Montgomery (1887–1976). "Monty" atop one of his American-made Grant tanks observes his own armored division moving forward in the desert. The prickly Montgomery was one of the Allies' most effective generals. He commanded a division of the British Expeditionary Force

during the French campaign; Eighth Army during its final victory drive in North Africa, Sicily, and Italy in 1942–43; and Twenty-first Army Group during the campaign in northwestern Europe 1944–45. The Americans often viewed Montgomery as overly methodical, but his approach was linked to the realities of the British army—its lack of manpower, mediocre equipment, and less than fully modern doctrine. *National Archives*

Erwin Johannes Eugen Rommel (1891–1944). Rommel was without doubt the best known German general of the Second World War. He was even the focus of a 1951 Hollywood movie—*The Desert Fox*—starring James Mason. Rommel was an aggressive and often successful commander. But as he rose within the command hierarchy, so, too, did his problems. As the postwar decades passed, the image of Rommel that developed was more balanced, and often critical. In the end, the Nazi regime whose propaganda machine had helped make him a hero, turned on him when his name was linked to the plot to assassinate Hitler in July 1944. Rommel, because of his celebrity, was allowed to commit suicide, thus sparing himself and his family the humiliation and suffering inflicted upon others. *National Archives*

Karl Dönitz (1891–1980). Dönitz served as chief of the German U-boat force from 1936 until 1943, and commander-in-chief of the entire Kriegsmarine from 1943 until the end of the war. Dönitz drew many important lessons from the German experience with U-boats during the Great War, but he remained too wedded to his concepts when confronted by developments related to technological change as the Second World War at sea progressed. By May 1943, the German U-boat arm stood little chance, yet Dönitz continued to send his boats and their crews on patrol, and to their deaths. Following Hitler's suicide in April 1945, the trusted and ever-loyal Dönitz became the second and final führer of the Third Reich. *Popperfoto/Getty Images*

Bibliography

THE HISTORIOGRAPHY OF THE SECOND WORLD WAR is vast, too expansive to simply list. The approach I have taken in developing the lists for further reading for the chapter covering the war, and the other chapters, is highly selective. What follows are suggested readings, organized by chapter. The books and articles listed fall into four categories: first, sources mentioned in the text; second, some of my personal favorites; third, a handful of works I consider classics; and fourth, citations that reflect some of the more recent relevant historical work. The most recent works on specific topics, generally, will provide more extensive lists of their own for additional reading. Please note that many books, although they may appear under the listing for an individual chapter, are relevant for several chapters.

INTRODUCTION

Angell, Norman. *The Great Illusion.* New York: Cosimo Classics, 2007.

Bloch, Ivan. *The Future of War in Its Technical, Economic, and Political Relations: Is War Now Impossible?* Ithaca, NY: Cornell Univ. Library, 2009.

Brodie, Bernard. *From Crossbow to H-Bomb: The Evolution of the Weapons and Tactics of Warfare.* Bloomington: Indiana Univ. Press, 1973.

_____. *Sea Power in the Machine Age.* Princeton, NJ: Princeton

Univ. Press, 1943.

Citino, Robert M. *The German Way of War: From the Thirty Years' War to the Third Reich.* Lawrence: Univ. Press of Kansas, 2005.

Millis, Walter. *Arms and Men: A Study in American Military History.* New Brunswick, NJ: Rutgers Univ. Press, 1981.

I. THE WARS OF ITALIAN AND GERMAN UNIFICATION

Barry, Quintin. *The Road to Koniggratz: Helmuth von Moltke and the Austro-Prussian War 1866.* Solihull, England: Helion and Company, Ltd., 2010.

Bucholz, Arden. *Moltke and the German Wars, 1864–1871.* New York: Palgrave Macmillan, 2001.

Craig, Gordon. *Koniggratz: Prussia's Victory over Austria, 1866.* Philadelphia: Univ. of Pennsylvania Press, 2003.

Dupuy, Trevor N. *A Genius for War: The German Army and the General Staff, 1807–1945.* Englewood Cliffs, NJ: Prentice-Hall, Inc., 1977.

Goerlitz, Walter. *History of the German General Staff, 1657–1945.* Brian Battershaw, trans. New York: Praeger Publishers, 1967.

Horne, Alistair. *The Fall of Paris: The Siege and the Commune, 1870–1871.* New York: St. Martin's Press, 1995.

Howard, Michael. *The Franco-Prussian War: The German Invasion of France, 1870–1871.* New York and London: Routledge, 2001.

McElwee, William. *The Art of War: Waterloo to Mons.* Bloomington: Univ. of Indiana Press, 1974.

Taylor, A. J. P. *Bismarck: The Man and the Statesman.* New York: Vintage Books, 1955.

Wawro, Geoffrey. *The Austro-Prussian War: Austria's War with Prussia and Italy in 1866.* Cambridge: Cambridge Univ. Press, 1997.

_____. *The Franco-Prussian War: The German Conquest of France in 1870–1871.* Cambridge: Cambridge Univ. Press, 2005.

II. THE ROAD TO SARAJEVO

Clark, Christopher. *Kaiser Wilhelm II.* London: Longmans, 2000.

Cox, Gary P. "Of Aphorisms, Lessons and Paradigms: Comparing the British and German Official Histories of the Russo-Japanese War." *Journal of Military History,* vol. 56 (July 1992): 389–402.

Herwig, Holger. *Luxury Fleet: The Imperial German Navy, 1898–1918.* Amherst, NY: Humanity Books, 1987.

Kennan, George F. *The Decline of Bismarck's European Order: Franco-Russian Relations, 1875–1890.* Princeton, NJ: Princeton Univ. Press, 1979.

Lambert, Nicholas. *Sir John Fisher's Naval Revolution.* Columbia: Univ. of South Carolina Press, 2002.

Maurice, Frederick. *The Russo-Turkish War 1877: A Strategic Sketch.* New York: Thomson Press, 2009. (Reprint of the 1905 edition.)

Pakenham, Thomas. *The Boer War.* New York: Random House, 1979.

Shirer, William L. *The Collapse of the Third Republic: An Inquiry into the Fall of France in 1940.* New York: Simon and Schuster, 1969.

Taylor, A. J. P. *The Struggle for the Mastery of Europe, 1848–1918.* New York: Oxford Univ. Press, 1974.

Van Creveld, Martin. *Supplying War: Logistics from Wallenstein to Patton.* Cambridge: Cambridge Univ. Press, 1977.

Von Schlieffen, Alfred. *Cannae.* Leavenworth, KS: U.S. Army Command and General Staff College Press, 1992. (Also available online at: www.cgsc.edu/carl/resources/csi/Cannae/cannae.asp.)

Warner, Peggy. *The Tide at Sunrise: The History of the Russo-Japanese War, 1904–05.* New York: Routledge, 2004.

III. THE GREAT WAR

Dowling, Timothy G. *The Brusilov Offensive.* Bloomington: Indiana Univ. Press, 2008.

Foley, Robert T. *German Strategy and the Path to Verdun.* Cambridge: Cambridge Univ. Press, 2007.

Fussell, Paul. *The Great War and Modern Memory.* New York: Oxford Univ. Press, 1977.

Gordon, Andrew. *The Rules of the Game: Jutland and British Naval Command.* London: John Murray, 1996.

Horne, Alistair. *The Price of Glory: Verdun, 1916.* New York: Penguin, 1994.

Hough, Richard. *The Great War at Sea, 1914–1918.* Edinburgh, Scotland: Birlinn, 2001.

Junger, Ernst. *Storm of Steel.* New York: Penguin, 2004.

Keegan, John. *The First World War.* New York: Alfred A. Knopf, 1999.

Kennedy, Paul. *The War Plans of the Great Powers, 1880–1914.* Boston: Unwin Hyman, 1985.

Kennett, Lee. *The First Air War, 1914–1918.* New York: The Free Press, 1991.

Mumford, Lewis. *Technics and Civilization.* Chicago. Univ. of Chicago Press, 2010.

Showalter, Dennis. *Tannenberg: Clash of Empires, 1914.* Dulles, VA: Potomac Books, 2004.

Stone, Norman. *The Eastern Front, 1914–1917.* New York: Penguin, 2004.

Strachan, Hew. *The First World War.* London: Penguin, 2005.

Terraine, John. *Douglas Haig: The Educated Soldier.* London: Cassell, 2005.

Tuchman, Barbara. *The Guns of August.* New York: Macmillan Publishing Co., Inc., 1962.

Wavell, Archibald. *Allenby, A Study In Greatness:* The Biography of Field-Marshal Viscount Allenby of Megiddo and Felixstowe. Whitefish, MT: Kessinger Publishing, 2008.

Weber, Frank G. *Eagles on the Crescent: Germany, Austria and the Diplomacy of the Turkish Alliance, 1914–1918.* Ithaca, NY: Cornell Univ. Press, 1970.

Williamson, Samuel R. Jr. *The Politics of Grand Strategy: Britain and France Prepare for War, 1904–1914.* Cambridge: Harvard Univ. Press, 1969.

IV. THE INTERWAR YEARS, 1918–1937

Barnett, Corelli. *The Swordbearers: Studies in Supreme Command in the First World War.* London: Hodder & Stoughton, Ltd., 1986.

Biddle, Tami Davis. *Rhetoric and Reality: The Evolution of British and American Ideas about Strategic Bombing, 1914–1945.* Princeton, NJ: Princeton Univ. Press, 2002.

Citino, Robert M. *Path to Blitzkrieg: Doctrine and Training in the German Army, 1920–1939.* Harrisburg, PA: Stackpole Books, 2008.

Corum, James S. *The Luftwaffe: Creating the Operational Air War, 1918–1940.* Lawrence: Univ. Press of Kansas, 1997.

————. *The Roots of Blitzkrieg: Hans von Seekt and German Military Reform.* Lawrence: Univ. Press of Kansas, 1994.

Doughty, Robert A. *The Seeds of Disaster: The Development of French Army Doctrine: 1919–1939.* Hamden, CT: Archon Books, 1985.

Glantz, David M. *Soviet Operational Art: In Pursuit of Deep Battle.* London: Frank Cass, 1991.

Kiesling, Eugenia C. *Arming Against Hitler: France and the Limits of Military Planning.* Lawrence: Univ. Press of Kansas, 1996.

Millet, Allan R., and Williamson Murray, eds. *Military Effectiveness, Vol. II: The Interwar Period.* London: Allen and Unwin, 1998.

Ogorkiewicz, Richard M. *Armour: The Development of Mechanized Forces and Their Equipment.* London: Stevens & Sons, Ltd., 1960.

Palmer, Michael A. *Command at Sea: Naval Command and Control since the Sixteenth Century.* Cambridge: Harvard Univ. Press, 2005.

Paret, Peter, ed. *Makers of Modern Strategy: From Machiavelli to the Nuclear Age.* Princeton, NJ: Princeton Univ. Press, 1986.

Posen, Barry R. *Sources of Military Doctrine: France, Britain and Germany between the World Wars.* Ithaca, NY: Cornell

Univ. Press, 1986.

Winton, Harold R., and David R. Mets, eds. *The Challenge of Change: Military Institutions and New Realities, 1918–1941.* Lincoln: Univ. of Nebraska Press, 2003.

V. WORLD WAR II, 1937–1945

Barnett, Corelli. *The Desert Generals.* Bloomington: Indiana Univ. Press, 1982.

Blair, Clay. *Hitler's U-Boat War: The Hunters, 1939–1942.* New York: Random House, 1996.

_____. *Hitler's U-Boat War: The Hunted, 1942–1945.* New York: Random House, 1998.

Bryant, Arthur. *The Turn of the Tide: A History of the War Years Based on the Diaries of Field-Marshal Lord Alanbrooke, Chief of the Imperial General Staff.*
Vol. I: 1939–1943. New York: Doubleday & Company, Inc., 1957.

_____. *The Turn of the Tide: A History of the War Years Based on the Diaries of Field-Marshal Lord Alanbrooke, Chief of the Imperial General Staff. Vol. II: 1943–1946.* New York: Doubleday & Company, Inc., 1959.

Costello, John, and Terry Hughes. *The Battle of the Atlantic.* New York: Dial Press, 1977.

Doenitz, Karl. *Memoirs: Ten Years and Twenty Days.* Annapolis, MD: Naval Institute Press, 1990.

Freeman, Roger A. *The Mighty Eighth: A History of the Units, Men and Machines of the US 8th Air Force.* London: Cassell, 2000.

Gilbert, Martin. *The Second World War: A Complete History.* New York: Holt Paperbacks, 2004.

Glantz, David M., and Jonathan M. House. *The Battle of Kursk.* Lawrence: Univ. Press of Kansas, 1999.

_____. *When Titans Clashed: How the Red Army Stopped Hitler.* Lawrence: Univ. Press of Kansas, 1998.

Horne, Alistair. *To Lose a Battle: France, 1940.* Boston: Little, Brown & Company, 1969.

Howard, Michael. *The Mediterranean Strategy in the Second World War.* New York: Praeger, 1968.

Keegan, John. *Six Armies in Normandy: From D-Day to the Liberation of Paris, June 6th–August 25th, 1944.* New York: Viking Press, 1982.

Lewin, Ronald. *Ultra Goes to War.* Barnsley, England: Pen and Sword, 2008.

Liddell Hart, B. H. *History of the Second World War.* New York: G. P. Putnam's Sons, 1970.

Montgomery, Bernard Law. *The Memoirs of Field Marshal the Viscount Montgomery of Alamein, K.G.* New York: The World Publishing Company, 1958.

Murray, Williamson. *Strategy for Defeat: The Luftwaffe, 1933–45.* Dulles, VA: Brassey's, 1996.

Murray, Williamson, and Allan R. Millett. *A War to Be Won: Fighting the Second World War.* Cambridge, MA: Belknap Press, 2000.

Overy, Richard. *Why the Allies Won.* New York: W. W. Norton & Company, 1995.

Saward, Dudley. *"Bomber" Harris: The Story of Marshal of the Royal Air Force Sir Arthur Harris, Bt, GCB, OBE, AFC, LLD, Air Officer Commanding-in-Chief, Bomber Command, 1942–1945.* London: Sphere Books Limited, 1990.

Taylor, A. J. P. *The Origins of the Second World War.* New York: Atheneum, 1962.

Van Creveld, Martin. *Command in War.* Cambridge: Harvard Univ. Press, 1985.

———. *Fighting Power: German and U.S. Army Performance, 1939–1945.* New York: Praeger, 2007.

Von Manstein, Erich. *Lost Victories.* Novato, California: Presidio Press, 1982.

Weigley, Russell F. *Eisenhower's Lieutenants: The Campaigns in France and Germany, 1944–1945.* Bloomington: Indiana Univ. Press, 1990.

CONCLUSIONS

Hitler, Adolf. *Mein Kampf.* Michael Ford, trans. London: Elite Minds, Inc., 2009.

Keeley, Lawrence H. *War Before Civilization: The Myth of the Peaceful Savage.* New York: Oxford Univ. Press, 1997.

Van Creveld, Martin. *The Transformation of War.* New York: The Free Press, 1991.

Weigley, Russell F. *The Age of Battles: The Quest for Decisive Warfare from Breitenfeld to Waterloo.* Bloomington: Indiana Univ. Press, 1991.

Index